PENGUIN BOOKS

APPRENTICED TO A HIMALAYAN MASTER

Born Mumtaz Ali in Thiruvananthapuram, Kerala, Sri M is a spiritual teacher, author, social reformer, educationist and global speaker. His memoir, *Apprenticed to a Himalayan Master: A Yogi's Autobiography*, published in 2011, became an instant bestseller; the sequel, *The Journey Continues*, was published in 2017.

He is the author of various other books on philosophy, yoga and Indian mysticism. Sri M established The Satsang Foundation twenty years ago and his mission has resulted in several initiatives in areas of education, community health, environment and the oneness of humanity.

Among the many awards and honours he has received, Sri M was conferred the Padma Bhushan by the Government of India in January 2020 for distinguished service of high order in spirituality.

APPRENTICED TO
A HIMALAYAN
MASTER

∽

A YOGI'S
AUTOBIOGRAPHY

SRI M

PENGUIN BOOKS

An imprint of Penguin Random House

PENGUIN BOOKS

USA | Canada | UK | Ireland | Australia
New Zealand | India | South Africa | China | Singapore

Penguin Books is part of the Penguin Random House group of companies
whose addresses can be found at global.penguinrandomhouse.com

Published by Penguin Random House India Pvt. Ltd
4th Floor, Capital Tower 1, MG Road,
Gurugram 122 002, Haryana, India

Penguin
Random House
India

First published by Magenta Press, 2011
Published by Westland Publications Private Limited in 2019
This edition published in Penguin Books by Penguin Random House India in 2022

ISBN 9780143458586

Typeset by R. Ajith Kumar
Printed at Gopsons Papers Pvt. Ltd., Noida.
Text is Printed on Recycled Paper

www.penguin.co.in

Dedicated to my Guru without whom I could have been lost.

Contents

Acknowledgements

I EXPRESS MY DEEP SENSE of gratitude to the following friends without whose help this book would not have been possible.

To Kaizer Karachiwala, who painstakingly and with great care made sense of my often unclear scribblings and turned them into a readable manuscript.

To Balaji and Sreedhar, who from the start, took charge of the publishing and business aspects so selflessly and efficiently.

To Shobha Reddy, who from the beginning took upon herself the responsibility of photographs and building up a formidable photo-archives in spite of my reluctance to approve the enterprise, and who with great attention and dedication helped me sort out the pictures that you'll find in here.

To Roshan, my son, and friend; Radha Mahendru, who specially helped in selecting the photographs and working out the layout of the pictures.

To Vijay Bhasker, who looked after the office work.

And to all my dear friends, whose great longing to know the hitherto secret and unknown chapters of my life moved me to begin this book in the first place.

Thank you one and all.

Sri M

Foreword

BEFORE I TAKE YOU with me on this adventurous journey, from the southern coast of India to the snowy heights of the mystical Himalayas and back—meeting extraordinary individuals, and sharing unusual and incredible experiences—I would like to say a few words that will put everything in its proper perspective.

Until now, I have held most of the experiences I have written about in this book close to my heart, not letting even my closest friends persuade me to come out with anything more than a hint of what lay hidden in the depths of my consciousness.

Why was I so secretive in these matters, and why have I now spilled the beans, as the expression goes?

Let me answer these questions now:

My Master Babaji, although he had hinted that I would at some point write an autobiography, did not send the green signal, which I was expecting from him, till two years before I sat down to write. Even after that, I deliberated a great deal for over six months before reluctantly beginning to write, mainly for two reasons:

One, I was afraid that the sincere spiritual aspirant, caught in the fantasy of the fascinating saga, might miss out the practical and necessary aspects of the spiritual journey.

Two, that the critical reader, finding some parts of the narrative unbelievably strange, might dismiss the whole book as a cock-and-bull story.

However, what clinched the issue in favour of writing this autobiography were the following factors:

First, it occurred to me that it was my business to write what I experienced and leave it to the small minority of skeptical readers to accept or reject. I felt I was being unfair to the majority of readers by hesitating to tell my story for fear of this minority.

Second, after the appearance of *The Autobiography of a Yogi*, very few authentic spiritual biographies have appeared, and the writers of even those are no longer alive and available for discussion. Also, however authentic Swami Yogananda's autobiography is, he hadn't personally spent much time in the Himalayas. Therefore, I thought it was important that I relate my experiences, especially those I had in the Himalayas, so that I would be available to the reader for an interaction.

Third, I wanted to prove the point that great teachers like Babaji and Sri Guru influence the tide of spiritual evolution silently, behind the scenes, even though very few know of their existence.

I appeal to the readers to ignore those parts that appear to them as too fantastic to be real, if need be, and read the rest so that they don't miss the great teachings of Sri Guru and Babaji. About my guru, I can only repeat what Swami Vivekananda said about his own guru, 'A particle of dust from his blessed feet could have created a thousand Vivekanandas.'

Substitute 'Vivekananda' with 'M' and you'll know what I mean.

So, come with me on this wonderful journey, dear readers, and may the blessings of the masters be with you.

Let us begin the journey

1

The Beginning

FORTY YEARS AGO, a young man of nineteen from Kerala, the southernmost state of India, was deep in meditation in the cave of Vyasa, up in the Himalayas near the Indo-Tibetan border. Even in those days, a teenager going away to the Himalayas to meditate was not a common occurrence. What made this case almost unbelievable was that the young man in question was not even born a Hindu.

How this young man became a yogi, and the mysterious and fascinating world of unimaginable power and grandeur that opened up for him, is the story of my life. I was this young man.

If you will allow me, I shall start at the very beginning. Let us, as quickly as possible, walk together to the abode of the eternal snows. There, among the ice-clad Himalayan peaks, dwelt my friend, philosopher and guide—my dearest teacher and master by whose kindness and grace, I learnt to fly high into the greater dimensions of consciousness.

Words fail to do justice to the glory of those spheres, but then, words are the only tools at our disposal. Let us, therefore, begin our journey, good friends, walking in the deep woods, talking about the wonderful sights, the bright flowers swaying gently, the sweet-singing birds, the great river gushing along, the tall trees standing silent and so on until we turn the corner and all of a sudden come across the towering great whiteness of the snow-covered Himalayas and are rendered speechless with wonder. Didn't the ancient rishis sing *Yad vaacha na abbhyuthitham*: 'the power and the glory that even words cannot comprehend'?

I am as eager as you are to bring you face to face with Parvati, the demure daughter of Himavan, Lord of the Mountains. But, we must gather and pack up a few essential pieces of luggage before we begin the ascent. I shall do that without wasting any time and stick to the bare essentials.

I was born in Thiruvananthapuram, 'the city of Lord Vishnu who sleeps on the serpent *Anantha*.' *Anantha* also means, in Sanskrit, 'without end, infinite.' Trivandrum, as it was renamed by the British when they ruled India, is a coastal city and the capital of Kerala. Back then, Kerala was like an overgrown village, with its hills and rivers and abundant greenery.

I was born on November 6, 1948, in an emigrant Pathan family whose ancestors had come to Kerala as mercenaries and joined the forces of the powerful Marthanda Varma, then Maharaja of Travancore. This is, to use a familiar expression, a 'rags to riches story' in a different context—an ordinary boy reaching the Himalayan heights of expanded consciousness by dint of sincerity, one-pointed attention, a willingness to take risks, and unwillingness to accept failure.

Of course, there was one more factor, which I consider the most important. The guidance and blessings of a great teacher whose unfathomable love and affection helped me undertake this journey through largely unexplored territory; a teacher who never curtailed my freedom to question, never held my hand too long lest I turn lazy and dependent, and forgave all my shortcomings and conditioned responses. Can I ever forget that great being—father, mother, teacher and dear friend, all rolled in one?

Was it compassion that led him to walk into my life when I was barely nine years old, or was there a link beyond the mundane reckoning of life spans? This, I leave to you to decide for yourselves after the story is finished.

Babaji (father), as I called my teacher, often said, 'Keep things simple and direct. No mumbo jumbo. Live in the world like anybody else. Greatness is never advertised. Those who come close, discover it themselves. Be an example to your friends and associates of how you can live in this world happily and, at the same time, tune in to the abundant energy and glory of the infinite consciousness.'

I cannot however refrain from stating certain facts before coming to that fateful day when the kind master walked into my life, six months after my ninth birthday.

(i)   From the time I was born, I had the tendency to cross one leg over the other. You will see the posture in the first ever photograph of mine, taken just two months after my birth. The habit continued, and as I grew up, I found that the classic, cross-legged posture of the yogis was the most comfortable seating position for me. Even today, wherever I go, I love to sit cross-legged on the dining chair, if the hosts have no objection.

(ii) Since the age of five-and-a-half to about the age of ten, I suffered from terrible nightmares which were identical. Around midnight, I would see in my sleep a gigantic semihuman monster with sharp, long canines and claws looking somewhat like a Kathakali dancer, trying to grab me and carry me away. Still asleep to the outside world, I would scream and run out of the house, with the monster in hot pursuit, shouting 'I have to go away there.'

My parents often ran after me, and my father was the only one who could wake me up from the trance-like state by shouting my name loudly in my ears. However, never once did the apparitions succeed in laying their hands on me.

Various cures were tried, including the wearing of talismans, but to no effect. The dreams finally disappeared after my first meeting with the Master. It took me many years to understand what I was fleeing from and where I wanted to go.

(iii) My maternal grandmother, who had Sufi connections, kept me enthralled with stories of the Sufis. Her favourite story (and mine as well) was the story of the life of the Sufi saint

Peer Mohammed Sahib, who lived a hundred years ago in a little hamlet called Tuckaley in the erstwhile kingdom of Travancore. Like the well-known saint from Banaras, Kabir Das, Tuckaley's Peer Mohammed Sahib was also a weaver. As he worked on his hand-operated loom, he sang songs of devotion and mystical insight in Tamil. Known as the 'Paadal', the songs are still popular among certain Sufi groups in Tamil Nadu. As he grew older, he went blind and had to be helped around by a young boy who was his disciple.

One incident in the story of this Sufi saint's life that my grandmother was very fond of retelling, and I was very fond of listening to, goes like this. On learning that there lived a saintly man in the south of India, two Arab doctors of divinity came to visit him. They liked everything except the fact that this man seemed not inclined to undertake the pilgrimage to the holy city of Mecca—an act which every able-bodied Muslim was expected to perform as part of his religious duties. The Tuckaley saint excused himself from the pilgrimage saying that he was blind and could not possibly go so far, but insisted that he had witnessed the pilgrimage and that Mecca was right there where he lived.

This was blasphemy according to the Arab visitors, and they put it down to the ravings of a madman. But Peer Mohammed Sahib would not give up his claims. He ordered his disciple to bring the old, clay water pot and requested the Arab visitors to look into the water. One by one, each beheld the whole scene of the pilgrimage to Mecca in the water pot and, wonder of wonders, saw themselves circumambulating the Kaaba, accompanied by the blind weaver saint. They fell at his feet and became his disciples.

Close to this saint's tomb is also the grave of one of my paternal ancestors, who was his disciple.

(iv) Between the ages of five and nine, I was exposed to Hinduism and Christianity. Even at that age, I began to notice how prejudiced people belonging to one religion could be about other religions.

For instance, my grandmother, who would go into ecstasy talking of Muslim saints, abhorred the Hindu religion and Hindu gods. She warned me to be careful about eating food in any of our Hindu neighbours' houses for fear that it might have been offered to the Hindu gods whom she considered to be unholy. She often referred to Hindus as idolaters and believed that the advent of Islam was the best thing that ever happened to mankind. Good Muslims were assured of a place in heaven.

I was sent to an elite English-medium school run by nuns belonging to a certain order. Here, we were not forced but encouraged to cross our hearts when we passed the chapel and the grotto of Virgin Mary, and were taught many a Christian hymns. I loved the bearded, kind face of Jesus Christ as the shepherd depicted in pictures that hung all over the place and was surprised to hear one of the nuns teach us that Muslims were sun-worshippers and Hindus worshipped hobgoblins.

Our neighbours were all Hindus and, while visiting their houses, I was fascinated by the great variety of gods that they worshipped. I always wondered why a lady from an orthodox Brahmin household was so fond of me and loved to feed me sweets, whilst my grandmother forbade me from eating them. Of course, on the other hand, there were Hindu neighbours who looked forward to the tasty mutton biryani which my mother made and distributed to our Nair neighbours during Ramzan and Bakri Id. As for myself, I longed for idli, sambhar and the traditional Malayali vegetarian meal, served on fresh banana leaves.

My first major contact with Hindu devotional practices—apart from the images and pictures of gods worshipped in little private shrines in our neighbours' houses—was a *kirtan* party which appeared unexpectedly on the road in front of our house one Sunday morning. I was sitting near the kitchen trying unsuccessfully to put together a mechanical toy that I had dismantled to see how it worked, when the soul-stirring rhythm (rhythm *vadishyaami*) of the mridangam's beat accompanied by the sweet tinkling of cymbals completely overwhelmed my mind.

I was wearing shorts, while my upper body was bare. I threw away the toy and ran towards the gate, my heart beating fast. A strange sight met my eyes. There were four middle-aged men singing and dancing on the road. All except one wore yellow loincloths, called *kaupin*, wrapped around the lower part of their bodies. The exception was a tall, fair and handsome man, with a flowing beard and long hair and a garland of pure white flowers around his neck. He wore only a thin ochre kaupin that barely covered his genitals and was otherwise bare-bodied.

All four were barefoot. One had a mridangam hanging from his neck, and as he drummed with both hands, eyes closed, he periodically broke into ecstatic laughter. Another seemed totally absorbed in playing a pair of tiny cymbals, and swung his head from side to side. The third one was walking from door to door, collecting fruit, vegetables, rice, and sometimes money, which was offered with great respect by some of our neighbours who stood at their gates.

Now the fourth person, the tall, handsome bearded man, seemed to be the leader of the group. He led the chorus as he danced and sang 'Hare Rama, Hare Rama' to the beautiful rhythm of the mridangam and the cymbals, his eyes closed and tears streaming down his cheeks. He was in some kind of semi-conscious state. I saw some of the neighbours go close to him and prostrate at his feet.

A strange happiness filled my heart, and I remember that I too started laughing. Then, I ran inside and finding a coin whose denomination I cannot remember now, ran back to the gate, walked across the road to drop the coin into the small bag the collector of offerings held in his hand. It was then that I heard my grandmother's voice calling me. As I hurried back, feeling guilty that I had perhaps done something that ought not to have been done, I turned around to take a last look at the strange, almost naked man dancing in the street. His eyes opened and our gaze met for a brief moment before I was inside the house.

The party moved on. The music faded away slowly and a strange silence took over. My grandmother did not approve of what I had done, but I was let off after being given a little bit of religious advice. Many years later, I came to know that the ecstatic man I had seen was

Swami Abhedananda who lived in an ashram not very far from where I lived. As a college student, I had many pleasant encounters with him but more of that later.

Around this time my mother's maternal uncle, who was a keen photographer, took me to see the Aratu festival inside the East Fort. The old fort was built by the Maharajas around the grand temple of Anantha Padmanabha Swamy, their tutelary deity. As I mentioned earlier, Trivandrum's original name Thiruvananthapuram is derived from the name of this deity who is described as 'one from whose navel grows the lotus.' Every year, the compound of the temple is decorated with festoons, flowers and lights and the entire Hindu pantheon is on display in the form of life size or even bigger idols, complete with colourful costumes and jewellery. As I gazed at the Gopuram towers of the ancient temple, something seemed to stir inside my navel and I was seized by an irresistible urge to go inside, although at that age of six or so, I had no idea what was inside the temple. My mother's uncle said that we would not be allowed in because we did not belong to the Hindu religion.

I remember clearly his pointing to the white-painted signboard and reading in Malayalam and English: 'No entry for non-Hindus.' The differentiation between the two communities consisting of the same human beings thoroughly puzzled me. At that time, I had no option but to accept defeat and return. How was I to know then that as time passed and as I grew older, I would see terrible communal divides that religious zealots brought about between human beings in the name of religion?

My mother's uncle got me peppermints to cheer me up and took me to the southern gate of the Central Secretariat building, four kilometres away. There, not far from the entrance, a slightly plump man with graying hair and an unshaven, pleasant face was lying on a cot, bare-bodied except for the Kerala mundu which covered the lower half of his body. He spoke to me softly, shook hands and gave me a sweet. He said that he was happy to see me wearing red shorts.

I came to know later that he was the veteran communist leader A.K. Gopalan who was on a fast-unto-death protest against the Congress government of that time. My mother's uncle, who had leftist leanings, had taken me to visit the communist leader whom he held in high esteem. Perhaps there was some magic in Mr Gopalan's soft eyes or his gentle touch that drew me to Karl Marx and *Das Capital* in my college days.

Speaking of magic, I also distinctly remember the magical moments I had on many an evening sitting in the backyard of my house and looking at the clouds. To my imagination, they appeared to be snowy peaks waiting to be discovered. Much later, when I saw a picture of the Himalayas in a coffee-table book, I said to myself, 'Haven't I seen them before in the clouds, sitting in the backyard of my house when I was barely six?'

To conclude this chapter, here is a story my master told me as I sat with him in a quiet spot on the banks of the river Bhagirathi as it wound its way down the Himalayas. I think it would be relevant to say it now, before we go to the next chapter of this journey, as I would like to repeat what the master said to me, 'Draw your own conclusions from the story I am going to tell you but don't be in a hurry to do so.'

Behind the famous temple of Badrinath, the sacred Himalayan shrine that stands 13,000 feet above sea level, there exist a few large and small caves perched on top of nearly inaccessible cliffs. The temple is open to pilgrims only during the summer months. The rest of the year, the whole area is snowbound. Even the Namboodiri priests from Kerala who have been officiating there since the time of Shankaracharya (a saint who renovated the temple hundreds of years ago and was himself from Kerala) go down to the village of Joshi Mutt and wait for the next season. Only a few extraordinary beings continue to live and meditate in the caves even during winter.

A hundred years ago, one such extraordinary yogi sat in one of the caves, bare bodied except for his cotton loin cloth, absorbed in deep meditation. He was fair and handsome with flowing black hair and a black beard, and while his eyes were closed, a peaceful smile lit his face as he enjoyed the inner joy of soul communion. This young yogi, who was just nineteen, came from a distinguished family of Vedic scholars from the holy city of Varanasi.

His ancestors had been disciples of a legendary yogi called Sri Guru Babaji, who it is believed has maintained his physical body in a youthful condition for many hundreds of years, even to this day.

This young man's father, himself a disciple of Sri Guru Babaji, had handed over his son to the great yogi at the tender age of nine. Since then he had wandered with his teacher (who had no fixed abode), the length and breadth of the Himalayas. A year ago, at the age of eighteen, he had graduated to the level of an independent yogi and since then had been wandering alone amongst the snow-covered peaks of Kedar and Badri.

While our young yogi sat perfectly still in the yogic state called samadhi, a strange drama was unfolding before his closed eyes. Clawing his way up the steep, rocky ledge, an old man of the kind rarely seen in those parts pulled himself up on to the flat rock in front of the cave. His dirty green turban and soiled robe—now almost torn to shreds—the rosary around his neck and his hennaed beard clearly indicated that he was a Muslim fakir.

There were cuts and bruises all over his arms, legs and other exposed parts of his body and blood oozed from his wounds. Cold and hungry, he was on the verge of collapsing, but as soon as his eyes fell upon the young yogi sitting in the cave, the pained expression on his face was replaced by a smile, which expanded into hysteric laughter. 'Praise be to Allah,' he cried, and with a deep sigh, forgetting all his pain and suffering, he moved towards the still meditating yogi and fell prostrate. He then did something no Hindu would ever dream of doing to a yogi—he hugged him. The yogi, crudely shaken out of his trance, opened his eyes and shook off the old man who was clinging to his body. He blew his nose to clear the stench that came from the travel-worn and bleeding body of the strange creature and shouted in anger, 'How dare you? Keep away from me.' Anger, that powerful poison that is sometimes difficult to control even for *rishis*, had entered this young yogi's heart.

'Please, Sir,' pleaded the fakir, 'Give me a chance to tell you my story.'

'Go away,' said the yogi, 'I need to have a dip in the Alakananda and resume my meditation. Your kind of person, a meat-eating barbarian, has no place here. Get lost.'

The fakir would not give up. 'Please listen to me, O great yogi. I am a Sufi and am the chief disciple of a great Sufi master of the Naqshabandiya order. Just before my master passed away, six months ago, he told me, "Friend, you have now reached the level of spiritual attainment that I was able to take you to. I am leaving my body soon and there is no Sufi master at this point who is willing to guide you to the next and higher level. But don't worry. There lives a young Himalayan yogi near Badri in the Himalayas. Find him and seek his help." You are the one he referred to and you alone can save me now.

'For two months, I have suffered incalculable travails and misfortunes before finding you. I might drop dead due to exhaustion, but just accept me as your disciple and my soul will depart in peace. Please, I beg you.'

'I know nothing about your master or the Sufis as you call them. I have received no such instructions, and moreover, I don't accept disciples,' said the young yogi, still angry. 'Now move out of my way and don't delay me from having my bath in the Alakananda and resume the meditation that you so rudely interrupted. Get out!'

'All right, O Great Yogi,' said the fakir, 'if that is your final word, I don't wish to stay alive anymore. My life's only dream has been shattered. I shall jump into the river and take my life. May the Supreme Lord of the Universe guide me.'

'Do what you want,' said the yogi firmly, 'but I can do nothing for you. You are lucky that in my anger I did not curse you. Go your way and let me go my way.'

The fakir bade farewell by prostrating at the yogi's feet and, with tears in his eyes, made his way to the river that flowed several feet below. With a prayer on his lips and seeking guidance from the Supreme Being, he plunged into the swirling waters and ended his life.

The young yogi, confident that he had done the right thing and having no remorse whatsoever, climbed down to a lovely spot on the banks of the river and, chanting the appropriate mantras for purification, had a dip in the extremely cold waters of the sacred river. He came out of the water and rubbed himself dry with the only towel that he possessed. Sitting on a rock, he thanked the sacred river for purifying his body and mind and was about to start his climb to the cave when he heard the familiar sweet voice of his master calling him, 'Madhu!'

From behind a rocky ledge appeared his great master, Sri Guru Babaji. It looked as if the darkness of the approaching dusk was suddenly lit by his glowing presence. Tall, fair with an almost European complexion, Babaji had long flowing brown hair and very little facial hair. He looked around sixteen years of age. The well-built, unadorned muscular body was bare except for a white loincloth. He was barefoot, and walked with great grace and dignity.

His large, meditative eyes fell on his young disciple Madhu. 'What a terrible thing you have done, my boy,' he said softly.

Instantly, the gravity of what he had done a few minutes ago, hit the young yogi like lightning. 'Babaji' was all he could utter before breaking into tears and prostrating at his feet.

'Control yourself, my boy, and come. Let us climb up to your cave.' They climbed up swiftly, reached the cave, and sat down facing each other. 'Haven't I always told you to think before you speak about what you are going to say, to whom, and under what circumstances? You could have had a little more patience and listened carefully to what the old man was trying to say. Is a holy man judged by his outward appearance? Like my great disciple Kabir said, would you give more importance to the scabbard than to the sword? You have hurt and pained a great devotee of the Lord. All the fruits of your many years of austerities, you have destroyed in a flash. A minute of kindness is more precious than a hundred years of intense austerities. You have to compensate for it.'

By then the young disciple had controlled himself and become calm. 'Whatever you say, my master, I am prepared to do,' he said.

'As for the fakir,' said Babaji, 'I shall take care of his spiritual needs. You have arrested your spiritual progress by your arrogant behaviour and the only way to get back on track is to go through the same or similar pain and privation that the fakir went through. Prepare to do the last kriya—total *khechari mudra*—and let your prana exit through the Ajna centre. We shall then guide your soul to be born in such circumstances that you go through pain similar to that suffered by the poor man. Do it now.'

'Your wish has always been a command for me, Babaji, and I will do so immediately, but I have a last wish.'

'Express it, my son,' said Babaji.

His voice breaking with deep emotion and hands clasped in prayer, the young disciple said, 'Master, I love you with all my heart. Promise that you will not let go of me, that you will keep track of me and not let me be carried away by the whirlpool of worldly thoughts and concerns. I beg you to please promise me that you will watch over me and bring me back to your blessed feet.'

'That, I promise,' said the great teacher, tender compassion tangibly flowing from his glittering eyes, 'My foremost disciple, Maheshwarnath, whom you have not met, shall come to you quite early in your future life. He shall be your guide. At some point in your future life, you will also see me and talk to me as you are doing now. But now, you must hurry, for this is the right time to go.'

By then, the sun had set and the beautiful silvery moon parted the clouds to bear witness to the sacred play that was being enacted. The young disciple, with tears in his eyes, prostrated once more at his guardian's feet. Babaji stretched forth his right hand, placed it on his head, blessed him and instantly merged into the night. Madhu, now alone, adopted the lotus posture, took a few deep breaths, and performed the khechari mudra, which forcibly stops the breathing process. Concentrating on the centre between the eyebrows, shook off his body.

That is the end of the story that my master Maheshwarnath told me.

2

A Visit from the Himalayan Master

NOW, IT IS TIME to tell you about the rather strange manner in which my guru contacted me and re-established the link.

I was a little more than nine years old at that time. We—my father, mother, younger sister, my maternal grandmother and myself—lived in a fairly large house on Ambujavilasam Road. The locality was Vanchiyoor, a quiet place though not very far from the main thoroughfare. The house was called Palliveedu and my father paid what in those days was considered a princely rent of Rs 40 per month.

There was very little space between the front door and the gate which opened on to the road, but our backyard was quite spacious—about half an acre filled with many coconut and jackfruit trees and flowering shrubs. My mother also kept hens in the courtyard and it was a delight to see the mother hens walking along with their fluffy chicks, dyed pink. This was to prevent them from being carried away by kites. We also had a couple of goats.

My father, in addition to being a building contractor, did some kind of business with waste paper. To stock sacks of waste paper collected from printing presses, a big shed was built on one side in the backyard. This was a favourite haunt for me and my sister, who was two-and-a-half years younger. Here, we played hide-and-seek or just sat on the sacks and had great fun inventing new words and nonsense rhymes.

The compound wall that surrounded the courtyard was very low, barely three feet in height, and was built of mud. Almost in the centre of the courtyard, from the branch of an old jackfruit tree, was suspended a sturdy swing. We enjoyed swinging on it and were often joined by children from our neighbourhood, who would easily climb over the low compound wall. There was also another jackfruit tree, a larger and perhaps older one, which stood at the far end of the courtyard on the right-hand corner. This was the tree under which the drama that changed my life completely took place.

Both my sister and I went to the Holy Angels' Convent, which was walking distance from home. As soon as we came back from school, it was our usual practice to wash up, eat something light, and play in the backyard till sunset. At sunset, we were supposed to wash our faces, hands and feet and sit for a short Arabic and Urdu prayer with our grandmother. After that, we would finish our school homework and have dinner. Sometimes my grandmother would tell a few stories from the Arabian Nights, or her own experiences, and then off to bed.

That particular day, my sister who was more studious than me (no wonder that she became a senior Indian Administrative Services Officer), cut short her playtime and went back into the house earlier than usual. I was wandering around the courtyard doing nothing in particular. Dusk was not far from setting in. The light had mellowed to a soft golden yellow. I thought I would go home too and perhaps find some snacks in the kitchen. So I turned towards the house. However, for reasons I cannot explain to this day, I turned instead and walked towards the jackfruit tree at the far end of the courtyard. There was someone standing under the tree and was gesturing for me to come forward.

The normal instinct would have been to bolt, but instead I was surprised to find I felt no fear whatsoever. A strange eagerness to go closer to the stranger filled my heart. I quickened my steps and was soon standing in front of him. Now I could see clearly. The stranger was tall, extremely fair and his well-built muscular body was bare except for a piece of white cloth that was wrapped around his waist and reached just above his knees. He was also barefoot.

I was intrigued by this strange man who had slightly brown and thickly matted long hair gathered over his head in a big knot that looked like a tall hat. He wore large, brown, probably copper earrings and carried a black, polished water pot in his right hand. By far, the most striking of his features were his eyes: large, brownish black, glittering and overflowing with love and affection. He put his right hand on my head without any hesitation and his kind voice said in Hindi, 'Kuch yaad aaya,' which means, 'Do you remember anything?'

I understood the stranger's words perfectly, for although our family had settled in Kerala for generations, we spoke a peculiar dialect of Urdu known as Dakkhini, very similar to Hindi. 'Nai,' no, I said.

He then removed his hand from my head and stroked the middle of my chest with it, saying 'Baad mein maalum ho jaayega. Ab vapas ghar jao.' (You will understand later. Go home now.) I still did not understand what he was trying to convey, but instantly obeyed the command to go back home. As I hurried back, I felt as if his touch had made my heart lighter. Reaching the last step to the rear entrance of the house, I turned around to have a last glimpse of the stranger under the jackfruit tree, but he was gone. There was no one there.

It was also getting darker. I ran into the kitchen with great excitement. What an adventure to share with my mother and tantalise my little sister with. A lovely aroma wafted from the kitchen. My mother was cooking prawn curry for dinner. I opened my mouth to begin my story but no word would come out of my mouth. It was as if someone or something had locked my vocal chords. I tried again and gave up. By then, I was breathing hard. 'You are out of breath,' said my mother, 'What happened? Ran too fast?'

'Yes,' I heard myself saying, and realised at the same time that I could not talk only when I was trying to relate the strange experience.

On a few more occasions, I tried to tell the story and failed. Convinced that I was being prevented by some unknown power from exposing the incident, I gave up all attempts. It took ten years before I could speak about it to anyone at all. The first person I spoke to about it was none other than the stranger I had first met under the jackfruit tree—my guru, whom I met again in the Himalayas under completely different circumstances. At that meeting, I was formally accepted as a disciple; but we'll come to that later.

After the jackfruit tree incident, although outwardly I looked like any other boy of my age, my personality had undergone a profound change. A secret life went on within, side by side with the ordinary activities of day-to-day existence. The inner journey had begun, and the first sign of this was that I began to meditate without even knowing the word meditation.

It happened like this. Although I found myself unable to share the extraordinary experience that I had had, the image of those loving eyes never left my heart. One night, I fell asleep as usual beside my mother and sister thinking of this man with the kind glance. Normally I was a sound sleeper, and in the morning I had to be called many times before I would wake up. But that night was different. Around midnight, I suddenly woke up and sensed a lovely, blissful feeling in the centre of my chest. It was as if someone was tickling my heart with a soft feather. A tingling sensation began to move slowly up my spine. I wanted to sit up but felt that my mother might wake up and get curious. So still lying down, I closed my eyes and tried to look inward.

First the loving eyes appeared, then they vanished and in their place was a cool silvery light that came up my spine and filled my heart. If I had known then what an orgasm feels like, I would have called it a strange orgasm of the heart with no sexual connotations. But I was still too young to make the comparison. All I could understand was that the blissful feeling intoxicated me.

I do not know how long it lasted, this first experience of a trance. My mother's voice woke me up, 'Get up, son, it's time to get ready to go to school.' After a few gentle nudges, I opened my eyes and sat up. No bliss, no light, no tingling sensation, everything had vanished in a moment. I was off to wash, have breakfast, dress and get ready for school. Only the kind eyes still haunted me.

Every night since then, the meditation continued. I had some extraordinary experiences, which I shall relate presently. But more importantly, saintly men and evolved souls came into my life and the writings I needed to read fell into my hands, as if by providence.

a moment. I was off, to wash, have breakfast, dress and get ready for
school. Only the kind eyes still haunted me.

Every night since then, the meditation continued, I had some
extraordinary experiences, which I shall relate presently. But more
importantly, saintly men and evolved souls came into my life and the
writings I needed to read fell into my hands, as if by providence.

3

The Gayatri Mantra

I SHALL START WITH the first of my extraordinary experiences.

No one, other than those close to me like my mother and
grandmother, noticed the changes in my personality. I began to be more
introverted than I had been and my mother would often find me sitting
or standing under the jackfruit tree staring at the sky or nothing in
particular. She also used to say that I would sometimes talk in a strange
language in my sleep. However, she was relieved that I no longer suffered
from that strange malady I mentioned in the first chapter: the screaming
and running out of the house in my sleep. The ghoul-like creatures that
used to chase me and try to grab me had vanished without a trace from
the day I met the stranger under the jackfruit tree. I would also pester
my grandmother for stories of saints and Sufis. When her stock was
over, I did not mind the same stories being repeated.

I began to find great happiness while meditating at night. Many
times, I would drift into deep sleep while meditating and have vivid and
elaborate dreams. Some of these were forgotten, but some remained
deeply impressed in my mind and indicated important events that were
going to take place in my spiritual journey. One such dream occurred
three months after the jackfruit-tree incident.

I dreamt of a beautiful green valley surrounded on all sides by
towering, snow-clad mountains. At the foot of one of these peaks, there
was a cave. A melodious chant in a language I could not understand

came from inside the cave. Yet, it somehow sounded familiar. I moved towards the mouth of the cave and looked within. It was a fairly large cave. In the centre of the floor was an open fireplace with orange flames leaping from the burning logs. At the far end of the cave, on a raised platform, facing me and the fire, sat a bearded middle-aged man with long, dark hair. The lower part of his body was covered in a kind of brown tree bark and across his chest was slung a white girdle that looked like cotton rope.

He was leading a chant, which was echoed by a number of young boys—also long haired and wearing similar garments and girdles. The boys sat facing him and the fire in a semi-circle. Carried away by the chant, I suddenly found myself imitating them in a loud voice.

The chanting stopped abruptly. The eyes of the man on the platform came to rest on me. 'Come forward, young fellow,' he said. I was surprised that I understood him perfectly, although he spoke a strange language. I moved into the cave. By now, the heads of all the boys turned in my direction. I was embarrassed that I was dressed in shorts and a sleeveless vest and had close-cropped hair. The boys started giggling and whispering to each other.

'Stop!' shouted the man. The boys fell silent. 'You,' he said turning to me, 'chant.' I chanted haltingly knowing that I was totally off-key. The boys started to giggle again. 'Stop!' said the teacher, 'You have forgotten the proper way to chant. Go back home and learn how to do it.' Before I could say, 'But how?' the dream faded away and I heard my mother's voice saying, 'wake up, wake up.'

I woke up wondering about the dream. It was a Sunday and I was happy because I didn't have to go to school. I could wander around the backyard, or draw and paint, or tinker with old clocks and gadgets in the attic. After a breakfast of delicious appam, potato stew and an omelette, I sat on a big cane armchair in the hall and wondered what to do next.

My father used one corner of the hall as his office. In this corner, there stood a large rosewood desk, the drawer of which he would always keep locked. My eyes now wandered to this table and I saw that the key was sticking out of the lock. 'Perhaps the drawer was not locked,' I thought to myself. I had always been curious about what was kept inside. This was my golden opportunity. My father had gone out early in the morning for a medical checkup and the table simply beckoned to me.

In a trice, I was sitting in my father's chair, fiddling with the key. The drawer opened and I looked inside. There were all kinds of files, thick account books, bills, stamp pads, a lovely old Parker pen and some excellent pencils. Looking around to make sure that no one was watching me, I dug deeper and found, under a thick stack of files, two books. One was a small, orange booklet called *Japa Yoga and Gayatri* and the other was a well-illustrated book on yoga. It had a lot of photographs of a man in various postures, which I thought were gymnastic exercises.

I later learnt that the little booklet was by Swami Chinmayananda, a well-known teacher of Vedanta. At the time, however, I was simply fascinated by the books I had discovered. I had to find a way of appropriating them, and hoped that my father would not notice they were gone.

At this point, I must tell you something about my father. Apart from his livelihood, his main interests were body-building exercises, kalaripayattu (a Malayali version of unarmed combat and self-defense), Hindu philosophy and cinema. He had graduated in Malayalam literature from the Kerala University with Indian philosophy as his optional subject. He had an abiding interest in Vedanta and other related topics, and attended lectures on these by eminent experts. He was not overtly religious however, and the only demonstration of his Islamic roots was his joining the congregation in the Juma Masjid mosque twice every year during Ramzan and Bakri Id. Otherwise, he was a happy-go-lucky man who never missed the latest movie. Before taking to the practice of yoga, he was a heavy smoker as well. Even before he started yoga, he would be up early in the morning and exercise vigorously for an hour and a half. Sometimes he would wake me up and teach me a few simple exercises.

Of the two books I found that day in my father's table, it was the little orange booklet that interested me more than the book of exercises. But

I decided to take both of them out. Then I closed the drawer and locked it, making sure that the key was left just as I had found it. Tiptoeing down to the bedroom where I kept my schoolbag, I pushed the books into it and came out once again to the hall. Then I played and whiled away my time, waiting for an opportunity to read the booklet.

Soon after lunch, I quietly took the book out of my school bag and ran to the backyard. On the way, I saw my sister doing her homework—I would have no trouble from her. Reaching the jackfruit tree, I settled down under it and opened the book. And there it was, the mantra I had heard and tried to chant, albeit imperfectly, in my dream. I could not read the original Devanagari script well because we had just started to learn Hindi in school, but being an English-medium student, I could easily read the excellent transliteration in English:

Om Bhur-Bhuvah Svah
Tat-Savitur-Varennyam
Bhargo Devasya Dhiimahi
Dhiyo Yo Nah Pracodayaat

With the chanting of the previous night's dream resounding in my head, I could even get the right tone, pitch and cadence. Soon I was chanting as melodiously as the people in the cave from my dream and even enjoying it. I continued to practise whenever I could find a lonely spot. When there were people around, I would chant mentally. The book said it was a prayer to the sun god to illumine the intellect. Many years later, my guru interpreted the mantra for me. He said that the sun was the inner self, the core of one's consciousness, and that the last line could be more accurately translated as 'stimulate my intelligence'.

The only thing that caught my attention in the second book was a picture of the cross-legged posture called padmasana. In an illustrated children's history book, I had seen a painting of the Buddha in the same pose. I found it very easy to practise this posture and would secretly do so and imagine myself to be the Buddha. One day, my mother caught me sitting in padmasana on an old wooden chest in the storeroom.

'Who taught you this?' she asked. 'No one,' I said. 'That is yoga,' she said, and went her way.

Since my father never asked me about the books, I presumed that he had not discovered the theft. But I was waiting for a chance to put the books back, for I no longer needed them. The opportunity came when one day I saw that the key was once again in the lock. Finding no one around, I quietly opened the drawer and replaced the books exactly as they were before with a sigh of relief. My presumption, however, that my father did not know about what happened was proved wrong. One day at breakfast, my father said, 'Those books you took out of my table and read, they can only be understood with a guru's help. Don't practise anything without proper guidance. If you wish to do yoga, you can meet one Mr Sharma from East Fort who is going to come here tomorrow morning to help me with my yoga.' I was thrilled. 'Sure!' I said.

So the next day, I met Mr Sharma, a middle-aged, clean shaven Brahmin who readily agreed to teach me yoga asanas and pranayama. Within a few months, I was practising the exercises with ease. I overheard him tell my father one day, 'This fellow is good. He will go a long way if he practises daily.' I have been practising yoga since then, and perform a set of yoga asanas and breathing exercises for at least half an hour every day, even now. I attribute my good health, stamina and high spirits to the practice of yoga.

4

Meeting Yogi Gopala Saami

I WILL NOW TELL you about my encounter with a greatly evolved soul who lived not far from my house. By then, I had completed my fifth class, and since the Holy Angels' Convent did not allow boys beyond the fifth class, I was admitted to the Model High School.

The Model High School, founded by an Englishman and taken over by the government after independence, was built like an old English public school with red brick and granite, and it had extensive grounds. It was a boys' school and was well known not only for its academic excellence but also for its proficient music, drama, arts and crafts department.

The school was about three to four kilometres from my house and I was part of a large group of boys who walked to school every day and had great fun together. Two of those boys, who were senior to me, lived half a kilometre away from my house. They were brothers and were good fellows, although a bit too serious about their studies. They belonged to a Tamil-speaking emigrant family from neighbouring Tamil Nadu.

Their father was Ananthanarayana Pillai, a retired minor official in the police department. Their mother's name was Kamalamma, and she was a very loving person. The older of the two boys, Marthanda Pillai was called Periya Thambi (older boy) at home and the younger one, Sivananda Pillai, was called Chinna Thambi (small boy). Marthanda

Pillai was very studious and went on to become a neurologist—and at one time was the head of the department of neurosurgery at the Trivandrum Medical College and Hospital. He now has his own multi-speciality hospital called Ananthapuri on the outskirts of Trivandrum. Sivananda managed to become an engineer and retired as a senior engineer from the electricity department of the government of Tamil Nadu. This was remarkable considering they did not even have electricity in their home and did their homework under the light of kerosene lamps.

Periya Thambi and Chinna Thambi's family lived in a small house with a large compound, one part of which was converted into a timber shop, where firewood was sold. Mr Ananthanarayan opened the firewood shop after retirement, since in those days all houses used firewood for cooking. Initially, we only knew them because we bought firewood from the shop. But later, we discovered that the family came from a place in the Kanyakumari district in Tamil Nadu where my mother's grandfather also lived, and that the families knew each other.

The friendship was further strengthened because I went to their house almost every day to meet the thambis and walked with them to school and back. Their mother Kamalamma was a kindly soul and was very fond of me. Those days, I was very fair and had slightly chubby cheeks. I can still remember her concern when she saw my cheeks turn red when I walked to their house in the morning. Stroking them with her fingers, she would tell her daughter 'Aiyyo, look how red his cheeks have become, like tomatoes, poor boy.'

Theirs was a large family. Apart from three boys (there was a younger one called Gopal) there lived in that little house their parents and their two sisters, Syamala and Thangam. The eldest sister Shanta was married to Kolasu Pillai and lived in Suchindrum. Syamala, the older one worked as a typist in a private firm and Thangam was still in college. Syamala was married to her cousin, Mr Ramaswamy, who worked in the census department of the Government of Kerala and was an MSc in mathematics. In a way, Mr Ramaswamy was instrumental in my meeting Gopala Saami.

While in the Holy Angels' Convent, I was good in English, history and science but showed a lack of interest in mathematics.

In the new school, with the curriculum getting tougher, I had great difficulty with mathematics. Mr Ramaswamy volunteered to coach me, more for the love of his subject than for the small fee he reluctantly accepted to augment his income. The arrangement was that I would go to the Pillai residence thrice a week in the evenings.

One evening, carrying my books, I went for my tuition and saw Mr Ramaswamy standing outside the door. He told me that the class was off for that day. He had some other engagement and asked me if I could come back the next day. 'Sure,' I said, happy that I could go back home and play, 'but, where are Periya Thambi and Chinna Thambi?'

'They are inside doing something.' I was intrigued. Something strange was going on. From inside the house, came the strong smell of incense. By then, Syamala, her parents and Chinna Thambi had come out of the house, and everyone was talking in hushed tones. I decided to be direct. 'Incense smell?' I said, 'What is it?' Silence. Everyone looked at each other and finally the mother spoke, 'Saami has come. You want to see?'

Saami is the word used to address Brahmins in general. Other than that, those who took a vow, wore black and went to the Sabari Hills on pilgrimage were also known as saamis, Ayyappa Saamis. I did not know what kind of saami this was but decided to see anyway.

'Yes,' I said.

Mr Ananthanarayan said, 'wait,' and went in. In a few minutes, he came back and called me in. In the centre of a small room sat a big-built old man in an armchair, his feet resting on a footstool. He wore a blue-and-white striped half-sleeve shirt and a simple white, borderless mundu. I stood there and looked closely. His grey hair was cropped very short and his square-jawed striking face looked as if he had not shaved for some time. White stubble, a few weeks old, covered his chin, cheeks and upper lip. Everything looked quite ordinary except the ramrod-straight majestic pose. And then I saw his eyes. I had never seen such penetrating eyes before.

Involuntarily, I felt my clothes to see if they were still on me, for it felt as though I was being 'X-rayed'. Those eyes were seeing inside me, through me and I thought, 'God! This man knows all my secrets.' Then he smiled and gestured 'Varu. Come.' The voice was unexpectedly soft. I went closer and stood, almost touching the arms of the chair. He continued to smile and then stretched out his right hand and touched my forehead for a fraction of a second before he withdrew it.

Waves of indescribable bliss rose from my forehead and engulfed my body. This was different from the experience I was already having almost every night. The only way I can describe it is that it was as if the noisy waves of the ocean had suddenly been stilled and the ocean surface had become as placid as a ripple-less lake. I could hear no external sounds. From deep inside my mind rose a chant that I could not understand. Tears started flowing from my eyes. I had to get out and sit somewhere by myself. I turned and tottered out of the room. Suddenly, the silence was broken by someone saying, 'Bow down, touch his feet.' By then I was near the door, so I quickly touched the doorstep and then touched my head as I had seen others do and bolted.

I never saw this man again. I remember I ran fast and was home in minutes. No one saw me come in. Using the passage beside the compound wall, I hurried to my jackfruit tree and sat under it. By then the bliss had subsided, but the peculiar silence continued for a while until it was broken by my mother who shouted from the back door, 'What happened, no tuition?'

'No!' I shouted back.

'Come and eat something,' she said.

'Coming,' I said. My mother was fond of feeding me.

When I went the next day for tuition, Mr Ramaswamy and the others kept asking me what happened on the previous day, but I said nothing. It occurred to me that such secrets, like the ones shared by lovers, must be kept sealed like gold and precious diamonds in a treasury till the appropriate time when they can be displayed for the benefit of others.

I learnt from the Pillai family that his name was Gopala Pillai and that they called him Gopala Saami out of reverence. Many years later, I came across a collection of his teachings printed and published by one Mr Prabhu and titled *Arul Mozigal*—'Sweet Words of Wisdom.' When I turned the pages at random, the first page my eyes fell on contained Gopala Saami's favourite words, words that he repeated often: '*Anandoham, Anandoham, Achala Paroham, Achala Paroham.*'

That's when I realised that it was the same chant I heard the day I met him nearly six years ago. At that time, I could not make out the words clearly, but when I understood the meaning of the words, I felt I had experienced it, if only for a short while. It meant, 'I am bliss, I am bliss; undistracted I am, undistracted I am.'

Gopala Pillai was born in August 1900 at Kollemkode in South Travancore. His mother was Kunni Paramba Veetil Kocchu Kunjamma and his father Sri Narayana Pillai. He had two brothers and two sisters, all older than him. The family later shifted to Thiruvananthapuram (then Trivandrum). The eldest brother, Shankara Pillai, looked after the family.

According to Gopala Pillai's childhood friend, Vidhwan Sreevaraham E.V. Pillai, who retired as a headmaster, even as a student of Fort High School, Gopala Pillai's ways were strange. He would sit for long hours, meditating with open eyes and would frequently fall into a trance. Once, when he was twelve years old, he was found sitting cross-legged looking directly at the midday sun, his back bent backwards like a bow. When his elder brother Shankara Pillai was informed about it, he wrote back saying 'Don't interfere. Let him do whatever he wants.'

At twenty, when he had still not passed his secondary school examination, his mother tried to persuade him to study harder. Gopala Saami responded, 'If I want, I can pass easily, but why? Anyway, I have decided not to work for money or for profit. Somebody will look after me.' After that he stopped going to school.

In his youth, Gopala Pillai was fond of wandering in strange places. One of his favourite places was Muttathara. Before him, Sri Narayana Guru and Chattambi Swami (See 'The Story of Sri Narayana Guru', page 43), had frequented Muttathara. At Muttathara, first one walked through acres and acres of bright green paddy fields. Where the paddy fields ended, the pure white sands of the beach, with many sand dunes, began. Further up, one could see the deep blue Arabian Sea, its waves sometimes rising high and breaking noisily on the shores, and sometimes rolling gently into the sands, depositing seashells of all kinds.

His dear friend E.V. Pillai has said that he travelled with Gopala Saami to Muttathara many times. Gopala Saami talked a great deal about Vedanta while they walked through the paddy fields. Once beside the sand dunes, he would fall silent. In the Veerasana posture, he would sit motionless, with eyes open, for a long time. Before coming out of the trance, he would utter strange growling sounds and sometimes laugh loudly for no known reason, which would frighten E.V. Pillai.

E.V. Pillai also writes that beyond Muttathara, near Poonthura, there was a totally deserted forested area called Ottapana Moodu. The place was used at one time to dispose of bodies of murderers executed by the hangman of the Central Jail, and also as a dumping ground for unclaimed and decayed corpses from the government mortuary. One afternoon, he accompanied Gopala Saami there, and saw a wizened old man, with matted hair, sitting stark naked on the scorching sands. Gopala Saami and the strange creature embraced each other, and asking E.V. Pillai to wait under the shade of a tamarind tree, they walked away and entered a grove of palms at a distance.

After an hour, a tired and quite anxious E.V. Pillai went to the grove and saw both of them lying down next to each other as if in deep sleep. As he went closer, they jumped up with a start. Gopala Saami then went back home with E.V. Pillai. According to E.V. Pillai, Gopala Saami and the strange man met each other quite frequently, but any questions regarding the old man were met with total silence.

Many years later, Gopala Pillai, by then called Gopala Saami by a small circle of spiritual seekers, held classes in the middle of the night, usually at the clinic of a homeopath in the city. Here, the profound truths of Vedanta were discussed. These discussions were collected and published as *Arul Mozigal*.

Another one of Gopala Saami's haunts was Samadhi Thotam. This place was the tomb of Sri Ramdas Swami, guru of Jalandar Yogi Hari Hara Brahma Sastri, who lived during the reign of Ayyilyam Tirunaal, the Maharaja of Travancore (1805–80). It is considered a *jeeva samadhi*—a tomb into which the yogi enters voluntarily and while still alive. The yogi is sealed in by his disciples, as per their teacher's instructions. Samadhi Thotam was also the last place at which Gopala Saami conducted a formal puja. He is said to have told his close circle of followers that this was going to be the last time he would go there. The next day he had had severe abdominal pain and on the third day was operated upon. He had reluctantly agreed to the surgery after a great deal of persuasion and had said that if surgery was going to be undertaken, then it would have to be done again. As predicted, the surgeon decided that a second surgery was necessary.

While he was waiting for the second surgery, Gopala Saami is said to have sat up on his bed, taken a deep breath and fallen back. Those who attended on him thought that he was in a deep trance. When he was wheeled into the operation theatre, the surgeon and anesthetist declared him dead. That was on 8 March 1960.

5

A God-intoxicated Sufi

A MONTH OR SO after meeting Gopala Saami, my mother's uncle, my grandmother, and a distant aunt invited me to accompany them to Beema Palli.

Beema Palli is the tomb of the Muslim woman saint Beema Bibi, and is situated on the seashore not far from the Trivandrum airport. It is famous for exorcism. People who are believed to be possessed are brought from far and wide and kept there for some time—the violent ones even chained to stone or wooden pillars. Usually on Thursdays and Fridays, the poor souls go into a trance, which can at best be described as a frenzy, whirling their heads and rolling their eyes, shrieking loudly and begging Beema Bibi not to torture them; promising to quit the body they had temporarily occupied; and finally hitting their heads on the doorstep of the mausoleum and fainting. All these are supposed to be the actions of the spirit that has possessed the body of the victim. The exorcised person is said to be free of the spirit and comes back to normal once they have regained consciousness.

The Muslim fishermen who live in the locality believe that Beema Bibi was an Arab Muslim saint, whose direct intervention cured the possessed. Legend has it that the coffin with the bodies of Beema Bibi and her son was carried by the waves of the Arabian Sea and deposited on the shores at the place where her tomb now stands. The locals built a tomb for her when they discovered that people who were believed to be possessed were cured simply by touching her coffin. A mosque is attached to the tomb, which is called a dargah.

We reached the dargah on a Friday evening. The white sands of the beach were still hot as we walked across the sandy grounds towards it. Scattered across the compound were crudely built lodges for patients and their caretakers. A few coconut trees, stone and wooden pillars stood scattered here and there. We saw that a few of the sick were chained to some of the pillars and coconut trees, some of them in a pathetic state, reduced to skeletons with their desperate eyes staring out of their sockets. As we passed a woman thus chained, she bared her yellow teeth, rolled her eyes and growled at us. My aunt shrieked and jumped to the other side. Everyone laughed except me. I won't say that I was not scared, but more than fear, a deep sense of sadness filled my heart when I saw these unfortunate creatures.

We entered the dargah. The hall in front of the enclosure housing the tomb was filled with people. One side was reserved for the sick and the other for the devotees. We walked towards the tomb and waited at the door of the enclosure. The tomb was covered with bright green satin and the curtains on either side were of red velvet. The inside of the enclosure was lit with green and blue bulbs, which gave it an eerie look.

The mullah, the Islamic counterpart of the Hindu priest, received the bananas we had brought as offerings and recited verses from the Quran. We all stood with our palms held together in prayer, our heads covered with a cloth, saying 'Ameen Ameen,' till he finished. Then we rubbed our faces with our palms and received bits of consecrated dried rose petals and sugar from the mullah. We also bent our heads low and received a stroke each from the bunch of peacock feathers that the mullah used to transfer the blessings of Beema Bibi to us. My grandmother dropped some money in the box kept for the purpose and then we went and sat in the section where the non-possessed sat.

As soon as the call for prayer was heard from the adjoining mosque, many of the so-called possessed people were up on their feet as if galvanised into action. They began to make weird noises and weirder movements. The atmosphere became almost unbearable.

All of a sudden, a middle-aged man who was supposedly normal and was sitting beside us stood up and started behaving strangely. He swung his body in a circular motion and began to utter 'huum huum' just like the people on the other side. Then he stopped, turned to me and said mockingly, 'You! You! You found me out, you tried to burn me, but I won't go.' Jumping to the front, he ran towards the door of the enclosure where the tomb was. There he hit his head on the doorstep and shrieked, 'Okay, I will go. That boy found me. Bibi, I will go. Don't burn me. I am burning.' With that, he again let out a hideous howl and fainted. For the first time, I was filled with fear and loathing.

It was too much for my grandmother. "Saabjaan," she whispered to her brother, 'Let's get out of here now.' We walked out of the place with my grandmother holding my hand tightly as if she were afraid something might snatch me away. Coming out, we saw another strange sight. A naked old man with grey hair and a black scrawny beard was racing through the sands and approaching the place where we stood. He was smiling to himself, sometimes breaking into peals of laughter and gesticulating at the sky with his hands. His head kept turning up and down in a jerky motion and his body was covered in sand. White sand on a dark body!

Anyone would have mistaken him for one of the possessed but for the fact that a number of people, both men and women, were walking behind him respectfully with folded hands, trying to keep pace with him. He went past us, stopped abruptly, came back to where we were, and halted right in front of me. For a minute, his face turned serious, almost grave. Bloodshot eyes searched my face. Then he laughed again as if I looked funny and said in Tamil, 'Seri seri po po apparaon wa da' (Okay, go now come later, lad) and was off again. I was not frightened this time for some reason.

Of course, I took him to be a madman. I did not know then that the line between madness and religious ecstasy is extremely thin. Later, my mother's uncle told me that he was called Kaladi Mastan and was a man of great powers. He was inebriated by the love of God and was not fully conscious of the outside world. 'Some holy men are like that,' he said, as if that explained everything—but I understood nothing. 'But why is he naked?' I asked. 'I don't know,' said my uncle. 'Every now and then someone wraps a new dhoti around his waist and within minutes he gives it away to some poor beggar and is naked once more.'

That I understood. I hated wearing clothes, especially in summer and would have loved to give away my clothes to a poor beggar and walk around free and naked. But I knew I could not do that for I was expected to be civilised and proper.

The words he had uttered, 'Okay, come later lad,' came true years later. But I will keep that story for another chapter.

6

Inside the Subramanya Temple

SRINIVAS RAO WAS ONE of my classmates, and I was very friendly with him. He was instrumental in my entering a Hindu temple for the first time.

There were two ways to go to school: the main road which was shorter but had heavy traffic, and a windy side road, which was longer but had hardly any traffic. Some of my friends and I preferred the longer but quieter road. We would walk at leisure, throw stones to fell mangoes, and in general, satisfy our curiosity for life's new experiences.

On this road, as you climbed a slope and turned right, stood the temple of Subramanya Saami. It was on a hillock with a tiled roof, built in the Kerala style. Adjoining the temple was a large green pond with rough granite steps leading to it from all four sides. Devotees took baths in the pond, and on festival days the deity was bathed in it. Not far from the pond was the little tiled house where the priest lived with his family. Srinivas was the priest's son and he lived with his parents and his beautiful sister.

The priest, Rao, was a Tulu Brahmin from Karnataka. The Tulus speak a dialect which has no written script and is usually written in Kannada, the language of Karnataka. The Brahmins among them are called Potis in Kerala and they are very good cooks. 'Poti Hotel' is a synonym for a vegetarian restaurant.

One day, when just Srinivas and I were trudging along returning from school, Srinivas invited me to step into his house. 'You can see peacocks,' he said, for there were peacocks in their wooded compound. So I went. The garden was beautiful. The pond with its green-coloured water looked wonderful, and sure enough, there were many peacocks with long shimmering tails. Some were perched on trees, some were walking around the compound pecking at something that we could not see in the grass. One was dancing with its multicoloured tail spread out like a fan.

From inside the house, Srinivas's father came out. He was well-built, fair, wore a sacred thread across his bare chest and was in a cream silk dhoti. His hair was black and long, twisted into a knot which hung behind his neck. By far, his most striking feature was his nose—sharp, hooked and aquiline, like Julius Caesar supposedly had. His sharp eyes looked no less stern than a dictator. Honestly, I was a little intimidated.

My friend Srinivas said something in Tulu. The only word I understood was my name. His father was now looking closely at me, his expression grim. 'Muslim?' he asked.

'Yes.'

'Ummph, you like peacocks?'

'Yes.'

'God Subramanya uses the peacock to ride. He flies fast on the peacock.'

'You have seen him do that?'

He hesitated before saying, 'Everyone cannot see that, only good and holy people can. We worship his image in the temple.'

'Can I see it?'

This time his expression turned grave and I wondered if he was going to refuse. After a minute, he sighed deeply and smiled, 'I was going there anyway. Come, but you must stand outside the sanctum sanctorum and see it. No one except me is allowed to enter, okay?'

Srinivas went into his house and I went with the priest who left me in the hall and disappeared in the sanctum. After a while he threw open the heavy door. From where I stood, I could see a small idol with two smaller ones on either side. Once my eyes got accustomed to the dim light, I could see the young and chubby face of Subramanya on his peacock. He carried a spear in one hand and the other was raised in blessing. To his left and right were the images of beautiful damsels.

I felt happy that Subramanya had a clean-shaven, cheerful face in contrast to the morose, bearded God I had been accustomed to imagine, breathing fire at the slightest excuse.

'What is that weapon he is carrying?' I asked

'A *vel*, a kind of spear to protect mankind.' he said. 'Who are the two ladies on either side?'

'Wives,' said the tall priest, and added with a twinkle in his eye, 'like Muslims, our gods have many wives.'

That last comment I couldn't understand, because I didn't know that Muslims could marry more than once. But I let it go and ate the banana he threw into my hands, wondering what to do with the sacred ash he dispensed. 'You can eat it,' the priest said, 'Muslims are not supposed to rub it on their foreheads.' I ate the small pinch of ashes.

Coming out, I found Srinivas with a little coffee in a steel tumbler. 'My mother made for you,' he said. I drank the lovely south Indian coffee standing near the pond, returned the glass to Srinivas, and went on my way.

Not far away lived my friend, Shantikumar, who still happens to be a good friend. He had seen me come out of the temple. 'You went to the temple?' he asked me, sounding surprised. 'Yes,' I said, 'Srinivas called me home. I saw the deity too.'

That evening, while eating hot dosas and delicious sambhar, which my mother was serving, I asked, 'Do Muslims have many wives?'

'Yes, Muslims are allowed to do that,' she said, and then proudly declared, 'But in my family, for three generations, no one has had more than one wife.' I continued to eat, wondering how confusing it must be to have two mothers.

7

Preparation for the Ascent

I MUST LINGER A little longer at the foothills of my formative years, though I am eager to take you to the Himalayan heights. These were important years, when preparations were made for the great ascent.

Model High School was indeed a fun-filled and excellent learning experience. More than academics, which of course were in the hands of dedicated and well-trained teachers, my interests revolved around the arts and crafts, and sports and games.

There was a small group of us that progressed well in drawing, painting and carpentry (drawing and painting remain my favourite hobbies even today). Football and hockey matches were great fun too. Some of us who fancied ourselves to be tough played kabaddi in the sand pit. Kabaddi involved a lot of physical, hand-to-hand pushing and pulling and I enjoyed demonstrating the close-combat techniques that I had learnt from my father, an expert in kalari and ju-jitsu. You could throw off-balance and immobilise a bully double your size with the right technique. A small do-gooder-cum-protector group was already growing around me on account of my combat abilities and my predilection towards protecting the weak from bullies.

As I grew, so did my understanding of the new world that was unravelling before me. Old myths and stereotyped ideas were being slowly discarded. For example, most of the boys, except those whose houses were close to the school, sat together in the so-called common dining rooms situated far away from the classrooms.

These rooms were abandoned classrooms of many years ago, and with the passage of time, had become dilapidated. Inside, one would often find scorpions, centipedes and giant caterpillars which rolled themselves into tight rings if touched. At many places, there were huge cracks on the walls, and the cement flooring was damaged here and there. There were no chairs and tables, but a water tap stood outside in one corner.

For us, lunch hours were great adventures, for there were no teachers supervising. We brought our own lunches, packed by our mothers in small aluminum tiffin-boxes. My mother would pack my tiffin-box as tightly as possible with things like brain masala, liver fry, kidney fry, fish fry, omelette and so on to make sure that I had enough protein to make me strong and brainy. It was her belief that there was no substitute for meat and fish when it came to proper nourishment.

Many of my close friends those days were Palghat Iyers, Brahmins of Tamil origin whose ancestors settled in the border areas of Palghat and later migrated to other parts of Kerala. Known for their sharp intellect and resourcefulness, these Brahmins had, for generations, occupied key administrative, cultural and intellectual positions and had merged their cultural identity with the land on which they had settled to such an extent that even the Tamil language they spoke at home sounded like a Malayalam dialect. They took intense pride in declaring that they were Malayalis.

These friends of mine, Shankaranarayanan, Ananthanarayan, Vishwanath Iyer, Venkatesh, Krishnamani and some others had kind of adopted me as a part of their group. We sat together at lunchtime with our tiffin-boxes, swapped stories and had good fun while we ate.

Every now and then, one or more of these boys, attracted by the strong smell of spices that came from my tiffin-box, would peep into it, only to recoil in horror when I explained to them what was inside. I must say, to their credit, that they did not hold anything against me.

We were such fast friends that they continued to sit with me and eat their frugal fare.

I observed with wonder that their simple menu was invariably curd-rice, vegetable, and pickle, or sometimes idli and chutney or sambhar, all pure vegetarian. Simple vegetarian food day in and day out, and when the results of the annual exams or midterm tests were declared, they scored top marks in mathematics and science, while I and another friend Siddique barely managed to scrape through.

One morning when my mother was packing my lunch, pressing in as many pieces of fried fish, rice and fish curry as the tiffin-box could carry, I said, 'Ma, all your ideas about diet are bunkum. Curd-rice and pickle build as much brain power as your fish and meat.' Of course she was not convinced at all, and when I continued arguing, added that our Pakhtoon ancestors were strong because they ate meat.

I disagreed, and from then on my ideas of diet underwent a change. Proper nourishment, I believe, is necessary but vegetarian food by itself can do the job. You can eat meat if you like, but to think the human body cannot do without it is rubbish.

I must not forget to mention some of the teachers who influenced my life. On the top of the list stands Tiger Kuttan Pillai, the headmaster who taught us discipline, although he believed in the maxim 'spare the rod and spoil the child.' Others include Mr George, an Oxford-trained teacher who did an excellent job of familiarising us with the nuances of the English language; Harihara Iyer, who was actually a science teacher but whose dramatic rendering of Arthur Conan Doyle's *Hound of the Baskervilles* is still etched in my memory; Gopalkrishnan Iyer, who somehow managed to inject mathematics into my almost non-mathematical brain; Tarzan Damodaran Pillai, the biology teacher, who for the first time opened our eyes to the fact that this complex and seemingly complicated life started from a single-celled organism; Madhavan Nair, the National Cadet Corp commandant and social studies teacher, who always turned up in such spotless white and sharply creased clothes that he was nicknamed 'Ironbox'; Mr Nayakam, who became our class teacher in Class IX and who, with an almost uncanny intuition, predicted that the major interest in my life would be the search for Truth or God or whatever one called it.

On the first day he took charge of the class, he introduced himself briefly. Some of us were sniggering behind our desks for he was the first teacher we had seen with horizontal gray lines of ashes drawn across his forehead. He said that he believed in the god Shiva, and that ashes were the symbol of Shiva. Soon, the discussion drifted into religion, and after a while, he asked each of us to stand up and declare if we believed in God. All except one said that they believed in God. I was the exception. 'I don't believe in God,' I said. 'Why?' asked Mr Nayakam.

'Why not, Sir?' I said. 'I have not seen God and have no proof. When and if I do, I won't have to believe anymore. Facts don't need belief.'

After a short silence, he said, 'I had a classmate who did not believe in God. Thirty years later, I saw him with a shaven head and wearing ochre robes. He had become a monk of the Ramakrishna order. So we will see. Maybe this is the beginning of your search for God. I am glad you are honest. What's your name?' When I told him my name he looked perplexed. He probably never expected a boy belonging to my community to say that he did not believe in God. I longed to share with him what was happening to me internally almost every night, but an inexplicable force prevented me from sharing my experiences with anyone.

Last but not the least, there was Mr Kuttan Achari who taught social studies, drawing, painting and occasionally carpentry. But more than anything, he was the inspiration behind the school drama troupes. English and Malayalam plays were produced under his guidance. We, the English-medium boys enacted the court scene of Shakespeare's *Merchant of Venice*. I played the role of Antonio. Kevin Fernandez did such a good job of playing Shylock that the play was selected for the state youth festival and won awards. Kevin Fernandez later joined the Armed Forces Medical College and retired as an air commodore.

Being friendly by nature, I had many friends at school, but there were a few with whom I enjoyed a special relationship. One of them was Siddique, a Gujarati-speaking Memon whose ancestors came from Porbandar. His grandfather Abdullah Ebrahim, who owned the biggest wholesale textile shop at Chalai Bazar in Trivandrum looked like an Old Testament prophet with his flowing white beard and stern features. Siddique himself was a rather unhealthy, thin and frail boy, who even at that age suffered from a serious eye ailment and was almost going blind in one eye. I became close to him because I felt he needed protection from the bullies at school.

He lived with his parents and elder sister, not very far from my house. I visited his house often and developed a loving relationship with his mother, who loved to feed me, and detecting something in my mental makeup (although I did not utter a word about my inner life), kept me enthralled with stories of Sufi saints and healers.

Siddique travelled often to Mumbai during the holidays and I waited eagerly for his return to hear stories about the great and fascinating city of Mumbai and its forbidden pleasures, which he was an expert at recounting with great artistry. Hindi cinema's heroes and heroines, women who would sleep with you for a fee, the great Taj Mahal Hotel and the Gateway of India, were a few of Siddique's favourite themes and we, Ananthanarayan and I, found these stories quite stimulating to our adolescent minds.

There was one more minor but not so unimportant sympathetic factor. Both of us, Siddique and I, loved sambhar and idlis. Although my mother was herself an expert in making idlis and sambhar, we found our friend Ananathanarayan's mother a greater expert, being vegetarian herself, and a great host. She always welcomed us—the two Muslim friends of her son—with a smile into her orthodox Brahmin home, and fed us sumptuously with our favourite foods, topped with a great cup of hot filter coffee in a steel tumbler.

Ananthanarayan, son of Vishwanath Iyer, also had a Mumbai connection. He studied in Mumbai till his sixth standard, because his father, who worked in the Life Insurance Corporation, had been posted there. Vishwanath Iyer had come to Trivandrum with his family on being transferred.

I don't know if it was the tasty food or the attraction I felt towards his elder sister, aptly named Suvarna (gold), or both, that tempted me to visit Ananthanarayan's house frequently. I learnt many things about a Brahmin household; for instance, the fact that his mother would not be allowed to enter the kitchen when she had her menses. The food was tastier then, because Vishwanath Iyer was a better cook.

Apart from all that, something that would be of deep significance later on in my spiritual life took place in that modest little house of Vishwanath Iyer, a typist at the Life Insurance Corporation. They had a room kept exclusively for worship called the puja room. In it were pictures of many Hindu deities whose identities were explained to me with great patience. But the largest picture, which occupied a prominent position on the wall, was that of a man who looked like a Muslim fakir, wearing a tattered robe and a cloth tied round his head in a unique style.

That was the first time I was setting my eyes on a picture of the Sai Baba of Shirdi, who had passed away in 1918. Here in this Brahmin household, the fakir was being accorded all the respect given to the Hindu gods. They sang hymns in his praise, rang bells and waved the *aarti* lamps. I was intrigued, and on many Thursdays, a special day for Shirdi Sai Baba, I too joined the singing and even wrote my very first bhajan in Hindi: 'Hey Prabhu, hey Sainath.' Mr Vishwanath Iyer gave me a brief account of Shirdi Sai Baba's life and expressed his belief that he was God. I listened and wondered.

One night, while engaged in my secret spontaneous meditation, I saw the figure of Shirdi Sai Baba emerge from the customary light in my heart, stand before me and then transform itself into the figure of the strange yogi I had seen under the jackfruit tree. No one knew this for, as usual, I was unable to relate the experience to anyone. I shall reserve, for the time being, the story of my link with the Sai Baba of Shirdi, and how I visited Shirdi for the first time.

Vishwanath Iyer also played a role in my entry into the Guruvayur Krishna temple near Trichur, Kerala.

8

The Story of Sri Narayana Guru

I HAD SOME MORE close friends, like Narayana Prasad, who became a doctor, and Zakariah, whose father was an evangelist. Zakariah also became a doctor, settled abroad and went on to be personal cardiologist to the former US President George W. Bush and a fundraiser for the Republican Party. Then, there were Mohandas, Sudhir, Venkatesh (who, even then, fancied himself a scientist) and others. But the one with whom I had a special bond those days was Ranjit Sadasivan.

He joined the Model High School in class IX and was in a different section, but from the time we met, there was a mutual appreciation and affection which grew with the years. He was a brave boy who could not be cowed down by threats and was ready to fight against what he thought was injustice. He had come from a military-run school called the Sainik School and it was through him that I developed friendships with Velayudhan Nair who became an air commodore, Madhavan Nair who became a vice-admiral, Radhakrishnan who became an air vice-marshal and Mohan Chand who took voluntary retirement after the rank of wing commander and started a training school for young men who aspired to enter the portals of the Indian Military Academy.

Ranjit came from the Ezava community, which till a 150 years ago was at the lowest rung of the social ladder. Thanks to the inspiration and blessings of the great Sri Narayana Guru Swami, Ezavas shed their so-called inferior status and climbed the ladder of success. At the time

I am speaking of, they were already wealthy and educated and, socially and politically in an enviable position.

Sri Narayana Guru was born in an Ezava family in about 1854 in a village by the name of Chempazanthi on the outskirts of Trivandrum city. His father Madan Asan was not just a farmer, but also a scholar who was well versed in astronomy and Ayurvedic medicine. He was accepted as a teacher in the village. The villagers called him 'asan', the colloquial form of acharya, because he expounded the Ramayana and the Mahabharata.

One must remember that, in those days, the knowledge of Sanskrit was zealously guarded by the Namboodiri Brahmins, and non-Brahmins were barred from Vedic studies. However, Vaidyas, the practitioners of Ayurveda, learnt Sanskrit to study medical treatises—the *Charaka* and *Sushruta Samhitas*—but they were barred from going any further. Narayana lost his mother when he was fifteen or so and his father passed away when he was thirty years old. By that time Narayana, who was called Nanu, began to be addressed by some as Nanu Asan ('Nanu the Teacher'). He had turned into an itinerant teacher, living on alms, and coming home only once in many months.

He had dared to go beyond the study of Ayurveda, delving deep into the Vedic and Vedantic texts, and even taught Sanskrit to a few students who came to him. Although orthodoxy demanded the segregation of the lower castes, Nanu had found an unusual upper-class Sanskrit teacher called Raman Pillay Asan who treated everyone equally. Soon Nanu learnt poetry, drama, literary criticism and rhetoric, apart from the Upanishads, which he studied himself. He wandered far and wide, from Kanyakumari in the south to Mangalore in the north, studying, meditating and exploring his consciousness.

Two more teachers influenced Nanu. One was Kunjan Pillai, also known as Chattambi Swami, who was the head boy of the class where Sanskrit rhetoric was taught. Later on, Chattambi Swami accompanied Nanu in his wanderings. The other was a man of Tamil origin by the name of Tycaud Ayyavoo, who was the manager at the British

Resident's Bungalow in Trivandrum. From him, he learnt the esoteric yogic teachings preserved in the Tamil spiritual traditions. To sum up, he soon emerged as a man who had dived into the inner depths of his own consciousness and discovered the true all-pervading Self spoken of in the Upanishads.

The inner experience unfolded as spiritual teachings on the one hand, and social reforms on the other. Especially after his wife passed away after a brief illness (they had no children), Nanu became a full-fledged wandering monk with a large following. People called him Sri Narayana Guru. He helped renovate abandoned temples and installed deities himself without asking the Brahmins to install them, as was the custom. In one temple where the deity was missing, he installed a mirror instead, to demonstrate the Vedantic and Socratic maxim 'Man, know thyself'.

He founded an ashram at Alwaye, and another, called Shivagiri, on top of a hill at Varkala, a coastal town not far from Trivandrum. For the first time in the history of Kerala, Vedic studies were open to non-Brahmins and all castes at the Shivagiri Ashram. (I spent two months in the Shivagiri Ashram during my wanderings.)

Expressing the great Vedantic truth in simple language, he sang, 'One in kind, one in faith, one in God is man, of one same womb, one same form, differences none there are at all.' He exhorted his fellow men to shed their inferiority and rise to infinite heights. He passed away on 20 September 1928, at the age of seventy-four, leaving a rich legacy of spiritual and social wealth.

Going back to Ranjit, what endeared him to me was his ability to face even dangerous situations if it came to protecting friends. This was proved time and again even during the occasional streetfights we got involved in while we were college students, mainly to save decent friends from being harassed by anti-social elements.

Apart from that, Ranjit became what Sri Ramakrishna Paramahansa used to call a 'provider'. Later on, when I wanted to quietly disappear to solitary places, Ranjit would finance my trips and also be the only

person who knew where I was and how to contact me. He would
provide solace to my parents by saying that he was in touch with me
and could get me back in any emergency. He was always ready to help
and asked no questions. Incidentally, it was in his house that I first saw
a photograph of Sri Narayana Guru.

9

Strange and Timely Inputs

THE PROCESS OF INNER transformation had begun and, deep down, in the core of my being, the river of consciousness was silently giving birth to new tributaries which would eventually flow into the great ocean. The external inputs required for accelerating the process were provided for in strange ways.

If I needed clarification regarding the practice of yoga or the finer points of philosophy and religion, books that discussed precisely the same questions, would fall into my hands as if by magic. As I grew older and was allowed to move around on my own, I began to frequent the Trivandrum Public Library, an old Victorian building which was a virtual treasure house of ancient works on philosophy, religion and even ceremonial magic.

There was a long haired and bearded librarian whose name I don't remember now, who appointed himself my mentor and, wonder of wonders, suggested the right book at the right time. In this way, I read *The Complete Works of Swami Vivekananda*, *The Gospel of Ramakrishna*, *Isis Unveiled*, *The Secret Doctrine* by Madame Blavatsky, *The Zohar*, the Upanishads and the Bhagawad Gita, the Greek philosophers Aristotle, Plato and many others.

Two incidents were so strange that I find it hard to dismiss them as coincidences. One morning, I walked to the British Council Library, which was not too far from home, hoping to find something which would explain certain contradictions I encountered in the classic Vedantic text called *Panchadasi of Vidyaaranya*. I was browsing through the philosophy and religion section and found nothing particularly useful.

Then I saw a copy of Dr Radhakrishnan's translation and commentaries on the Upanishads in the bottom shelf and bent down to pull it out. At that exact moment, three hardbound books landed on my neck from the top shelf. After massaging my neck with my hands to get rid of the pain, I picked up the books. One was *The Perennial Philosophy* by Aldous Huxley, and the other two were volumes of *The Commentaries on Living* by J. Krishnamurti. That was my introduction to Krishnamurti, and I must say that—although I do not totally agree with Krishnamurti regarding various issues—*The Commentaries on Living* was certainly useful in resolving many a Vedantic conundrum. However, I cannot explain how the books fell, for other than me, there was nobody near that particular bookshelf.

The other incident was even stranger. I was fourteen years old and had by then read a lot of books on yoga, mysticism, religion and philosophy. The spontaneous night-time meditation on the light that appeared in the centre of my chest continued, but I was faced with a peculiar problem which was to me very serious. Different teachers and different texts gave different locations for the heart centre. Ramana Maharishi insisted that the heart centre was on the right side of the chest, the Kabir Panthis and even Ramakrishna Paramahansa mentioned the left side of the chest close to the actual heart.

Many yogic texts including the *Hatha Yoga Pradeepika*, located the heart centre in the centre of the chest and called it the 'Anahata Chakra' (the centre which had automatically been activated in me). What was perplexing was the fact that spiritual stalwarts like Ramana Maharishi and Ramakrishna Paramahansa, who one would think had reached great heights of personal spiritual experience should contradict each other on the location of a very important psychic centre. If one was right, then the other was wrong. I began to have serious doubts about the existence of these centres. Was it all imagination; mine as well as that of others?

I think that was the first serious crisis in my spiritual journey and I decided that I must sort it out immediately. I worked out a plan. My tuition teacher Mr Ramaswamy, had by then shifted to a place called Manacaud far away from my house. I had therefore stopped going there. One day, I informed his brother-in-law who was in school with me that I would like to consult Mr Ramaswamy regarding certain problems in mathematics. I then went home and told my parents the same thing, adding that if it got too late, I would sleep there and come home the next morning which was a Sunday.

That was going to be the first night I was spending outside my house. After initially expressing some apprehension, my mother finally let me go. Actually, I did have some problems with geometry, which I knew could only be solved with Mr Ramaswamy's help—but that was only half the truth.

The other half was that not very far from Mr Ramaswamy's house in Manacaud was an isolated grove called the Samadhi Thotam. My intention was to finish the tuition early and then walk up to the Samadhi Thotam and spend the night there. Before I continue narrating my nocturnal adventure, I must tell you something about Samadhi Thotam and why I wanted to go there.

In a remote and lonely corner of Manacaud, there was an untended grove of coconut and other trees, frequented by dogs and jackals. In it, under an ancient banyan tree, stood the samadhi of a great yogi, Sri Ramadasa Swami, who had lived during the reign of Maharaja Ayillyam Tirunal of Trivandrum, (1865–80). As mentioned earlier, a samadhi is a grave that holy men and yogis supposedly enter into voluntarily.

Jeeva Samadhis were even more special as the yogi is believed to have entered it while still living, sitting in the cross-legged Buddha pose while his disciples seal the grave. The samadhi at Manacaud was considered a Jeeva Samadhi, and I had heard that great yogis in the past, including Sri Gopala Saami had meditated in the Samadhi Thotam at night and had had illuminating spiritual experiences. I thought I would do the same, and perhaps get an answer to the problem that was confusing me. Of course, I did not mention anything about the Samadhi Thotam to my tuition teacher or his household.

I got into a bus and alighted at the East Fort terminus. Then I walked up to Mr Ramaswamy's residence. I must have reached there around 7 p.m. By the time the tuition was over, it was 8 p.m. Mr Ramaswamy's household insisted that I stay there for the night, but I excused myself saying that I could find a bus and managed to get out. That Mr Ramaswamy's household did not have a telephone was a great consolation. My parents would not know that I did not spend the night there.

My friend Marthanda Pillai walked with me some distance, but I managed to shake him off and proceeded alone to the Samadhi Thotam. I had to make a few enquiries before I finally reached the place. It must have been around 9.30 p.m. or so, but I could not say with accuracy because I did not have a watch.

The small gate was open. There were no lights inside except for an oil lamp in front of the cubical Samadhi structure. The flame flickered in the wind. I was quite scared. Jackals howled not very far away. There were no human beings in sight, and in the dim light, I imagined strange creatures lurking among the trees and bushes which swayed in the wind. I sat down at the back of the Samadhi, somewhat shielded from the wind which had suddenly begun to blow strongly. An otherworldly peace enveloped my being as the half-moon slowly came out of the clouds. I leaned against the Samadhi and soon fell asleep as I was quite tired.

I can't say how long I must have slept. I woke up with a start when I felt someone or something shaking my legs violently. As I sat up my hair stood on end and I had goosebumps all over. I was petrified for there, near me, sat a creature who can best be described as grotesque and frightening. I saw a thin, almost skeletal, dark-complexioned naked man, with large, sunken eyes, long matted hair and a long beard. His only redeeming feature was the strong smell of sweet incense that seemed to emanate from his unwashed body.

'Don't fear,' he told me in Malayalam, tapping my shoulder with his thin, long-nailed fingers, then broke into a spell of eerie laughter showing his yellow teeth.

'Who are you?' I asked emboldened by his friendly gesture.

'Me? Ha ha, nobody, nobody, only smoke and vapour.' I kept silent. 'So you have a problem, yeah? Don't know where the heart lotus is, yeah? It is everywhere, here, there, everywhere. Ha ha, manifested in different centres for different people. No controversy.'

Then he tapped me in the middle of my chest and said, 'Yours, right here, anahata—you stick to it, Babaji's orders.' A violet light that I had never seen before filled my heart centre. Even with my eyes open I could feel it. Before I could respond to his words in any way, he abruptly jumped up and ran into the darkness. I thought that, far away, a white flame leapt up from the ground—or was I imagining it? That was the last I saw of him.

My eyes still open, I enjoyed the joy of the violet glow. No more afraid. Slowly, dawn vanquished the darkness of the night. With that, the violet flame also subsided. I stood up. Not a soul in sight. I walked nearly three kilometres. Luckily, I found a bus, alighted near the tamarind-tree bus stop, and went home. No questions asked except for my mother's, 'How was tuition?' I said, 'Okay.'

'Go now, take a bath and have your breakfast. I have made iddiyappam and potato curry.'

As I had my breakfast, my mind was still lost in the adventure of the night.

10

The Mastan's Blessings

AT FOURTEEN-AND-A-HALF YEARS, I cleared my SSLC (high school) missing a first grade by nine marks; reason—instead of working hard on Mathematics and Hindi, I was fully immersed in reading an English translation of the *Panchadasi of Vidyaaranya*, a treatise on Vedanta.

I was amongst a small group of boys whose parents opted to send us to the Loyola College, which had just been established at Sreekaryam on the outskirts of Trivandrum. Others went to the government intermediate college, to the Mar Ivanius, and the Mahatma Gandhi College. Some old friendships faded and new ones were made. A few of my old friends stayed in the Loyola College hostel. I decided to be a day scholar. It took me more than an hour to reach college by bus.

I must not forget to mention my friends: Thomas Kurien, Raja Raja Verma, Johnny Joseph and Narayanan. I was beginning to be on my own, and was able to stay away from home for short periods, if I found it necessary, under some excuse or the other. It was during these years, from the age of fourteen to nineteen, that I was exposed and subjected to a host of experiences both mundane and supra-mundane.

In retrospect, I am convinced that all that was required to mature the mind and strengthen it to ascend to higher spiritual dimensions—which would have required a dozen years or more under normal circumstances—was concentrated to come my way in just five years.

At the mundane level, I was led to taste all that is considered forbidden; drugs, drinks and all the other things that many teenagers indulge in at that age, and yet, I was pulled out in the nick of time. Someone or something was watching over and protecting me. My teacher would later refer to this period as the tantric phase. Even today, I consider every friend and associate of mine who contributed to my experiences during that phase as an upa-guru or associate-teacher and thank him or her, wholeheartedly.

Little did I know then that later in life, drunks, drug addicts, Casanovas and deviants of various colours and shades would come to me for succour. If it had not been for those five years of intense exposure, I would not have been able to understand or help them in any way, and worse, might have even been tempted to fall into their terrible and miserable ways of life.

Regarding what happened at the spiritual level, I shall go into a little more in detail, since this is meant to be a spiritual biography.

First, I must tell you about my meeting with Kaladi Mastan. If you remember, I had mentioned in chapter five, how I met someone who appeared to be a madman, outside the Sufi saint's tomb at the seashore. He had looked at my face, laughed and said, 'Okay go and come later, lad.' I had not given much importance to it then, but nearly six or seven years later, I came face to face with the same person. This was our second meeting.

At sixteen, close to the end of my first year in college, I joined the National Cadet Corps and was selected for an army attachment camp at the Mahatma Gandhi College campus. After three days of attending the camp, I applied for sick leave, complaining of fever, headache and joint pain. The leave was granted, and I walked out of the camp. Just outside the campus, I discovered to my surprise that I was fine. At home, everyone thought that I would be back in a week. There was plenty of time and I decided to wander a bit. Changing two buses, I reached the seashore tomb and shrine of Beema Palli in the afternoon.

Standing before the entrance to the shrine I noticed that the influence of organised religion had penetrated even in what was once a remote seaside hamlet. In place of the little mosque beside the shrine stood a huge, colourful mosque, built probably with contributions from expatriates. It was a Friday, and sensing the commotion inside the shrine created by those who believed themselves possessed, I decided not to enter. Lugging my army style hold-all, I walked across the sands and crossed the road, looking for a tea shop. I thought I needed a strong cup of tea first.

There was one right in front called the Dargah Tea Stall. It was a thatched structure with a small raised verandah in front. As I walked towards it, I noticed that there was a small crowd of about a dozen people standing silently around the verandah, with their backs turned towards me. I joined the group and found that they were all looking at a dirty looking, thin, naked man, crouching on the floor and laughing to himself.

His grey hair was cut short in a summer cut and his dark face was framed by a trimmed white beard, but the eyes were fascinating, large and loving—and they were now glancing at me. A scene flashed in my mind's eye. I suddenly realised that this was the same man, and that I had come back as he had predicted.

His first words to me confirmed the same. Staring into my eyes, he said, 'Vanditaan, sonna madiri, vanditaan…' (He has come, just as I said), and burst out laughing. 'Big thief,' he said between guffaws, 'come to steal my treasure.'

Recovering quickly from the initial shock, I noticed that he was drinking tea from a glass tumbler and smoking a cigarette, which someone lit for him. He threw away the cigarette and gestured, 'Sit down, here.'

I threw the hold-all on the verandah and sat down on the floor. 'All go away,' he said in Tamil and the crowd melted away. The proprietor of the tea shop got him a fresh cup of tea. 'Give him money,' the old man said. I paid half a rupee. He drank half the tea and commanded me to drink the rest. Seeing his yellow teeth, which looked like they had never been brushed all his life, I hesitated. The tea shop owner whispered, 'Drink, drink, you don't know how lucky you are. Rarely does he do this.' Why not, I said to myself, and mainly out of love for those affectionate eyes, I closed my eyes and drank up the tea. By then, it was growing dark. The old man jumped up, shouted, 'Come, come!' and started running. Forgetting all about my regulation hold-all, I ran behind him.

Soon we came to the seashore. He stopped in front of an abandoned fisherman's hut with half its roof blown off, and sat down on the dilapidated verandah facing the sea. Sit,' he said. I sat cross-legged near him. Both of us faced the Arabian Sea. 'He came from the Himalayas, no?' he said.

'Who?'

'He touched your head, very fair, matted hair.'

'Yes,' I said, wondering how he knew.

'Okay, now I will touch your head. Big thief, come to steal my treasure.'

'Sorry,' I said angry this time, 'I am not a thief, I haven't stolen anything.'

'Like Kannan, Krishnan, stealing butter, stealing the hearts of gopis. Stealing loving glances. Stealing! Big Thief.'

'So?'

'Aha, Aha,' he said, and touched my chest and then my forehead with the fingers of his right hand.

First, a silvery light flooded my heart and then exploded into my head. I forgot everything except the presence of that light, which was flowing up and down between my forehead and my heart. Waves of ecstasy filled my heart and from there my entire body. My hair stood on end, and I wanted to embrace the whole world. I do not know how long I sat there or what happened in the outside world.

When the ecstasy subsided somewhat, I opened my eyes and found myself sitting inside the fisherman's hut. The old man was sitting near me and pouring a bucket of sand on my head saying, 'Enough, enough. Come back, poor little boy.'

Wiping the sand from my face, I stood up and realised that I was naked. Embarrassed, I asked, 'Where are my clothes?'

'All are here. You go and take a bath'. said the owner of the tea shop, who was standing beside me. He gave me a towel to wrap around myself and took me to his house for a bath. Dawn was breaking, and as I bathed, I could still feel mild waves of bliss in my heart centre. When I had finished, the tea shop owner, Hamid, gave me my clothes, which he had washed, ironed and kept ready. I wore them and stepped out.

Hamid told me that I had been in a mad ecstasy for four days, and had to be physically restrained from wandering around naked. On the old man's instructions, he had kept my hold-all and the money I had in my pocket safe. 'Mastan Sahib is waiting outside,' he said, 'hurry up.'

Kaladi Mastan Sahib, as Hamid called him, was sitting outside on the verandah of the tea shop. He never went into a shop or home. Seeing me, he burst out laughing and said, 'Puthu Maaplai'—new bridegroom—'Big Thief. Don't come back here. No more treasure. Go.' I bent down and kissed his dirty, holy feet. He stood up naked as ever and ran away. Circumstances prevented me from going to Kaladi Mastan after that, and when I finally went after several years, I could only see his tomb.

After serving me breakfast, Hamid told me what he knew of Kaladi Mastan, which was very little. He had suddenly appeared some years ago, naked and unwashed, like a newborn child, and had for a long time been mistaken for a madman. Once a big storm hit the area and the main high-tension electric line broke and fell on the flooded road. All traffic was disrupted and no one could move across the road. Anyone coming in contact with the water was sure to be electrocuted. Two people had already died, and the fire services, the army and the police had set up a barrier to prevent people and cattle from walking into certain death.

Onlookers were shocked to see Kaladi Mastan running fast, jumping the barrier and before anyone could prevent him, walk through knee deep water. What astonished them beyond measure was that instead of being electrocuted, he emerged unscathed and nonchalantly walked away towards the sea. A soldier was the first one to touch his feet and prostrate before him.

From then on, he became popular amongst locals. People started providing him with tea, which he drank frequently. He rarely ate, sometimes smoked, and resisted all attempts to clothe him. The ultra-orthodox Muslim kept away from him, for it was against Islamic law to walk around naked. Those who had some understanding of Sufi teachings compared him with Rabia and the naked Mansoor al-Hallaj and accorded him all the respect due to a saint. The Hindu fishermen considered him an Avadhoota, an ecstatic saint who had freed himself from all social norms and customs.

In general, most of the people of that little village believed that feeding him brought them luck. Hamid claimed that Mastan Sahib—meaning intoxicated saint—was a great Sufi master who came from Kaladi in Tamil Nadu. Unknown to the general public, he had a small circle of disciples of which Hamid was one. He believed that the Mastan had specifically blessed me to prepare me for greater spiritual unfoldment. Hamid died a year after the incident I have described.

11

Three Monks

I WILL NOW TELL you about my association with certain special people. Three of these were monks, each quite different from the other. They were Swami Abhedananda, Chempazanthi Swami, and Swami Tapasyananda of the Ramakrishna Mission. If you remember, in chapter one, I had described my first encounter with Hindu devotional practices and how, overwhelmed by the rhythm of the mridangam and cymbals, I had run out of the house and seen a small group singing and dancing around a tall and handsome man with a flowing beard.

That was Swami Abhedananda.

Swami Abhedananda had his ashram in the East Fort area. Having by then acquired a bicycle, I celebrated my newfound mobility by cycling to East Fort quite regularly. The East Fort was built by the Maharajas of Travancore to protect the temple of Sri Padmanabha, and was a residential area, called the agraharam, for Brahmins. Eventually, it became a small township with shops, restaurants and large jewellery shops. The temple pond mercifully exists even today.

On the western side of the pond stood the Abhedananda Ashram. Those days, the only buildings in the ashram were the swami's modest dwelling, a few lodging units for the small number of permanent residents, an open-air auditorium, and a temple of Radha-Krishna facing a tiny hall used for kirtan.

Swami Abhedananda was a renunciant, a monk who had renounced everything including most of his clothes, and wore only a loincloth. When I went to see him, he was around fifty-five years of age and had settled down after wandering on foot to all the pilgrimage centres in India, including the Himalayan shrines.

He was tall, fair and very handsome, with curly hair touching his shoulders and a salt-and-pepper beard that gave him a royal look. He was the most tender-hearted human being I have ever seen, and his words were always soft and loving. He was not an intellectually inclined Vedantin, but a man soaked with devotion, a bhakta who loved the amorous cowherd-god Krishna and had surrendered totally to him.

It was from him that I learnt the concept of 'Madhura Bhava', which involves thinking of oneself as a female lover of Krishna, like the cowherding gopis of Brindavan. When he sang devotional songs, his voice turned female in tone and pitch. Shedding tears of devotion, he would fall into a trance.

Whenever I visited the ashram, I had free access to the swami, except when he rested. Sitting alongside a small group of his devotees, I enjoyed the discussions. Devotion was the main theme. The swami welcomed me always with a smile, and would not let me go without eating lunch with him.

One Friday, I went in at around 11 a.m. and found the swami all alone. He welcomed me as if he was expecting me. He then got up from the armchair in which he had been sitting and sat on the floor very close to me. With his eyes full of affection, he touched my chin and said, 'Love is all that is required. All arguments and discussions fail to reach the unlimited. Only love does. Open your heart and see Krishna. Love him like the gopis.'

Then, resting his hand on my shoulder, he fell into a trance. Tears rolled down his cheeks. After a while, his body shuddered all of a sudden, and with that he was back to normal consciousness. 'You will travel far to the Himalayas,' he said, 'The Guru awaits you. Take care, and may Radha-Krishna protect you.' He wept and blessed me, placing his hands on my head.

That night, during my customary meditation, I had an unusual vision. I was in a beautiful wooded countryside with a river flowing by. From far away came the incredibly sweet music of a flute. Hearing female laughter, I looked around and found half-a-dozen lovely damsels barely in their teens, colourfully dressed and ornamented standing near me. 'Go,' said one of them teasing me, 'the God of love, your lover Krishna is summoning you with his flute.' The others giggled in excitement. I looked at my bangled wrists and jingling anklets and suddenly realised that I was one of the damsels.

'Here,' said one of my companions, 'take a look at the mirror and touch up your make-up.' She handed me a round mirror. I looked and saw a pretty, bejeweled young girl smiling at me. Suddenly, I was embarrassed. In the mirror, I could see my cheeks blushing. 'She's blushing!' my companions said, giggling. I looked at my arched eyebrows, heavy lashes and red lips. Everything was fine. I was ready to meet my beloved.

I trembled, shy and excited. Then the music stopped. A strong scent of sandal paste filled the air. Someone held my shoulders from behind. The girls ran away, their anklets and bangles jingling. I turned and looked into the lotus eyes of my dark lover Krishna, and fainted. When I woke up, it was morning. Only once more in my life did I have a similar experience. That was in Brindavan many years later.

Swami Abhedananda was the first to introduce Nagara Sankirtan, or congregational singing, in the city of Trivandrum. He was also the first to start Akhanda Nama Sankirtan, the chanting of the holy names of the deity without pause. It continues even today. People chant in shifts at the Abhedananda Ashram. The chanting never stops.

It is not for us to discuss the merits or demerits of such practices; perhaps it is useful for some. But Swami Abhedananda's simple, child-like, devotional temperament invoked a deep, devotional attitude in me, which was hidden so deep in the recesses of my consciousness that I was not aware of it myself.

Chempazanthi Swami was different. He was quite unimpressive to look at. His body was thin, almost skeletal, and his matted hair was wrapped around his head like a strange hat. He was not handsome in the conventional sense of the term and hardly spoke. Anyone meeting him on the street would have mistaken him for a madman. He usually wrapped a white towel around his waist and squatted in a small thatched shed.

Chempazanthi is the name of a small village on the outskirts of Trivandrum city that was already well-known for being the birthplace of Sri Narayana Guru. Loyola College, where I did my pre-degree, was not far from Chempazanthi, so one afternoon I went there to see if I could meet the swami.

We had by then shifted to a new house and one of our neighbours had mentioned the swami's name. From this neighbour, whose name I have now forgotten, I learnt that the swami previously ran a tea shop in the village of Chempazanthi. One night, a wandering sadhu from the north initiated him into the mantra of Sri Rama. Chanting the name continuously, Chempazanthi Swami found that soon the name took over, and he became too intoxicated to do any physical activity. He gave up the tea shop and spent a long time living in the woods nearby.

Sometimes, the mood of Hanuman—the monkey god and devotee of Rama—would take over him. He would start behaving like a monkey, living on branches, eating nuts, and swinging from one tree to another. It is said that after having a vision of his deity Rama, he came down from the trees and started living in the thatched hut beside a tiny temple of Rama. That was where I went to meet him.

There was just one man outside the hut, and when I explained my intention, he went into the hut and came back in no time. 'You can go in,' he said simply. On a raised mud and cow-dung plastered platform, I saw the frail, matted-haired Swami. He was squatting on a bamboo mat. "Come," he gestured without any fancy introductions. I went near him. 'Sit,' he said. I sat down in front of him.

'Ramayanam,' he said, looking sharply at me.

'I have read it,' I said, 'but I...'

'Not enough,' he said, cutting me short.

'Then?'

'Raa-maayanam,' he said.

This time I got it. The emphasis was clear. He was not talking of the epic Ramayana. He had split the word into two: 'raa' and 'maayanam'. He added, 'Raa means night, darkness, "irrtu". That darkness must go. Then you will see Rama.'

I could not believe my ears. Here was an illiterate former tea-maker presenting the great truth of Vedanta in such simple terms. The darkness of ignorance must go before one saw Rama, the Truth. Was this the same man who jumped from tree to tree, ate nuts and behaved like a monkey?

He went into silence. I waited for well over half an hour before deciding to leave. I stood up to bid farewell and touched his feet. He produced a distinctly monkey-like sound and touched my forehead with the index finger of his right hand. I walked out of the place and hurried to the bus stand for it was already quite late. Sitting in the bus, I kept thinking, the darkness must go, yes, the darkness must go.

Swami Tapasyananda was quite different from both these souls. He was then the President of the Ramakrishna Mission situated at Sasthamangalam. The Ramakrishna Mission also ran a free hospital. I had read about the great Saint Ramakrishna Paramahansa and his illustrious disciple, the incomparable Swami Vivekananda, but did not know of the existence of a branch of the Ramakrishna Mission in Trivandrum. This is how I discovered its existence.

Not far from the Trivandrum Public Library, where I had first read the wonderful set of books called *The Complete Works of Swami Vivekananda*, is a beautiful garden called the Museum Garden. It was my habit to walk from the library to the gardens and sit quietly on one of the benches there. One day, I met a young ochre-clad *sanyasin* with a shining face. Curious, I asked him who he was. He laughed like a child and said that he was from the Ramakrishna Mission. It was not too far away. I asked him if I could visit the ashram.

'Sure. You should,' he said laughing again, 'and you must meet our head, Swami Tapasyananda, great soul. Come sometime. My name is Golakananda.'

So one Sunday morning, I went. Swami Golakananda introduced me to Swami Tapasyanandaji. He was dressed in an ochre kurta and dhoti like all monks of the Ramakrishna order, and the first impression one got was that of sternness and discipline. Over time however, I sensed a tenderness and affection that was well hidden by a deliberately constructed facade. I learnt many things from him, especially about the Ramakrishna–Vivekananda movement; and for the first time, I understood Swami Vivekananda's dictum that service to mankind is service to God. I realised how the loving heart of the great monk Vivekananda bled for suffering humanity. Tapasyananda enlightened me about the Ramakrishna movement and the stalwarts who worked tirelessly under the command of Swami Vivekananda, the greatest among Ramakrishna's disciples.

He himself was a disciple of Swami Shivananda, better known as Mahapurush Maharaj, a direct disciple of Sri Ramakrishna Paramahansa. He had also served Sarada Devi, the spouse of Sri Ramakrishna, for many years and had been blessed by her many times.

It was Swami Tapasyanandaji who introduced me to Professor Balakrishnan Nair who, according to him, had ascended the dizzy heights of Vedanta even whilst leading a family life with wife and children. Many a Sunday, on my way to the Shangumukham Beach to practise kalari, I would drop in at Professor Balakrishnan Nair's house, and listen to him expounding the Vedantic teachings in simple language, mostly using the parables of Sri Ramakrishna Paramahansa.

Many years later, when Swami Tapasyananda was the head of the Ramakrishna Mission at Chennai and also the vice-pesident of the Ramakrishna Order, he graciously initiated me into the Ramakrishna mantra, which had evaded me even though I had spent some time as an acolyte of the Ramakrishna Order at its different centres. I am eternally obliged to him for this.

12

Mai Ma

NOW, I MUST TELL you about that strange, naked being, Mai Ma, and my meeting with her. I first heard of Mai Ma from Mr Ananthanarayana Pillai in whose house, if you remember, I met Gopala Saami for the first time. He said that she was an Avadhoota, a spiritually advanced person, who cared nothing for the niceties of social behaviour, and lived naked on the sands of the Kanyakumari beach with a number of stray dogs for companions.

Two days after getting this information, I boarded an early morning bus from Trivandrum bound for Kanyakumari. It was a hot summer Sunday. The bus reached Kanyakumari a little before noon. Kanyakumari, Cape Comorin, lies on the southernmost tip of India. The Bay of Bengal, Indian Ocean and the Arabian Sea all mingle here.

It is a beautiful place, especially at sunset, sunrise, and on full moon nights. At the time of which I am speaking, it was still free of man-made brick and cement structures that rob a place of its natural beauty and sanctity. One could still, at low tide, swim across to the large boulder in the ocean called Vivekananda Rock and meditate amongst the majesty of the thundering waves. It was while meditating here that Swami Vivekananda received the inspiration to work for the poor and downtrodden.

The legendary temple of the virgin goddess, Kanya Kumari, stands facing the sea. It is said that in the olden days, a precious diamond set in the deity's nose ring served as a beacon, helping sailors navigate their vessels. Like all legends, we have no way to prove or disprove this story. Perhaps there was such a precious diamond then, but now it has disappeared. Even goddesses can be victims of human greed.

I decided to first visit the temple, since I knew that it closed at midday. I found the deity very beautiful even with the lowly, artificial diamond in her nose ring. As usual, the priest eyed the money in my pocket and waved the lamp in front of the goddess. I dropped a rupee into the plate held out, picked up the jamanthi flower and sandalwood paste, and bowed low before walking out.

Now I had to find Mai Ma. But then I was suddenly feeling very hungry, as I had not had breakfast. I thought I would go to a restaurant, eat something and also make enquiries. I entered the first restaurant I saw, Hotel Murugavilas, and sat at the table nearest to the cash counter. As I tucked into delicious dosas, I spoke to the grey haired, spectacled man at the counter who had a walrus moustache and a gold wristwatch and seemed to be the owner of the restaurant. 'Yes,' he said, 'I know of Mai Ma.' I asked him if he knew where she came from. 'Nobody knows,' he said, 'she just appeared in Kanyakumari some thirty years ago.' He said that she had looked the same since he first set eyes on her in his childhood. She rarely wore clothes and was always surrounded by a cordon of stray dogs with whom she shared her meals.

We were then joined by a middle-aged waiter who claimed that she was the mother of the universe in human form. I asked him how he knew this, and he said that he had had many experiences that he could not take lightly.

I asked where she got food from. They told me that at first, people thought she was mad, and refused to feed her. She is said to have walked to the sea, caught fish with her bare hands, heaped wet seaweed on the fish, and blown a few times into the heap. Lo and behold, fire burst forth and the fish was roasted enough to be eaten.

After this, some people began to give her food. Many restaurant owners now believed that if she went to a restaurant and begged for food, that was a sure sign of good luck for them, and they fed her sumptuously. However, she rarely did this.

I asked where I could find her and was advised to walk down the rocky ledge beyond the temple. She was usually found sitting with her dogs, hidden by the boulders scattered across the shoreline.

I parcelled some dosas as advised by my informants, and set out to find the elusive Mai Ma. By then, the sand was burning hot and I was glad that I was wearing sandals. I walked down the shoreline, sometimes on sand and sometimes climbing up and down the rocks, until I heard the snarling of dogs and stopped.

Half a dozen dogs of all colours and sizes stood in a semi-circle in front of a large boulder and snarled at me, baring their teeth. I could do nothing but stop and stare at them, hoping that they would not attack me. From behind the boulder came the sound of a musical, singsong female voice. I could not understand the words but the sounds were soothing. The dogs stopped snarling and slunk away behind the rocks. Emboldened, I moved forward and looked behind the boulder.

There she sat, leaning against another rock, naked as a babe. I could not help wondering how beautiful that sunburnt and darkened face must have been at one time. Her grey, unwashed hair was thick and abundant. When she smiled her face shone brightly. Her eyes... Oh! How can I describe them?

'Aao,' she said, like a doting mother calling her child.

I surprised myself by bursting into tears and crying like an infant. My whole body shook as the sobs seemed to push forth from some deep cavity in my heart. I wanted to suck those breasts and drink the milk of human kindness, but my upbringing prevented me.

Mai Ma put forth her hands and caressed every inch of my body lovingly. She kept saying something unintelligible in that musical voice of hers. After a while, I felt light, as if the shedding of the tears had washed all the burdens away. I pulled myself together and, remembering the dosas I had brought, offered them to her.

She opened the packet and, keeping one dosa for herself, distributed the rest to her dog companions. One piece she put into my mouth, patted my face and said one word which I understood. 'Jao, Jao.' Go. Taking that as a signal of dismissal, I prostrated full length at her feet, got up, and walked away.

As I walked towards the bus stand, I could see the Vivekananda Rock far away, washed repeatedly by the waves of all three seas. I wondered if Swami Vivekananda had felt similar emotions when he met his beloved Sri Ramakrishna. A Trivandrum-bound bus was waiting.

I reached home quite late. My mother was still awake. She heated dinner, placed the food on the dining table, and went back to the bedroom. No questions were asked. All she said before leaving was, 'It's late. Eat and sleep now.'

That night, I had a vision. At the centre of a junction stood a gigantic banyan tree. I sat under it, cross-legged in the Buddha posture. I was thin and bare-bodied except for a kaupin, and had matted hair and a black beard.

From one of the roads, came someone with a crude walking stick. As she came closer, I recognised her as Mai Ma, but now she was dressed in a purple sari. As I looked at her, she suddenly grew tall, almost as tall as the banyan tree. She smiled down at me and said, 'I am hungry, give me something to eat.' I was in a fix, because I did not remember having any food with me.

'Look in your begging bowl,' she said. I looked and found one grain of rice which I offered to her apologetically. She ate it with great relish and then touched my forehead with her right hand. 'Close your eyes,' she said. A wave of indefinable bliss entered my body from my forehead and permeated every single cell. Then I woke up. It was well past dawn and, wonder of wonders, my body was still pulsating with such bliss that, like a drunk, I could hardly stand steadily on my feet.

Somehow, I tottered towards the bathroom, relieved myself and went back to bed. I told my mother that I wasn't feeling well and I would not be able to go to college. She felt my forehead and thought I had high temperature. I got only kanji for breakfast that morning. By evening, the sensation had subsided and I was back to normal. The memory remained forever.

13

Understanding Holy Madness

I MUST MENTION ONE more strange encounter before we move along. I heard from a carpenter known to us that a strange holy man who kicked people lived in Poonthura, not far from Beema Palli, where I had met Kaladi Mastan. One Friday, during the Christmas vacation, my curiosity overcame my reluctance to visit an eccentric, and I took a morning bus to Poonthura. Arriving there, I found a small group of people standing around a weird man who squatted on the sand.

His emaciated dark body, naked except for a loincloth, had layers of dirt on it. His matted hair and beard were so long that they touched the ground, and his wild eyes were frightening. They shifted constantly, like those of a trapped animal. I too joined the group. After a while, just as I was thinking it was wiser to leave, the strange man gestured for me to come closer. I hesitated, and someone standing near me said, 'Go, go, good fortune.'

Reluctantly, I moved forward and stood close to him. He gestured for me to bend down. I knelt and bent my head towards his face expecting to be hit by a concentrated whiff of foul odour. Surprisingly, all I got was the scent of incense. But something else hit me, and hit me hard too.

Without warning, the strange man leaned on his elbows and landed a solid kick on my right cheek. I saw a flash, fell to the ground, and rolled over once. Then I stood up and rubbed my cheek. No words were exchanged between us. The swami seemed to have lost interest in me and was looking elsewhere. Seeing that there was no point in hanging around, I walked away and went to the bus stop.

As I got on the bus, I realised that the ache I had on the right side of the lower part of my back, which I had developed a few months ago because of falling while practising the topsyturvy Sirshasana, had vanished completely. I debated going back to thank him, but the bus started moving. I thanked the strange man mentally, and never saw him again. What effect Poonthura Swami had on my spiritual evolution I cannot say, but being skeptical by nature, I wondered if the back pain cure was a mere fluke.

Having read the above descriptions of my encounters, you will probably wonder why many of these characters I met seemed to lead abnormal lives—naked, dirty, behaving in strange ways. In the Hindu tradition, such seemingly insane holy men and women are called Avadhootas, and in the Sufi tradition they are called Masts or Mastans.

The Avadhootas and Mastans are said to be a category of spiritually advanced beings who, by virtue of their communion with Unconditional Truth, have freed themselves from all conditions imposed upon human beings by so called civilised society. Breaking free from all norms of normal social behaviour, they are more like the insane than the sane. One of them, when questioned about his insane ways, is said to have remarked that he is yet to find a sane person anywhere on the earth. 'Everyone,' he said, 'is mad about something or the other.' According to him, the only difference between those inside an institution for the insane, and those who are not in there is that they are 'inside' and the others are 'outside'.

There is also a category of holy men who, imitating the natural state of the Avadhoota, go about naked or behave in strange ways. The Naga Sadhus and Digambar Jain monks however, explain their nakedness as a symbol of renouncing everything including their clothes, and going back to the natural simplicity of the child.

The Masts of the Sufi tradition are called this because they are said to be always in an intoxicated state of the ecstasy of love and communion with the beloved. Now, the dividing line between the ordinary madman and the holy madman is so thin that in many cases an insane person may be mistaken for a saint or vice versa. In fact, this is not an uncommon occurrence and there are very few guidelines by which one can distinguish between the two. For most seekers, it is preferable to seek guidance from someone who appears sane.

There is one more category of holy men who behave in odd ways. They are absolutely balanced in their private moments, but behave in strange and scandalous ways to keep worthless people away. One such group is the Sufi order called Malamathis.

At this point in life, I was on the threshold and raring to go—to break the bonds of the familiar, of the dear and the near, and explore vaster vistas. Two important factors that could have prevented me from taking the plunge, or could have turned me in the wrong direction, had been resolved to my satisfaction. I shall explain.

First, orthodox Islam frowned on mystic practices. Had I been indoctrinated in the Wahabi tradition, I would not have thought of leaving home and abandoning my social commitments even for a short while. Fortunately, the teacher who was engaged to teach my sister and me the Quran and the Shariat, Ebrahim Bhai, turned out to be a Sufi. I am eternally indebted to him for teaching me the inner mysteries of Sufi teachings.

On many a day, especially when for some reason my sister was absent from class, he held forth beautifully on the teachings of the Travellers on the Path, thereby inspiring and encouraging me to seek the spiritual treasure personally, no matter what sacrifices I had to make.

Second, one important warning sounded by greatly evolved souls to all spiritual seekers is that they should be wary of being attracted by so-called miraculous powers and the desire to acquire them. Ramakrishna Paramahansa even went to the extent of saying, 'If a holy man exhibits magic powers, run away from him as far as you can.' Having had an interest in magic and so-called supernatural powers since childhood, I had by then become familiar with a great deal of literature on the subject of both conjuring tricks and ceremonial magic. Not only that, I had met several magicians and personally learnt the tricks of their trade, so much so that in college and other small gatherings, I could perform a full-fledged magic show, which included levitation, the great Indian rope trick and sawing a lady in two.

Little tricks—like producing holy ash from thin air, or producing gold rings and crystal lingas—were child's play to me. I had angered many a holy man by displaying these feats in the presence of their disciples. What is relevant here is that, having studied magic and so-called miracles in depth, I was no longer overwhelmed by them and considered the exhibition of these as no big deal. I was therefore free from the danger of being attracted and misled by 'holy men' who used these as bait, and exploited the credulous. I was prepared to seek out a genuine spiritual teacher no matter how difficult it was to find one, and not be fooled by ochre-robed magicians.

14

Trial Run

BY NOW, I WAS dying to go. The pull of the Himalayas had become irresistible. Every time I saw a grand cloud formation, my imagination conjured up snowy peaks. Even bare rocky hills, I painted white with my snow-obsessed mind. In my dreams, I saw great yogis meditating in caves beside lofty, silver-hued cliffs. In one particular dream, I saw a yogi who I was convinced was the same person I had seen under the jackfruit tree, when I was nine-and-a-half years old. He was standing near a cave somewhere in the Himalayas, waiting for me.

That was it. I read all the literature available on the Himalayas, including travelogues and railway guides, and charted out a plan of action.

The practical part of me intervened to suggest that I take a trial run before the actual rendezvous. A short ten days of going away from home would serve the purpose. First, I would learn if I could survive all by myself for that period. Second, I would come to know, when I returned, how my parents—especially my mother who loved me dearly—would take it. And third, I would find out how separation from my little second sister, who was barely five-and-a-half years old, and of whom I was very fond, would affect me.

I had heard from a relative of ours, a retired magistrate, that on the banks of the Tamraparni River, a little way from Tirunalveli, there was a mausoleum in the tiny hamlet of Pottalputhur. A pair of sandals believed to belong to the great Sufi Saint Abdul Khader Gilani were housed there, and a small community of Sufi fakirs of the Qadariya order resided there as well.

I was also told that not far from there, in the deep forest, was a cave on a hill with the tomb of an unknown saint, frequented by this Sufi group. It was rumoured that strange beings visited the cave on certain nights.

I chose Pottalputhur as my destination. It was not very far from Trivandrum. I had enough pocket money to buy the tickets and keep some for expenses. I boarded a bus to Nagercoil and from there got another bus to Tirunalveli, reaching Pottalputhur by evening. I only had the clothes I wore, a white shirt and a white dhoti, and a large white towel wrapped around my neck. No one at home had any idea where I was going.

In Pottalputhur, I lost no time in trying to locate the Sufi group I' had heard of. I was told that the Sheikh, or Inamdar—the hereditary head of the order—resided in a massive, whitewashed bungalow not too far from the mausoleum and the little mosque attached to it. I visited the bungalow and, after a little bit of waiting, was ushered into the Sheikh's presence.

I was surprised. He looked normal and wore ordinary clothes: a white shirt and white pants. He was middle-aged and fair, and sported a neatly shaped black beard and a thin moustache. No turban, not even a cap.

Behind his chair, on the wall, was a portrait of a distinguished man with a flowing beard, wearing a green robe and saffron turban. 'My father,' he said, seeing that I was looking at the portrait. We discussed quite a few matters informally. He politely declined my request—that I be initiated into the Sufi order—stating two reasons. One, the initiation was possible only after the seeker turned forty; and two, a Sufi leads a complete life and therefore the experience of a married life is essential. I was unmarried and therefore had to wait.

Short of initiation, he was ready to discuss anything about Sufism. He reluctantly agreed to the idea of my sleeping in the dormitory attached to the mosque, but insisted that I have my meals with him.

I retired to the mosque and had a good night's sleep. Early the next morning, I woke up to the prayer call of the muezzin and, although I did not believe much in the formal ritual of namaz, fell in line with the few people who assembled. Then I meditated, sitting in Vajrasana. The pigeons that lived on the roof of the mosque kept up their constant cooing chorus.

I had breakfast with the sheikh and then met some of the fakirs of the Qadariya order. Unlike the chief, they were dressed in the traditional robes of Sufi fakirs, complete with saffron turbans and long beards. The sheikh introduced them to me and told them about the discussions we had had on the first day.

I met the sheikh again at mealtime, and learnt a great many things about Sufi theory and practice. He lent me a good English translation of *Kasf-al-Mehjoob* (*Revelation of the Veiled*) by Ali Hujiwiri, the great classic of Sufi teachings, and *The Sufis* by Sardar Iqbal Ali Shah. He also instructed a fairly senior member of the order to discuss the teachings with me freely. And so time passed, and I had lovely and blissful meditations night and day. The food was good too.

After seven days, I broached the subject of going to the cave in the forest and asked for directions. The directions were given, but the sheikh would not agree to my going alone. He said the jungle was thick, there were leopards around, and also the path to the cave was not so easily found. So arrangements were made and a senior member of the Halqa (community), a tall sturdy man with a white goatee called Ebrahim, who had gone there many times, was asked to accompany me. Along with us came his assistant, a young, dark, stocky man who uttered few words.

One afternoon, we boarded a bus which dropped us an hour later near an isolated village. The sheikh was right. It was indeed a thick forest and, at many places, the young assistant had to cut away thorny bushes to clear the way. Here and there, we saw huge, ferocious-looking idols worshipped by the tribals who were reputed to be expert black magicians. In some places, we found heads and entrails of animals decapitated and offered as sacrifices to these *vana devatas* or deities of the woods. It was quite frightening.

We reached the hillock around dusk. Steps had been cut into the rock and we climbed up to the cave in just ten minutes. Gigantic old trees stood all around as if guarding the cave. Darkness was fast approaching and the young man, Hassan, busied himself with gathering firewood. Meanwhile, I explored the mid-size cave. It was empty but clean, as if someone had recently tidied it up.

At the entrance to the cave was the grave, which Ebrahim Sahib explained was the grave of a wandering Sufi saint called Malang Baba. He lit incense sticks and closed his eyes in prayer. By then, a great fire was lit on the large, flat, rocky area near the cave. Hassan had procured drinking water from a natural spring, a little beyond the cave. My companions had brought some provisions in cloth bags. While Hassan busied himself making chapatis directly on the fire and grinding together a chutney of tamarind, onion, coconut scrapings, red chillies and salt, Ebrahim Sahib and I washed our hands, face and feet and meditated.

After a while we sat together and had our fill of roti and chutney, deliciously spiced with the hunger we felt.

After the meal, Ebrahim Sahib and Hassan took out their tambourines and sang two beautiful Sufi songs in Urdu—both expressions of love and yearning for the beloved. We stretched ourselves on the grass mats which the duo had carried with them. The fire was still burning bright. Just before I fell asleep, Ebrahim Sahib said to me, 'If anyone other than us wakes you up in the night, just call me. Don't commit the mistake of going out into the forest in the dark. If you have to relieve yourself at night, go only till the edge of this rocky ledge.'

After this, for some time, I could not sleep out of fear. But eventually fatigue, assisted by the cool breeze that had started blowing, lulled me into deep sleep. I can't say how long I slept but some time before dawn, I was woken up by something or someone tugging my right arm. The first thought that occurred to me was that it must be some wild animal trying to chew my fingers, but when I turned to the right and focused, what I saw froze me with fear.

Kneeling beside me, with a broom tucked under her armpit, was an old, toothless hag with a sad face. With her bony fingers she continued to tug at my right hand and whispered in a moaning voice, 'Come, son, come with me. I am an old sick woman. Come and help me. Come, come...'

Ebrahim Sahib's warning suddenly came into my mind, but although he was sleeping quite close, I could neither move my left hand to touch him, nor shout for help. It appeared that my whole body, including my vocal chords, was paralysed. It was terrifying. The old woman was moving her face closer to mine. The stench of decaying flesh smote my nostrils. I closed my eyes and decided to make one last, desperate effort.

I fixed my attention on my heart centre, and visualised a glowing cord of silver light coming out of it and going towards Ebrahim Sahib. It worked. I heard a shout from my left side, and Ebrahim Sahib sprang up and jumped towards me, holding a blazing log which he had picked up from the camp fire. He pointed it towards the apparition that I guessed was visible to him too, and chanted something loudly in Tamil.

It disappeared, and I sat up, no longer immobilised. Hassan had woken up too and looked a little shaken. When I asked what had just happened, Ebrahim Sahib simply said, 'One of the disembodied beings of the forest. Evil ones,' and would say no more.

At dawn, we washed, meditated and set out on our return journey. I had wanted to stay two nights but the scary experience of the night was enough to clinch the issue. I went back with the others.

After one more day at Pottalputhur, I took leave of the Inamdar, and boarded a bus that reached Trivandrum around evening. Since I had no money left to pay for the local bus, I walked all the way to my house and arrived there wearing the same clothes I had set out in. The clothes were quite dirty and my face was unshaven. I looked every bit a vagabond.

My mother was the first to see me. She hugged me and wept. My little sister was very excited. Now she could once again come to my bedroom and play with me. My other sister did not show any outward emotion but I guessed she was happy. My father did not speak to me for a month but afterwards thawed.

I began to spend more and more time meditating in a small attic upstairs in the new house we had shifted to. The house was named Chandra Vilas, or Moon House. I had many new adventures in meditation.

Now that I had had a taste of living away from home, and had passed the self-imposed test of freeing myself emotionally from my family and friends, I was longing to fly away, into the distant Himalayas. Someone was waiting for me. The call was becoming stronger each day and I was looking for the right opportunity.

The opportunity presented itself in the form of money given to me to pay for my examination fees. I decided that it could be utilised instead to pass a different—and to me more important—examination. My friend Ranjit, the only one who knew that I was planning a long journey, chipped in with a little more cash. I was ready to go.

15

Towards the Himalayas

ONE FINE FEBRUARY EVENING, I boarded the Chennai Express. The journey to the Himalayas had begun. I was almost twenty years old.

Those days, it took more than twenty-four hours to reach Chennai. I avoided talking to my fellow passengers as much as I could. The train steamed into the Egmore Station sometime the next evening. From there, I took a bus to Chennai Central. At the booking office, I managed to book a second class sleeper ticket to Delhi for the day after the next. I found a small, cheap hotel nearby and checked in.

My maternal grandfather lived in Chennai, and having been there thrice during vacations, I was fairly familiar with the place. The bus services were quite good, and I knew how to go to the Theosophical Society, the Ramakrishna Mission, and the Kapaliswara Temple in Mylapore. I spent the next day visiting these places.

I had read the teachings of J. Krishnamurti, who broke all connections with the Theosophical Society and dismissed theosophical masters as figments of the theosophists' imagination. I personally held a firm conviction in the existence of great spiritual masters, and had once before, while visiting the sprawling Theosophical Society campus near the sea, felt a tangible presence and great feeling of peace. This time, as I sat on the bench, near the big banyan tree, a deep sense of vastness and stillness overwhelmed me. It was reassuring, and put to rest all my anxieties about the adventurous journey I had embarked upon.

I then visited the tomb of a well-known Sufi saint called Moti Baba, before returning to the hotel. After eating and before sitting for my meditation, I read from a volume of the works of Swami Vivekananda.

The silver light that invariably appeared in my heart centre during meditation changed that night into orange, and then a deep violet. The violet disc expanded and then split in the middle to reveal a Himalayan scene. At the foot of a snow-clad peak, I saw a small cave, and someone standing outside it. I could not see the figure clearly. It was hazy and I thought I heard a voice calling me by some strange name, which I could not comprehend. Soon, I fell asleep.

The next day, early in the morning, I was seated in the three-tier sleeper bogey of the New Delhi Express. It was an uneventful journey, and I kept mostly to myself. Forty-eight hours later, at dawn, the train reached New Delhi. This was my first trip to Delhi, and I was not enamoured of the modern edition of Indraprashta, the ancient city of the Pandavas.

Enquiries revealed that the train to Haridwar started from the Old Delhi Railway Station. I got into a cycle-rickshaw and soon reached the station in the older and dirtier part of the city. Many of the buildings, and of course the imposing Red Fort and Jama Masjid, were relics of the long period of Islamic rule.

At eight in the morning, I boarded the train to Dehradun, which stopped at Haridwar. It took most of the day and reached Haridwar in the evening. I was told that the train to Rishikesh left only in the morning, so I decided to spend some time in Haridwar.

Haridwar is thus named because it is the doorway (dwar) to the upper Himalayas, where Hari—the deity of Badrinath, and Hara— the deity of Kedarnath— are established. For the first time, I set my eyes upon the great river Ganga, flowing majestically at Hari ki Pawri. It was breathtaking. Of course there were many tourists and pilgrims going about their business but nothing could distract me from the clear and cool, ever-moving waters.

I did something that came into my mind all of a sudden. I bought myself a yellow dhoti, a yellow short-sleeved knee-length kurta, and a yellow cloth bag. Then I went to a barber's shop and tonsured my head and my moustache, save for a small, round portion of hair, at the back of my head. This was the pigtail like shikha, which acolytes belonging to the Hindu tradition have worn for hundreds of years.

Looking at myself in the barber's mirror, I liked what I saw. A young and bright looking brahmachari (acolyte), ready to set out on a journey to the distant and difficult to reach snowbound peaks in search of a great teacher, who he believed lived there.

At Hari ki Pawri, I had a bath in the Ganga and changed into the yellow dhoti and kurta. The rubber slippers I had on were okay, for I saw many sadhus wearing them. The traces of my immediate past, namely the shirt and pant I had been wearing, I stuffed into my airbag and left near the ghats, hoping that someone who needed them would find them.

Now I looked like the rest of the sadhus. In the cloth bag slung on my right shoulder were a few books, a towel, a pencil and a toothbrush. On my left shoulder hung a woolen blanket that I could use to meditate as well as to sleep. All I needed now was a water pot or kamandalu. This I purchased from a shop nearby, a nice brass one. I examined my cash reserve. There was still quite a bit of money. This I kept in the side pockets of my kurta.

I noticed the Enicar watch my grandfather had gifted me two years ago, and thinking how ill-suited it was to the general appearance of an itinerant seeker of the truth, I removed it and quietly left it near the steps of the bathing ghat. It was time to explore Haridwar. Perhaps I would meet a great yogi right here.

From Hari ki Pawri, I could see the Shivalik hills and the roofs of the numerous temples and ashrams. As I walked up the road, I saw a little temple of Hanuman, the mighty monkey god from Ramayana. The old Brahmin priest touched a red tilak on my forehead and seemed disappointed that I had not given him the customary dakshina. I quickly gave him a rupee and he blessed me with long life and happiness.

I visited many temples and ashrams and saw sadhus and seekers of all varieties. Vaishnavas with vertical sectarian symbols drawn on their foreheads, Shaivaites with horizontal ash stripes, Shaktas with blood red tilaks, and others with strange markings that I had never seen before. The robes they wore ranged from the exotic and the outlandish to ordinary saffron dhotis—and some had just narrow strips of cloth wound round the loins.

Then there were the matted-haired Nagas, who were Digambaras (sky-clad), which means stark naked. They walked around nonchalantly holding trishuls and revelling in the attention they got from the public.

At one of the ashrams presided over by a *Mahamandaleshwar* (chief abbot) belonging to the Nirvani Paramahansa Akhada, I met a man from Kerala who claimed to be a close disciple of the abbot. Probably from my accent, he found out that I was a fellow Keralite and took me into the dining hall, where I was given a large glass of hot cow's milk. Afterwards, we talked a great deal. He was a retired Government of India bureaucrat and had settled in the ashram of his guru after retirement. His wife had died and he lived in the ashram with his beautiful daughter, who taught in the ashram school.

When I told him my real name, he was taken aback, but after talking to me for a while, he was convinced of my genuine interest and serious involvement with Hindu philosophy. 'You seem to be a serious seeker,' he said, 'and if you reveal your real name, you might not be able to pursue your studies or get initiated into spiritual practices because, unfortunately, a certain level of orthodoxy, still prevails. My suggestion is that you adopt a Hindu name. Even Hindu neophytes change their names when initiated. Which among the Hindu deities is your favourite?'

'Shiva,' I said, 'the meditating yogi God who sits on Mount Kailash.'

'Good,' he said, 'If I may suggest, Shivaprasad is a great name. Adopt it right now, and when you meet the swami, I will introduce you as Shivaprasad. Is that all right?'

'Do you really think it would help in my search?' I asked.

'Yes,' he said, and calling his beautiful daughter Sridevi, introduced me saying, 'This is brahmachari Shivaprasad.' From that time and for the greater part of my spiritual journey, I stuck to that name, and it helped in many ways.

I met the abbot (I will not name him) in the evening, and after I was introduced by my friend Mr Iyer, he suggested that I stay on in the ashram, do a little bit of work in the school and meditate. He would initiate me into meditation, if I so desired, the next day. 'Haridwar is a holy place,' he told me, 'and you can pursue your spiritual interests by staying at the ashram. Only when you go out, be careful. This is *kaliyuga*, and most of the sadhus and sanyasins are frauds. They will promise you shortcuts to the "Truth" and you will end up frustrated.

'The modern ones who own helicopters and have air-conditioned meditation cells for their foreign disciples are the worst. They are on the lookout for young, educated disciples, and before you know it, you will be caught in their trap. Then, there are the *ganja* addicts, who earn their living by pretending to be sadhus. What will you learn from them? Now go. Mr Iyer will show you to your room.'

Mr Iyer showed me my room. It had a window facing the river Ganga and I stayed there happily for a few days. The ashram had a large shelter with over sixty cows, and the food was good, with lots of milk, fruit and ghee. Mr Iyer and his daughter Sridevi were very friendly, and soon I realised I was getting too close to the beautiful Sridevi, and she to me.

Before things got too complicated, I decided to move out and stick to my original plan of travelling to the upper Himalayas. I didn't want to let anything distract me. So one morning, I collected my meagre belongings and headed for Rishikesh.

That train journey to Rishikesh was quite an experience. Most of the passengers were *sadhus* belonging to different denominations. I was probably the only one with a ticket. The Travelling Ticket Examiner walked up and down the train, paying his obeisance and greeting the sadhus, never asking for tickets. When I enquired with a Bairagi Bawaji, who was sitting close to me, why the ticket examiner never asked for a ticket, he guffawed and said, 'Child, you are obviously new to this place. This is Bhagwan's train'—God's train—'It is meant for us. Who can ask for tickets?'

Getting off the train, I followed the other *sadhus* to Muni-ki-Reti, where most of the ashrams were located, on either side of the

Ganga. It was evening, and I walked up the one-hundred-odd steps to enter the famous Divine Life Society, founded by Swami Sivananda Saraswati. He was no more, and the ashram was presided over by Swami Chidananda, one of his foremost disciples. A *satsang* was going on in the open-air auditorium.

Swami Chidananda sat cross-legged on a raised seat, leading the prayer meeting. He was tall and very thin and sat ramrod straight. There were about fifty people, some of them Westerners. He was answering someone's question in English. I went quietly and sat in a corner.

He stopped midway, and turning towards me with a kind smile, asked, 'When did you arrive?' as if talking to an old friend. Caught by surprise, I stammered, 'Just now.'

'I think you should go and have a bath and take rest,' he said, 'You can attend the satsang tomorrow.'

He whispered something to a young brahmachari who stood beside him. The brahmachari told me to come with him. I bowed to the swami as I left the room. '*Hari Om*,' chanted the Swami in a melodious voice.

I was shown a room further up, near the foothills. It was basic, but neat and clean. The brahmachari, who was from Tamil Nadu, was happy to learn that I could also speak Tamil. He gave me two cotton towels and explained where the dining room was located. 'Sharp seven-thirty dinner,' he said, 'I'll see you there,' and hurried away.

I had a cold-water bath, and after my shivering ceased, changed into my other new pair of yellow dhoti and half-sleeved kurta, and walked down the steps. One had to cross the road to reach the dining hall. Since there was plenty of time, I went to the ghat and sat down on one of the steps, watching the Ganga flow by. Boats regularly plied across the river between the ashrams on either side.

It was dusk, and people were performing aarti on both banks, worshipping the river goddess by lighting tiny lamps and sending them floating on the surface of the water while singing hymns. It was a beautiful evening. From the ashrams across the river came the hypnotic chants in the ancient Sanskrit language.

Suddenly, the dining hall gong rang, and I jumped up from the steps. My soul was filled with the food it needed, but the body was hungry. Inside the large dining hall, *sadhus* and *dandi swamis* sat on one side, and others on the other. Everybody squatted on the floor and ate from steel plates. The brahmachari from Tamil Nadu was there, serving food with some others. The fare was South Indian: rice, vegetables, sambhar and a laddu each. I was hungry and ate two full servings.

My stomach full, I felt very sleepy and tired. After enquiring from the brahmachari about the daily routine, I went up to my room and sat for a while, meditating on my cot with the windows left open. Then I stretched myself on the bed and almost instantly fell asleep.

I dreamt that I was walking along a path in a valley, through which gushed a stream with pure, crystal clear water. Near the banks of the stream was a small thatched hut. As I approached the hut, a man with a white veil covering his face emerged. I was somewhat frightened and froze.

'Don't be afraid,' he said, 'I am a friend. They call me "M" like they are going to call you. Don't be complacent. Don't stay at the foothills. Walk, climb up into the mountains. He is waiting for you.'

Then everything vanished—the valley, the stream, the hut and the veiled figure. I was alone, and there was only a glacier stretching on all sides around me. It was cold and I started to shiver. 'Help me, lord,' I shouted, and then I woke up and found myself actually cold—for I had not covered myself with the quilt that was provided. Dawn was just breaking and someone was blowing a conch.

The morning routine at the ashram started quite early. After the temple service, there would be *yoga asana* class at 6 a.m., then meditation for half an hour, then a break for bathing, and so on, with light breakfast at eight. After that, one was free to do self-study or *swadhyaya* at the library or in one's own room till 10:30 a.m. At this time, there would be a class on the Upanishads, conducted by Swami Krishnananda, the General Secretary of the Divine Life Society and a prominent disciple of the founder, Swami Sivananda. Lunch was at noon followed by rest till 3 p.m. The evening satsang was at 6:30 p.m.

and dinner at 7:30 p.m. Inmates were discouraged from going out after dinner and wandering aimlessly.

At nine-thirty, the brahmachari, who had by then become a good friend, told me that Swami Chidanandaji would like to talk to me in an hour at his residence. I was very excited and waited for the brahmachari to take me to the president maharaj's residence. I would miss Swami Krishnananda's Upanishad class, but then this was more important, and a great privilege. Promptly at 10:20 a.m., the brahmachari came to fetch me. 'Prostrate on your knees when you see the Swamiji Maharaj,' he told me.

After making preliminary inquiries about me—where I came from, how old I was, how many siblings I had and if the room allotted to me was alright and so on—Swami Chidananda suddenly asked, 'And what's your name?'

'Shivaprasad,' I said, sticking to the newly adopted name.

'Practised yoga before?'

'Yes Maharaj, from the age of eight.'

'Sanskrit? Do you know?'

'Not much, but I can read Devanagari. Hindi was my second language.'

'Ummph. Meditation?'

'Some kind of meditation comes naturally to me. You know Maharaj, as a small boy I met a yogi who blessed me...' I was shocked that I could say even that much, without my vocal chords getting locked up as they normally did whenever I had attempted to relate the story of my encounter with the yogi under the jackfruit tree. But no more information would come forth. The lock was on again. I gave up trying.

Swami Chidanandaji looked into my eyes with great attention. He sighed deeply and chanted, 'Hari Om,' in his deep voice and patted my head. 'Ummph, past birth influences. God bless you, and what's the name you were given at birth?'

Before I could recover from my second shock of the day and speak, he said, 'It's alright. You don't have to say it. Learn asanas and a little more pranayama from our asana acharya and spend as many days as you like here. I know you are irresistibly attracted by the upper Himalayas. Whenever you feel like it, you are free to go. Perhaps your destiny is linked to the mountains. If you have any problems, let me know. God bless you. Hari Om.'

I spent a wonderful month in the ashram. I joined the yoga class, attended the really thought-provoking Upanishad sessions of Swami Krishnananda, used the well-stocked library, and was present for most evening satsangs of Swami Chidananda. There was still plenty of time for me to explore Rishikesh. Very often, I crossed to the other side by boat and visited the many ashrams there.

One of the oldest, the Swarg Ashram, was started by the great Baba Kalikambliwala, who was so named because his only possession was a black woolen blanket. The cheap boarding and lodging called Kalikambliwala Kshetras, which exist all along the Himalayan pilgrimage route for wandering sadhus, owe their origins to this remarkable ascetic who lived during the early 1900s. Many stories are told about him, but I shall confine myself to relating just one.

There lived a notorious Gujjar dacoit called Sultana, who plundered the caravans of rich pilgrims and looted wealthy ashrams. The very mention of Sultana, it was said, made the rich men tremble with fear. His unique technique was that he robbed in broad daylight after sending word in advance that he was going to strike. Once, it seems, he sent word to Baba Kalikambliwala that he was going to descend on Swarg Ashram with his gang and plunder the treasury at a certain appointed hour. All the ashram staff as well as the devotees were filled with fear, all except the Baba. He had an elaborate lunch made for Sultana and his gang, and waited for him on the porch of his cottage.

The dacoit came with a gang of six, all armed with swords and guns. As he got off his horse, the Baba went towards him and welcomed him. He invited him and his gang to sit on the porch, drink water and relax. Then he handed over the keys to the treasury and said, "You may take what you desire, but I don't want violence and bloodshed. If ever you feel like killing someone, spare everyone and kill me instead. Life and death are the same to me. The police chief of this locality is a devotee of mine and I could have sought his help, but then there would have been violence, lives would have been lost. I want none of that.

'After you have taken all that you require from the treasury, don't ride away immediately. I have arranged a feast for you. You and your friends should enjoy the lunch, rest for a while, if you are tired, and then leave. I have no animosity towards you or any other living creature. Now, do what you think is proper.'

The dacoit, having never encountered a man like that, is said to have bowed low, apologised, and instead of plundering the treasury, contributed a small amount of gold coins and left, after profusely thanking the Baba for the sumptuous lunch.

Some of the ashrams I visited included the Yoga Niketan, Paramarth Niketan, Gita Bhavan and the air-conditioned caves that Mahesh Yogi of Transcendental Meditation (TM) fame had constructed for the Beatles, who were his disciples. Behind the air-conditioned caves was a thick forest, through which ran a trekker's path to Neelkant Mahadeva temple on top of the hill.

A narrow path passing through the jungle led to Laxman Jhula. On either side were tiny cottages and thatched huts where sadhus, yogis, and monks lived in solitude in close proximity to the ever-flowing waters of the Ganga. There was a cosy little cave facing the river, surrounded by large boulders. There lived Mast Ram Baba, a chubby little man who seemed to be perpetually in ecstasy and appeared drunk with joy. His devotees gathered in a log enclosure near the cave and sang devotional songs. Mast Ram Baba hardly spoke.

A little beyond, if one walked over the boulders and skirted a rocky hillock, there was a small stretch of hidden sandy beach not visible from the road. That was one of Babaji's favourite places when he came to Rishikesh. I have spent many an evening sitting there with him, watching the crystal clear waters flow by, or engaging in a serious discussion, or meditating in silence.

Laxman Jhula was also full of ashrams and sadhus of all varieties. The place was named after Laxman, the brother and faithful companion of Rama, the hero of the Ramayana, and called Jhula meaning a swing, because the bridge across the Ganga is a suspension bridge. Crossing the bridge, one came to the main road from Rishikesh that leads to the Badrinath shrine in the upper Himalayas.

At Laxman Jhula, I met Tatwale Baba, a sadhu with long matted hair, who lived in a cave near the forest. Many of his devotees claimed that he was the deathless Mahaavatar Babaji. I wasn't impressed. I heard years later that he was shot dead while walking to his cave. It was a gruesome, unsolved murder that was reported extensively in the newspapers.

Rishikesh in those days was a great place for the spiritual seeker, except during the season when pilgrims going to the four holy places—Badrinath, Kedarnath, Gangotri and Yamunotri—descended in hordes, desecrating the sacred stillness with their city-bred, harsh cacophony.

Otherwise, one could visit a number of ashrams, meet all varieties of sadhus and wandering ascetics, and imbibe what one could from the panoramic vastness of Hindu culture. The place was still clean. No one used soap while bathing in the river. The water was crystal clear. The numerous resorts which one finds today were non-existent, and one could hardly find the plastic cups and other indestructible rubbish that is dumped in heaps by the riverside. The few foreigners one encountered were either serious seekers or trekkers and mountaineers fascinated by the Himalayan heights.

Yet, I was not satisfied. These were mere foothills, however beautiful, and I longed for the snow-clad peaks. Also, none of the sadhus and ascetics I met fit the vision I had of a Himalayan yogi. Some were indeed great scholars, some headed large monasteries, some were experts in yoga, and there were, of course, the itinerant, cannabis-addicted Bairagis, many of whom were merely holy beggars, usually quite ignorant of the deeper aspects of Hindu religion and philosophy. With this last lot, I was thoroughly disgusted.

However, I continued for a while, meditating, spending long hours watching the Ganga flow past, practising yoga, reading as much as I could, and still seeking something I could not define.

Full moon nights were especially beautiful beside the river, and as I sat one night fascinated by the scene and the sound of the flowing waters, an old South Indian monk who had been quite friendly with me, came and sat beside me. After agreeing with me that the scene was indeed beautiful, he said, 'You know I wanted to talk to you for some time. Can I talk now?'

'Yes,' I said reluctantly, sad that the magic of the night was going to be destroyed by mortal speech.

'You see, I have been in these parts for many years. In the beginning, it was quite thrilling; the satsangs, the emotion-laden singing, the saffron-robed monks, the river, the hills and so on. I gave up a good job, my wife and children, and came away here, fascinated by the lofty picture of renunciation, painted by the big Swami who is no more.

'And then, slowly and surely, the veils dropped when I saw the hypocrisy—the power struggle in the ashrams, the caucuses among the inmates and so on. But it is too late. My children hate me and my wife is happily married to someone else. In meditation, I see nothing. I am still the same desire-filled and angry person I was. I have taken sanyas and I can't discard the role. I have become a social misfit. So, I just carry on hoping to die one day. At least, I have food and shelter.'

'Why do you tell me all this?' I asked, shaken by the words of the old monk, who I had thought was a senior and advanced disciple of a great swami.

'No, no, you see, you are so young, handsome and educated, and I felt I must warn you before it's too late. You'll find nothing here except a bit of Himalayan adventure. So after wandering a little, go back and write a book. There is another alternative.

'If you don't want to live an ordinary life and work nine-to-five, you can set yourself up as a guru and make millions. You have all the makings to attract foreigners. Just give them a simple formula and they are hooked. You must have seen the air-conditioned caves?'

Now I was filled with anger. This old man seemed to me a personification of Satan come to tempt me and misguide me. 'Please stop,' I said, 'and I don't want to hear another word.'

'Aha! The great yogi cannot control his anger. Very well, it's your funeral. I was only trying to help.' With that he got up and left, never to bother me again. But what he had said bothered me a lot. I could no longer accept any of the sadhus and sanyasins I met at face value. Doubts began to unsettle my hitherto straightforward and innocent mind. I felt I had to go, walk up the pilgrim's path. Perhaps, I would find a real wandering sage, not attached to an institution and its hierarchical trappings.

I requested another interview with Swami Chidananda. It was granted. I did not tell him about the conversation I had with the old monk, but I told him I was not happy and, in any case, I wanted to go to Badrinath and other Himalayan shrines and would like to start the next day. I needed his blessings. Swami Chidananda touched my head and blessed me. He said he had felt all along that I would leave the ashram. Perhaps there were greater experiences in store. 'Take at least two blankets,' he said, 'and do you need some money?' I declined the money, because I still had some with me, bowed down to him, and came away feeling free and light-hearted.

16

The Cave of Vasishta

I SET OUT THE next day at five-thirty in the morning. I had resolved the previous night that I would not use any kind of transport, and would walk to Badrinath like some of the wandering sadhus I had met.

The road to Badrinath winds its way along the bank of the beautiful river Ganga. On the other side were rocky mountains and forests. Those days, one could see peacocks dancing among the trees and hear their loud calls. That was before dams were built in Uttarakhand, and the rivers manipulated to provide power stations to enlighten its inhabitants. The peacocks have all but disappeared now.

I enjoyed the freedom of walking alone without a care. I had just one blanket and a towel strapped on my back, and a small copper water pot. In my cloth bag were a matchbox, a writing pad, a penknife and two pencils. I wore the yellow dhoti, tucked in Brahmin style. With a tuft on my otherwise tonsured head, and armed with a spiked trekking stick, I looked the quintessential jijnasu, or seeker of truth.

My aim was to reach Vasishta Guha, the cave of Vasishta, by nightfall. The cave was twenty-two kilometres away, and that is the distance I hoped to cover every day. Badrinath is 240 km from Rishikesh.

As the day advanced and the sun got brighter and harsher, I began to feel less light-hearted. First, my feet were beginning to give me trouble. The strap of one of the rubber slippers I wore broke, and I had to abandon my slippers. By midday, the road had become quite hot and the soles of my feet were getting burnt. Having never walked much barefoot, I found it quite painful to walk on the rough and uneven ground. The sun beat down mercilessly and I covered my head with a towel and trudged along. I avoided the veteran sadhus who walked merrily along, barefoot. They would stop from time to time under a shady tree, prepare a chillum and smoke something which I suspected was charas or some other narcotic. They would invite me to join them but I refused. I hadn't come to the Himalayas to end up a drug addict.

Hunger now besieged me. I still had a little money, and seeing a roadside dhaba, hurried to appease the mortal want. The Garhwali Dhaba owner had no respect for sadhus, and he over charged me for the two chapatis and potato curry that I had. Now I had only thirty rupees left.

The place, however, was quite well shaded. So, I allowed myself a short nap on one of the wooden cots rented out to truck drivers at five rupees an hour. I slept deeply.

When I woke up, the sun was not so severe and the shadows had begun to lengthen. I washed my feet in cold, soothing tap water and continued my journey. As the sun prepared to set, anxiety gripped my mind. Vasishta Guha was not in sight and every step was becoming more and more painful. The soles of my feet were cut and bruised. My calf and thigh muscles were aching badly.

Finally, when I thought I could proceed no further and was praying fervently for help, a jeep coming from Rishikesh stopped beside me. 'Where to Maharaj?' asked the driver in Hindi. 'Badrinarayan,' I said, 'but right now, looking for Vasishta Guha.'

'Two kilometres,' he said. 'Climb in and I'll take you there in five minutes. There are no lights there and it's getting dark. No signboard either.'

I thought for a second. It was becoming difficult to walk. True, I had vowed not to use any kind of transport but circumstances were now different. The words of Ramakrishna Paramahansa came to my mind— 'To be religious is not to be foolish.'

'Okay,' I said and climbed into the jeep.

It was an old Willys Jeep and it rattled along pretty fast. The young driver was an expert in hill driving. Soon, the jeep stopped to the side of the road. 'Maharaj, get down,' said the driver. 'I'll take you to the ashram. There is a young brahmachari maharaj from Kerala there. The big swami passed away some years ago.'

I got off the jeep, and guided by the young man, painfully descended down the rather steep path which led to the ashram. The place had no electricity. In the subdued light of the hurricane lanterns, I could not see anything in detail. A young man wearing white, with a brahmachari's tuft on his head came out of a room and said, "Hari Om, I am brahmachari Atmachaitanya. Who are you?'

'Maharaj,' said my companion Rajesh, 'I found this young sadhu hobbling along on the road. He is going to Badrinath and I gave him a lift. He said he was looking for Vasishta Guha.'

'Hari Om, Maharaj,' I said. Knowing from his accent that he was the Keralite brahmachari my companion had spoken of, I spoke in Malayalam. 'Going to Badrinath,' I said. 'Heard about Vasishta Guha and wanted to visit. But it got very dark and my feet are all bruised. I...'

The brahmachari was a kind soul. 'Okay,' he said in Malayalam, 'no problem. You can spend the night here. Where are you from?'

'I'll take your leave, Maharaj,' said the young Garhwali. 'I live in Byasi, a short distance away, and own a small shop and roadside *dhaba*. Do come by whenever you like.' He then touched the brahmachari's feet, then mine, and went away. In the silence of the night, we heard him fire his engine and drive off.

'You must be tired,' said the brahmachari. He showed me to a tiny room with a cot. 'Have a bath and rest for a while. In half an hour, food will be served there on that verandah. In the morning, I'll show you the cave of Vasishta.' Lighting a lantern for me, he walked away saying, 'We shall meet at dinner time.'

Dinner was a simple affair: chapatis, dal, rice, and potato curry. After dinner, we talked for a while and the brahmachari seemed convinced that I was a genuine seeker. 'You sleep now,' he said, 'We'll meet in the morning.' I felt that he was happy to have met a fellow Keralite.

By then, there was a chill in the air. I wrapped myself in the blankets and, tired as I was, fell fast asleep. The last sound I heard was the music of the cicadas. I slept like a log.

The next morning I woke up, and finding that it was well past dawn, jumped out of the bed in a hurry, then screamed in pain. I realised that the soles of my feet were full of blisters and my ankles were swollen. Some of the blisters had burst and the pain was severe. My whole body ached, especially the calf muscles. But I was eager and determined to get up and explore.

Hobbling out of the tiny room, I was relieved to find a water tap not far away and the toilet, a simple hole in the ground, at a little distance. After washing up, I walked slowly to what I thought was the brahmachari's room. The brahmachari was there and after a light breakfast of beaten rice and cow's milk, we talked in Malayalam for some time.

Concerned about my physical condition, he said I should stay on till I feel fit to travel on foot. I agreed gladly. Then he took me on a guided tour of the Vasishta Cave, his guru's samadhi, the rocky banks of the river, and a small cave on a rocky ledge called Arundhati Cave. Little did I realise then that I would later spend some days in the Arundhati Cave with Babaji.

The Vasishta Cave is a large natural tunnel that ends in a fairly spacious cavern. It is pitch-dark inside until your eyes get accustomed to the dim light that comes in through the entrance.

A black Shiva linga has been installed at the far end of the cave. Legend has it that the tunnel once continued beyond the cave and opened near the river. Sitting inside the cave, one is completely cut off from all the sounds and activities of the outside world. The profound silence is only broken by the occasional cicada registering its presence. One needs to just sit quietly and the mind falls into meditation all by itself.

Although known to be ancient and used by the great sage Vasishta for his penance, in recent times the cave was the abode of Swami Purushottamananda, whom the Malayali brahmachari served for many years. Swami Purushottamananda was himself from Kerala and had been a disciple of Swami Nirmalananda, a senior monk of the Ramakrishna order, and a direct disciple of the great Ramakrishna Paramahansa. Later in life, he had a difference of opinion with the Ramakrishna Mission and started his own independent Ramakrishna Ashram in Ottapalam, Kerala.

Born on 23 November 1879, Swami Purushottamananda was directed by Swami Nirmalananda to take his initiation in 1916 from Swami Brahmananda, the first President of the Ramakrishna order. In 1923, he was ordained as a monk by Swami Shivananda (popularly known as Mahapurush Maharaj), another direct disciple of Ramakrishna. Arriving at Vasishta Guha in 1928, Swami Purushottamananda spent many years in the cave, and his samadhi stands in the courtyard outside it. The swami passed away on 13 February 1961, at 10:50 p.m. on the auspicious Mahashivratri night, at the age of 82.

At the time that I was at the ashram, there were only a few kutirs—simple rooms used by spiritual aspirants—and a small kitchen. Apart from the brahmachari, a cook and his assistant, and one or two visitors, the place was usually quite solitary and conducive to contemplation. So I spent fifteen days there, bathing in the cool waters of the Ganga, doing my yoga exercises and meditating in the cave.

The food was simple, just enough, and it was wonderful. The brahmachari was happy to talk occasionally in Malayalam and told me stories about his life with his guru and the other wandering sadhus and monks who had visited and sometimes stayed there.

In fifteen days, my blisters had healed, and I did not want to stay another day. The place was indeed great, but I had to find my own way. Doubts tortured me. The old monk's cynical words kept coming back to my mind every now and then. I had to find a real teacher who would clear my doubts and answer my questions. Did such a teacher exist?

'You have just started,' I told myself, 'have patience, don't give up. Walk the path, the journey has just begun.' One early morning, I thanked the brahmachari, bid goodbye and started out once again towards Badrinath.

17

The Naga and Learning the Mahamantra

THE PATH FROM RISHIKESH to Badrinath passes through five *prayags*, the confluences of the sacred rivers of India. At Devaprayag, the Bhagirathi, flowing down from Gangotri meets the Alakananda, which flows down from Badrinath. In the little town beside this confluence is a temple dedicated to Sri Ram, who is believed to have performed penance there in his old age. The confluence of the rivers as they roar down the ranges is a wonderful sight.

Further on is Rudraprayag, where the Mandakini, coming from Kedarnath, joins the Alakananda. Next is Karnaprayag, where the Pindara meets the Alakananda. Then come the Nandaprayag and Vishnuprayag. Near Vishnuprayag is the famous Jyothirmath, locally known as Joshi Mutt. The great Vedantin Adi Shankara is believed to have founded the Joshi Mutt—making it the northernmost monastery he established. The other monasteries Adi Shankara founded are the Dwarka, Puri and Sringeri Mutts in the west, east, and south of India.

Further up in Pandukeshwar is the trailhead for the trek to the Valley of Flowers, and Hemkund Sahib, the holy lake of the Sikhs situated 15,000 feet above sea level. Beyond Pandukeshwar is the holy mountain shrine of Badrinath. The head priest of Badrinath spends the six cold months in Joshi Mutt.

I covered the roughly 220 km from Vasishta Guha to Badrinath in twenty-five days. I was proud that I had walked the entire distance without using any form of transport. I had become a seasoned wandering sadhu. Despite facing difficulties in obtaining food at times, having to sleep in abandoned sheds, and shivering with cold, nothing could diminish my enthusiasm and eagerness to continue my journey.

Physical inconveniences became the least of my problems. It was my mind that would become agitated in times of solitude, and at times disillusioned. The beauty of the hills and rivers, and the hope that there was someone up there in the snowy heights who would help me find the answers to my questions, kept me going.

I had two experiences during the course of my journey that deserve a mention.

Darkness was fast approaching as I reached Devaprayag, and I was wondering where to find food and rest when I was accosted by a tall, dark, naked Naga sadhu. 'If you are looking for a place to stay, come,' he said.

Living with a Naga would be a new experience, so I agreed. He lived close to the banks of the river, not far from the Rama temple, in a small kutir. In front of the kutir, a sacred bonfire, or *dhuni*, was burning brightly. I washed myself in the river and came back to find him sitting in front of the dhuni. 'Sit down,' he said, 'pray to the fire god, and bow down to him. We will eat and then have *siddhi*.'

'Siddhi?' I asked, because siddhi is the word used for supernatural powers which yogis are supposed to possess.

'Yes, yes, you'll see,' he said.

While we ate hot chapatis and potato curry, he asked me questions about my life and where I was going. I said that I was a spiritual seeker, Shivaprasad by name, and was going to Badrinath, looking for a proper teacher. I felt him sizing me up, and I was right. As soon as we finished eating, he went in and brought out a clay chillum, filled it with a mixture of ganja and tobacco, and lit it. He then sat cross-legged, shouted loudly, '*Bhum Bhole, Har Har Mahadev Shambhu*,' and took a deep puff. Then, he slowly exhaled the smoke and stretched the chillum towards me.

'Siddhi,' he said, 'With this you will travel to the world of Shiva and gain all powers. I can be your guru. Shiva Mahadev has sent me a handsome disciple. Smoke, smoke. You know how to do it.'

From the odour of the smoke, I knew it was ganja. Some of my friends in Trivandrum smoked pot, and I had tried it a few times, but was not particularly attracted by it. It does put you into a meditative mood, but only temporarily, and the dangers of addiction were great. I declined. He got very angry. 'No one refuses siddhi offered by a Naga in front of the fire,' he shouted loudly. 'Take it!'

Reluctantly, I took the chillum from him and took a few puffs. After a few minutes, he suddenly said, 'Dakshina. You have to offer me dakshina, money, for having initiated you into the mysteries of meditation. Give!' Not wanting to argue with him, I gave him ten rupees. 'More, more,' he roared.

I gave him ten more and said, 'That's all I have.' He grinned happily. 'Enough, enough,' he said, 'now you are blessed.' He placed his hands on my head. 'Have some more siddhi.' I declined.

'You may sleep on the verandah or inside,' he said. I was tired and the ganja made me feel drowsy. I wrapped myself in my blankets, used my bag as a pillow, and fell asleep. I had a few more rupees in my bag and I wondered if the Naga would try to steal it. That night, my usual meditation before falling asleep was not smooth and bright. It was as if my being was enveloped in darkness and my soul fettered by thick, heavy ropes. The Naga was still smoking his potion.

The next morning, I woke up much before dawn and was relieved to discover that the Naga was still fast asleep and snoring loudly inside the kutir. Without making any noise, I rolled up my blankets, picked up my bag, water pot and stick, and quietly walked out in the semi-darkness. By dawn, I had already walked far away from Devaprayag and the Naga Siddha.

A few days later, not far from Rudraprayag, I wandered into a thick forest and soon realised that I had lost my way. It was growing dark, and I was again wondering where to spend the night when I saw a middle-aged man walking in my direction. He carried a bundle of firewood on his back. 'Maharaj, where are you bound?' he asked. 'Badrinath,' I said, 'but I think I have lost my way. Do you know some place where I can rest for the night and get some food?'

'Come with me,' he said, 'Bawaji's ashram is not far away. He is my guru. Come.'

I had read about a mysterious, ever-living yogi called Babaji who lived somewhere in the Himalayas, so I got really excited. 'You mean the great Babaji is your guru?' I blurted out.

He did not know which Babaji I was talking about. His guru was a Vaishnavite Babaji. Vaishnavite sadhus were called Bawajis.

We climbed down a steep pathway that descended to the bank of the river. Very close to the river, surrounded by fruit trees and flowering plants, stood a small temple made of granite. Around the temple were small cottages, and what appeared to be a dining hall and a kitchen. Bells and gongs were being rung, and I realised that the evening puja was going on.

Both men and women were attending the service. A tall, well-built man—bare bodied except for his loincloth and a sacred thread across his chest; clean-shaven with his head tonsured except for a long, thick tuft tied in a knot—was waving a lit lamp in front of beautiful images of Krishna and his consort Radha, and simultaneously ringing a small bell.

As he finished and turned to pass the lamp to others, I noticed that he wore the elaborate U-shaped insignia of a Vaishnavite, drawn with sandal paste, on his forehead, neck and upper arms. Around his neck was a small necklace of tulsi beads. The man who brought me there touched his feet and whispered to him. The Bawaji smiled and came towards me. I touched his feet as was the custom.

'Jai Sri Krishna, blessings,' he said. 'Go have a bath in Ganga maiyya'—mother Ganga. 'First, we'll eat prasad and then we'll talk. Namo Narayana.'

The Bawaji sat a little away, cross-legged on a flat wooden seat, and the rest of us sat cross-legged on the floor of the dining hall. They chanted the fifteenth chapter of the Bhagawad Gita, then we were served simple but delicious vegetarian food. The women sat in one row and the men in another. There were four young women and six middle-aged men, all wearing white clothes and the U-shaped marks on their foreheads. Only the Bawaji wore an ochre dhoti.

After dinner, the Bawaji invited me to his little cottage for a chat. He made quite a few enquiries about my childhood and spiritual quest, and I answered him as well as I could. Not once did he ask me what religion I was born into, which surprised me a bit because I guessed they were all orthodox Brahmins. I learnt from him that they were a community of Krishna devotees and followers of Sri Krishna Chaitanya.

They believed that devotion was the only way to serve God and that Krishna was the Supreme God. They danced and sang in front of Krishna and Radha, and worshipped them regularly. They were pure vegetarians and believed that anyone who was initiated into their cult immediately became a Brahmin. They hated the Advaita Vedantins belonging to the order of Shankaracharya, who they called Mayavaadins or those who considered the world an illusion, maya. According to these Vaishnavites, the world was no illusion. It was real, and Krishna was its Supreme Lord and controller.

What really seemed quite reasonable to me was the Bawaji's idea of formal renunciation, or becoming a monk. 'I know,' he said, 'that you are keen to renounce the world, wear ochre and gatecrash into the state of mukti, but young man, be careful. If you fall from a short height you will not be badly injured. You can get up and get treated and be on your feet again. But if you fall from the lofty height of sanyasa, a monk's life, you might be severely or even fatally injured. You may not even be able to stand up again. So be very careful before you take a decision.

'As for us, we follow the Vedic principles of first going through grihasthashrama—married life—before attempting sanyasa. All of us are married. A married man can find God, with God's blessings; without God's grace even a monk cannot find God. I was married too and became a renunciant after my wife died.

'And one more thing—don't mix with ganja-smoking sadhus, however learned they may be, for I am sure your eyes are set on the upper Himalayas and you might find them there too. I would have loved to have you live with us and engage in devotional practices but I know you are eager to go forward. So be it.

Finally, he said, 'You are a pure soul, and if you so desire, I can give you our Mahamantra. Recite it regularly and do come back to us whenever you wish. God bless you. Jai Sri Krishna.'

I touched his feet, thanked him, and requested him to initiate me into the mantra, 'Om Namo Bhagavathe Vasudevaaya.' I went to my allotted room, chanted the mantra silently for a while and went into a deep, peaceful sleep.

I woke up early in the morning, had a dip in the ice-cold Ganga and sought the blessings of the Bawaji. He laid his hands on my head and blessed me with great affection. 'May Sri Krishna guide you to spiritual fulfillment. Jai Sri Krishna.' Bidding farewell to my friend Damodar, who had taken me to the Bawaji, I set out again, my face turned towards Badrinath.

18

The Cobbler and the Monk

ONE COLD EVENING, SOME days later, I reached Karnaprayag. On the outskirts of the little town, I saw a Shiva temple beside the river from which a Brahmin priest emerged. I made enquiries about a suitable place to spend the night and he recommended that I spend the night in the temple premises. There was a nice room meant for pilgrims, presently unoccupied, he said. The only problem was that, for food I had to be satisfied with two bananas and a piece of jaggery, for that was all he could offer me. He was going home to the town and would bring me food the next morning.

I said that was fine, tired and hungry as I was. I lit the single kerosene lamp and sat on the mattress that was laid on a wooden plank. As I started eating the bananas, I heard a voice outside saying, 'Ram Ram, Maharaj.' Outside the door, stood a darkish man of diminutive structure, wearing a long white kurta and pyjamas, and a typical white Gandhi cap on his head. His hands were folded in salutation.

'Maharaj,' he said in a soft, subdued voice, 'I am Ramprasad, a cobbler who lives in the town. My wife dreamt yesterday that a holy man would come to our house and have his meal. I am an untouchable, you know, and this is a Brahmin's temple. I am not supposed to come here but I saw you come and the Brahmin go away, and I summoned the courage to step in. Please don't get angry or curse me.

'Maharaj, do you think I can bring you food? My wife has cooked *luchis*, dal and halwa and is waiting for the holy man she dreamt of. It would be too much to invite you home, but we could bring the food here.'

He was almost in tears. I stood up and said, 'I'll go with you to your house. Let your wife serve me.' Hardly believing his ears, he led me to his house in the Harijan section, separate from the rest of the village. 'Please wait here, Maharaj,' he said pointing to the verandah of his house. Hurrying in, he shouted excitedly to his wife, 'Leelavati, a holy man has come.'

Together, they washed my feet, not listening to my protests, and served me hot luchis, dal and delicious vegetables cooked in ghee. As I sat enjoying the food, they stood looking at me shedding tears of joy. Ramprasad kept shaking his head and telling his wife, 'Leelavati, I can't believe this is happening. Your dream has come true, we are blessed. Now, you will surely have a child. Maharaj, bless us that we have a baby.'

After eating the hot and sweet halwa for dessert, I went back to the temple, escorted by Ramprasad who held a flashlight. My hunger appeased, I meditated for a while and fell asleep.

Early in the morning, I was woken up by the Brahmin priest, who was shouting loudly. I found him livid with anger. 'What kind of a sadhu are you?' he screamed, 'Eating in an untouchable's house. Couldn't you wait for the morning? What kind of a brahmachari are you, sitting in a cobbler's house, Eating food prepared by low-caste untouchables? You have now polluted yourself and the temple premises. Get out before I get someone to beat you up and throw you out. Go and take a dip in the holy river to purify yourself. I'll have to wash this room with holy water now. Go, get out!'

Without a word, I took my belongings and walked out of the place. There was no point in talking to him. My heart was filled with pain. How could one human being call another untouchable? Is this the holy land where great yogis lived? Doubts assailed me, but I was determined to go the whole way and find out for myself. Would I find a great yogi somewhere who would show me the light that dispelled the darkness of ignorance?

The last important religious centre before Badrinath was before me. At four o'clock one evening, I reached Joshi Mutt. It was cold. From nearby Auli, one could see the great snowbound Himalayan peaks. I was told that the Shankara Mutt could provide accommodation only for Brahmin brahmacharis and sanyasins. Not far from the Mutt was a dharamshala. I managed to get a small room there, and went back to visit Joshi Mutt.

I saw the cave of Shankaracharya, the big crystal linga, and the so-called wish-fulfilling tree. A large number of brahmacharis and monks lived there, pursuing the study of Sanskrit and Vedanta. One of the students would one day become the next Shankaracharya. The Brahmin sanyasins known as *dandi* swamis moved about with staffs. As I stood wondering about the complexity of the caste system, and how deviant the human mind could be, a tall, austere, tonsured monk, came towards me and spoke.

'Where are you going?'

'Badrinath, Sir.'

'Staying where?'

'Dharamshala, Sir. I was told non-Brahmins are not allowed to stay here.'

'You are not a born Brahmin, but you look so much like one.'

'No sir, I am not a Brahmin.'

'You must be wondering about all this. Let me tell you, personally, I think it is all nonsense. I was a dandi swami, a Brahmin monk, but I threw my dandi away into the Ganga, and am now free. I am allowed to stay here when I come because the *mahant* knew me from the time I was a dandi swami.

'You know,' he continued, 'the founder of the Dasanami Order, to which this Mutt belongs, was one day walking back from the river after a bath when he was accosted by a tribal hunter, accompanied by numerous stray dogs. "Move out of my way! How dare you stand in front of me, you low-born, untouchable?" shouted Shankara. The story goes that the hunter, who was the great yogi god Shiva himself, suddenly transformed into his original form. He warned Shankara not to discriminate between human beings, based on birth.

'In everybody lives the same atman, the transcendental soul,' said the old monk, 'and I am pained to see what goes on in places like these. But I am powerless to change the system.'

I spent some time discussing Vedanta with him, and then went back to my room to eat and sleep. The next morning, I was back on the road. It took me four days to reach Badrinath via Govindghat and Pandukeshwar. Nothing worth mentioning happened on the way. However, my mind was troubled and unsettled. The rigours of the journey were also beginning to have their effect on the body. I was tired.

19

The Seeker at Badrinath

I REACHED BADRINATH IN the afternoon. The sight of the Nara Narayana mountains, the snow-covered Neelkanth and the clear waters of the Alakananda as they gushed down with great force past the Badrinath temple, momentarily washed away all my mental and physical troubles. I felt calm, peaceful and joyous.

Before exploring Badrinath, I decided to try and meet the Ravalji, the chief priest of Badrinarayan. I had been told that the Ravaljis, since ancient times, were all Namboodiri Brahmins from Kerala. The illustrious Shankaracharya, who had re-established the Badrinarayan temple after freeing it from Buddhist influence, is said to have stipulated that the chief priest would have to be a Namboodiri Brahmin from Kerala. I was longing to speak in Malayalam and was eagerly looking forward to conversing with the Ravalji, a fellow Malayali.

So, after a bath in the hot Tapta Kund, perennially filled by natural hot-water springs, I changed into my clean spare set of clothes. I bowed to Sri Badrinarayan from the entrance to the temple and walked across the road to the official residence of the Ravalji. After I had spoken to his assistant in Malayalam and waited in the anteroom for a few minutes, I was ushered into the presence of the Ravalji. His name, I had gathered, was Kesavan Namboodiri. The Ravalji was a very courteous and pleasant man, fair and good-looking. The conversation with him, mostly in Malayalam, went roughly like this.

'What's your name?'

'Shivaprasad,' I said, fearing how an orthodox Namboodiri Brahmin might react if I told him my real name.

'So what brings you here at such a young age?'

I explained about my spiritual quest and how, since childhood, I had been meditating and meeting holy men. I left out the meeting with the mysterious yogi under the jackfruit tree, fearing that any attempt to narrate that incident would prove futile.

I told him how I was irresistibly attracted to the Himalayas from a tender age and had now set out to search for a spiritual guide in the Himalayas. I had heard that great yogis lived in solitude in the Himalayan mountains. Could he guide me to someone he knew?

The Ravalji laughed heartily. 'Poor fellow,' he said, 'Do you know that a great yogi had to come all the way from Kerala to establish the Badrinarayan temple? You have come from the same state seeking a guru in Badrinath. Great!

'Anyway, I don't know anybody like that here. Well, there are sadhus and sanyasins who come here during the pilgrim season and go back in the extreme winter. Even we go down and stay at Joshi Mutt during the winter. Badrinath is 11,000 feet above sea level and everything freezes here.

'I have heard rumors that some mysterious mahatmas live in caves like Vyasa Guha and Muchukunda Guha throughout the year. But then, I personally think they are nothing more than rumours that help add magic to Badrinarayan.

'If you need guidance, it is better to read the great works of Shankara, the commentaries on the Upanishads, the Viveka Chudamani [Crest Jewel of Wisdom], etcetera from a competent Vedic scholar. Do you know Sanskrit?'

'Very little,' I said, 'but I have studied English translations of the books you have mentioned.'

'Ummph, that's not enough. They are not the same thing. You need to find a place to stay, right? The accommodation here is very limited but I can get you a small kutir across the Alakananda not far from here.

Food, you may eat here twice a day. I will leave instructions with my assistant. If you are hungry now, you can eat something in the outer room. With Badrinarayan's blessings, we are never short of prasad.

'My advice to you would be to stay for a while, explore this beautiful place and then return to Kerala. Pursue further studies, perhaps a PhD in Indian philosophy; look after your parents and lead a happy life. You can come here at times and spend a few days. So, don't waste your time and energy looking for a Himalayan master and all that. You will probably end up disillusioned and it will be too late to retreat.

'I am especially warning you because there are some pseudo-saints looking for young educated disciples. They might consider you a good catch. Then there are the ganja sadhus. Most of them are mere drug addicts. The visions they see under the effect of the narcotics, they consider real. Watch out for these and avoid them like the plague.

'Now you eat, and then my assistant will show you the kutir. I have to make preparations for the evening worship of Badrinarayan. Drop in at the temple for the evening aarti. Then come back here. We can talk some more, okay?'

I was given a good Kerala meal and then led across the bridge to the Kalikambliwala kutir. It was great watching the thundering Alakananda day in and day out. I went regularly to attend the temple service and had my food at the Ravalji's place. He was a very busy man and had to meet many visitors, but once or twice in three days, he gave me some time. From him, I learnt about Badrinath and the places around.

Badrinath falls within the area called Kedarkhand and is considered to be the place where Nara and Narayana did penance. It is the valley of the river Alakananda, between the two mountains named after them. The hot water springs of Tapta Kunda and Brahma Kapali are the two sacred bathing places. The temple of Badrinarayana is reputed to have been re-established by Adi Shankaracharya who is said to have replaced the image of the Buddha with that of the image of Narayana, the original idol that the Buddhists had abandoned in an old well. There is no historical evidence regarding this, but the possibility of Badri being a Buddhist centre once upon a time cannot be ruled out, as the Tibetan border is very close.

Six or seven kilometres from Badri, travelling along the bank of the Alakananda, one reaches the village of Mana which is the last village on the Indian side. This village is inhabited by tribes of Tibetan origin.

Two kilometres north of the Badri temple is the rock called Gaudapadasila. It is on the left bank of the Alakananda and is said to have been the seat of the great rishi Gaudapada, a disciple of Suka Deva. Gaudapada is said to have written his *Karikas* (explanations) on the *Mandukya Upanishad* there. Shankaracharya, it is said, met Gaudapada who entrusted him with writing commentaries on the *Karikas*.

The cave of Vyasa, where Vyasa the rishi, also known as Badaraayana (one who dwells in the forest of Badri trees), compiled the Vedas, is close to Mana. I was told that great mahatmas sometimes frequented the Vyasa Guha or several other caves in the vicinity, during the summer months. At Kesava Prayag, the Alakananda meets the Saraswati, which comes out of an underground tunnel. From there starts the path to Tibet over the Mana pass, 18,000 feet above sea level.

Further up are the Vasundhara Falls, and Swargarohini, from where, according to the Mahabharata, the great king Yudhishthira was lifted into heaven in Indra's chariot.

Badrinarayan was a beautiful place. Surrounded by snowy peaks and kissed by the rushing waters of the Alakananda, it was an ideal place for those who love solitude and contemplation. I say was, because now, everything has been spoilt by the heavy influx of irresponsible tourists, with little or no understanding of the sacred. Innumerable shops with greedy merchants waiting for the unwary traveller, are the order of the day. On a recent visit, I found a man trying to sell a beautiful young Garhwali girl, just for the night.

One of the indelible impressions of Badrinath that I carry with me, and which never fails to fill my heart with joy, was the day it snowed. It was a full moon night and the whole place glowed as if it were made of molten silver.

But the beautiful sights did not give me much relief. Doubts, made worse by the Ravalji's remarks that an educated young man like me will find nothing here, and that I should go back home, assailed my already shaken mind. One day, sitting in front of the kutir, I decided I would go to Mana village and search for a great yogi in one of the caves, and if I did not find a genuine mahatma there, I would throw myself into the Alakananda and commit suicide. Perhaps, I would be reborn under more conducive circumstances. I could no longer stand this torture of doubt and depression.

20

Meeting Babaji

EARLY THE NEXT MORNING, I set out towards Mana village. By noon, I had reached the village, inhabited by shepherds of Tibetan origin, who wove colourful, intricately designed woollen rugs on their handlooms. They were all Buddhist. I walked until I came to the Vyasa Guha. It was a medium-sized, natural cave.

I decided to explore the other caves in the vicinity and walking further up over the rocks, saw the Saraswati gushing out of a tunnel and joining the Alakananda. Another hour of walking through rocky terrain and I had reached the Vasundhara Falls. My idea was to reach Swargarohini. There must be something to the story of Yudhishthira being lifted into heaven. Perhaps extraordinary beings lived there?

It was then that I realised that it would soon grow dark. The wind was already icy cold, and there was no one in sight. Hunger was gnawing my insides. I decided to walk down at least to Mana village. I had to find some kind soul who would offer me a place to sleep at night, and maybe some food. I was filled with doubt, fear, hunger and a deep sense of failure. I had started on a quest and failed. There were no mahatmas, except in the imagination of fiction writers who pretended to be factual. Better to die than live like this. I decided to jump into the Alakananda, and commit suicide.

By then, it was almost fully dark and the icy wind was howling. I reached Vyasa Guha again, and to my surprise, found that a dhuni was brightly burning at the mouth of the cave. Flames leapt and danced as the logs burned brightly. In the freezing weather, the warmth of the fire beckoned. I went towards it, wondering who could have lit the fire. Perhaps a shepherd? Or was I finally about to see a yogi?

From inside the cave came a voice. Was it familiar? Was it a voice buried deep in the recesses of my mind for years, now becoming audible? I hurried towards the cave trembling. From inside emerged a long-haired, bare-bodied, tall man. 'Come,' the voice said in clear Hindustani, 'Where have you been, wandering Madhu?'

'Madhu?' Had I heard that name in a long forgotten dream? Who was this man? 'I am not Madhu,' I said, 'I am Mum…'

'Enough, enough, I know. From under the jackfruit tree in Vanchiyoor, to Vyasa Guha in the far north. Come and sit here, near the fire. First, I will get you some food, and then you can sleep. We will talk tomorrow.' With his right hand, he patted my left shoulder with great affection. 'Sit here.'

At that instant, I realised that this was the same person I had met in the backyard of my house, under the jackfruit tree, at age nine. That was it. Even the voice was the same. I had found my guru, my father, my mother, my teacher, all in one. As it turned out, I was not to leave him for the next three-and-a-half years.

He entered the cave and soon came out with his kamandalu (an oval shaped vessel, carried by sadhus to hold food or water). In it were two fresh wheat rotis and hot potato curry. He placed it in front of me and said 'Eat.'

I bent down and touched his feet. 'I'll call you Babaji,' I said, 'I know of no other Babaji. You are my Baba, father. I am indebted to you for life. You have found me when I was at the end of my tether.' Tears clouded my vision.

'All that is fine, you sit down now and eat,' he said affectionately.

Sitting there, in front of the fire, surrounded by the Himalayan ranges, I ate with relish under the affectionate gaze of my teacher. He went in again, and this time came out with a jalebi, a sweet, which he insisted he would hold while I ate. After the meal, I drank the clear, pure water of the Alakananda, which Babaji passed on to me, and immediately felt drowsy. It was as if I had not slept for ages.

Babaji took me into the cave, and in the dim light of the fire inside, I saw that he had made a bed for me, with a blanket spread on dry leaves and twigs. With a gentle wind blowing the heat of the fire into the cave, or so I thought, I fell asleep instantly, secure in the thought that Babaji would take care of me. The last thing I remember was Babaji sitting on a folded blanket, cross-legged, facing the fire, steady and motionless.

21

My First Initiation

THIS WAS THE BEGINNING of a new life and a new journey with a loving and caring guide. The next morning, Babaji woke me up many hours before dawn. '*Brahma muhurtha*,' said Babaji, 'this is the time when the air is clear for meditation. You don't have to be foolish and take a dip in the freezing waters of Alakananda. You will probably contract pneumonia, and there are no good hospitals close by. Take water from my kamandalu and clean your mouth and face. Do you have a brush?'

'Yes, Babaji.'

'So use it, and pick up some ash from the fire to use as a tooth cleaner.'

The fire was still blazing. I wondered if Babaji had stayed awake and fueled it through the night. This was also the first time that I saw how practical and matter-of-fact he was, and not prone to age-worn customs such as: one needs to have a bath before meditation even if it can kill you. The words of a great spiritual master, who wandered the streets of Jerusalem with no place to lay his head came to mind: 'The law was made for man, not man for the law.'

When I returned, he gave me a folded blanket and said, 'From now on, use this blanket. No one else should use it. It is yours.'

Then he corrected my posture and told me how to sit in padmasana properly, and initiated me into the mysteries of Kriya Yoga, the technique taught to him by his guru, who I was thrilled to hear was the legendary Mahaavtar Babaji. As I began to meditate, he touched my chest gently, and then my forehead. I went into a deep and blissful meditation. My mind travelled to dimensions I had not even dreamt of before and my consciousness expanded immeasurably. I came back to the waking state, hearing Babaji's voice saying, 'Come back, come back. Not everything at once, son.'

The sun had just risen and I found the scene unbelievably beautiful—the ice-clad peaks at a distance, the sound of the river and the diffused tranquil light. Babaji was smiling affectionately and, for the first time, I saw his features clearly. He was tall and very fair with an almost European complexion and light brown eyes. His thick, long brownish-black hair was kept tied in a bun on the top of his head. He had somewhat Nepalese features and his facial hair was sparse—a very light beard and moustache. The cartilage of his ears was pierced, and he wore large copper earrings. On his neck, he wore a rosary of big Rudraksha beads. His body was bare, even in the biting cold, except for a thick white cotton cloth wrapped around his waist. It stopped above his knees. He was barefoot, and his only possessions were a black wooden kamandalu, a meditation blanket, and a short axe, which he carried strapped to his back.

'These surroundings seem so familiar,' I said, 'as if I have been here before. Were you with me then?'

'Not I, but my great master, the legendary Sri Guru Babaji, who was your guru then. I am one of his earliest disciples, and my name is Maheshwarnath. Sometime in the future, people will call you "M", and you will be reminded of me constantly. Sri Guru Babaji has put you in my charge, until you are ready.'

'Will I see the great Sri Guru Babaji?' I asked eagerly, not able to contain my excitement.

'If and when you require,' said Babaji, 'but remember, that one meditates and practises kriya, not to meet Sri Guru Babaji, but to attain the high level of consciousness that will lead you to understand and experience with certainty what he stands for. We will see.

'Meanwhile, let us get going. I don't come here to Vyasa Guha often. Yesterday, I was here only to receive you. In Badri, I usually reside in one of the caves near Charan Paduka behind the Narayan Parvat on which the temple stands. After going there, we shall start your lessons. Come.'

So we set out, the young disciple, with the guru who, like the legendary Dakshina Moorthi, himself looked quite young. I realised how fast Babaji walked, and had to try hard to follow him. Occasionally, he would let me rest and encourage me, 'Young man,' he would say, 'walk a little faster. You have abundant energy. Good.'

We reached Badrinath, crossed over to the path behind the temple, and continued to climb up till we reached Charan Paduka. The Jains considered this a sacred place graced by one of their Tirthankaras. Beyond this, were grassy plains and a narrow valley with caves on either side. A small number of yogis occupied some of the caves. They greeted Babaji as he passed. Further up, we halted in front of a spacious cave. The fireplace, made of crude rocks at the mouth of the cave, was still smoldering.

'This shall be our residence for a while,' said Babaji, 'Go in and put your blankets and bag away. You will find a large, loose, thick woollen robe inside. Put it on. I don't want you to get sick. Also, wrap your head properly, covering your ears with the blue turban you will find in a bamboo basket. You can rest now. Our first lesson will start in the evening.'

Although there were fixed timings for formal lessons and discussions, living with Babaji was, by itself, a learning process. I learnt to clean up the cave, bring water from the nearby waterfall, which was sometimes full of ice pieces, collect firewood, which involved learning to wield the axe, go out to beg for vegetables, wheat flour and other provisions from the shopkeepers in the bazaar near the temple, or from *annakshetras*, and buffalo milk from the Gujjars.

Begging was a big blow to my ego, in spite of the fact that the merchants gave gladly, knowing I was Babaji's *chela* (disciple). I noticed how much respect Babaji commanded. When he walked past, many of the merchants stood up to show respect, and with their palms held together, greeted him with 'Ram Ram, Maharaj.' Babaji always returned the greetings with his head bowed and his right hand on his heart.

I also understood the value of food and was taught to cook for the first time. The food could be very simple, but it had to be perfect. No compromises—from cutting the vegetables properly to boiling just enough. 'If you cannot cut your vegetables properly or cook your rice to perfection, how on earth are you going to seek the ultimate perfection,' Babaji said to me once. 'It is like the man who speaks lies day and night, and says he is seeking the Ultimate Truth, Satya. Don't politicians swear by Truth? *Satyameva Jayate*'—Truth Alone Triumphs. 'Begin with perfecting your daily life. That's the way to perfection.'

The morning lessons came after meditation, yoga asanas and a light breakfast of milk and some fruit, usually guavas or litchis, and lasted for about an hour. Babaji said, 'Your attention span is only an hour right now, and also, it is better to digest your knowledge properly.' After the lessons, I would collect wood if required to keep the dhuni burning, and went about cooking a meal. After the first few days of coaching, Babaji, used to walk up towards the hills and come back when the food was ready. He ate very little.

After the meal, we would rest for a while, and then I was free to wander around on my own and sometimes with Babaji. At sundown, it was time for meditation, and wherever we were, we sat down and meditated. After that, a one-hour study session, then a simple meal, after which we would sit beside the fire and talk informally. Sometimes, we discussed things for hours, while the leaping flames danced freely and the firewood crackled. When I felt sleepy, I would lie down inside the cave and sleep. Babaji would sit near the fire and sometimes lie down with his eyes closed. But I wondered if he really slept.

The sessions we had were quite elaborate, and may be boring to you, the reader. So, I will confine myself to what I think are the important ones. Let me add, however, that all the knowledge that I possess was acquired in the course of those wonderful three-and-a-half years with Babaji.

22

Lighting the Kundalini Fire

THE VERY FIRST LEARNING session with Babaji took place in the evening just as it was turning dark. We sat facing the dhuni with the flames dancing in front of us.

'Fire,' said Babaji, 'has been sacred to all ancient civilisations. Agni, the God of Fire was invoked every day in the Vedic times. Have you thought about why fire is so important?'

'One needs fire to cook food,' I said, 'and in winter, fire keeps you warm and keeps wild animals away. So probably the ancients respected fire.'

Babaji laughed. 'Yes, yes, but there is much more to it. In ancient times, there were no matchboxes. To produce fire, one went through the elaborate ritual of rubbing dry sticks together with invocations to the fire god. When the spark appeared, it was indeed a miracle. Where was this fire before it manifested, asked the ancient thinkers. Surely, it was hidden in the wood always and needed the right conditions to manifest. So, fire became a symbol of the spirit, all pervading, yet manifesting only under certain conditions.

'Another reason fire was used as a symbol of the spirit, is that fire always burns upwards. Try holding the firewood downwards, the flames always move upwards. Also, just one spark is enough to set a whole forest on fire. You can light a thousand candles from one flame with no loss to the original mother flame. What better symbol of the spirit?

'When it turns destroyer, it burns everything to ashes, reduces everything to dust. The sacred fire of love and compassion burns all self-centredness to ashes. The ascetics apply ashes on their bodies, to show how they are free of limitations.

'It is not only the visible fire which is called Agni. All forms of combustion are Agni. Even the catabolic and anabolic processes that sustain the human body are called the digestive fires; as also, the fire of desire, higher or lower.

'If you had a lover, don't you call her your "old flame"? Nobody says "old water" or "old air". Because love, desire, inspiration, all these are a kind of fire. So also is imagination. Therefore, fire has been worshipped for ages. For us, who belong to the Nath tradition, fire is part of our Self. We light the dhuni and sit for hours looking at the flames. The fire becomes our friend and protector. Our minds merge with the flames and we are one. Believe me, fire, like all of nature, has a mind of its own, and our minds are linked intimately with Agni, the lord of fire, so much so that the flames fulfill any wish that we have.

'So, the inner fire, the kundalini, which is actually part of the universal power of combustion, identifies itself with the outer fire and manifests in the dhuni. Flames burst forth from it and reach the thousand-petalled lotus, and man becomes god. Vast dimensions of consciousness can now be accessed and tapped. Sorrow disappears. Watch carefully.'

Babaji then looked at the fire with intense attention and said, 'O Flame of my heart who dances in the dhuni, go higher and higher and reveal your majesty.' One of the tongues of the fire then began to grow tall. My skeptical mind was about to attribute this to the cold wind that had begun to blow when I realised that only one flame was growing. The flame went up like a swaying pillar of fire, almost as tall as the devadar tree that stood some distance away.

'Now touch this boy's navel, O Agni. May Madhu's inner fire be awakened by your blessings.' I trembled with awe as the tall tongue of fire curved towards me, and in a flash, licked my navel, setting my whole body on fire. The fire moved upwards burning all obstacles to ashes until it reached my brain, and exploded into a many-splendoured, multicoloured flash that surprisingly radiated a cool and pleasant feeling down my spine. A link had been established between the lower and the higher. The way was clear and I had to traverse it patiently with Babaji's kind encouragement.

When I opened my eyes the flames were back to normal, and Babaji was smiling happily, like a doting mother watching her child taking its first step. 'Good,' he said 'that's enough for today. You meditate quietly and then go to sleep.'

'Babaji,' I said 'I wanted to ask you this yesterday, do you ever sleep? I thought you were awake throughout the night. Were you?'

'Son, I don't need to sleep. You need to sleep because your body and mind get tired and need rejuvenation. I feel no tiredness, no fatigue. You will understand this for yourself as you go along, at least to some extent. After many years, when you are involved in many an activity, you will understand how it works.'

I meditated deeply that night. My mind ascended to hitherto unexplored dimensions, and came back with answers to various questions that had troubled me. Then I bowed down to Babaji and went into the cave to sleep. Babaji sat upright in padmasana, steady as a rock, his eyes on the fire.

23

The Old Tibetan Lama

ONE DAY, JUST AFTER meditation and breakfast, Babaji sprung a surprise. 'Today, you have no fixed schedule,' he said. 'You can wander around as you please. Perhaps you would like to walk up the hills and explore the caves? Just make sure you are back before dark, okay?'

There was nothing I liked better than trekking and exploring unknown territories. I set out, taking only my water pot and walking stick. I climbed up the steep and narrow path that I had seen Babaji go up on one or two occasions. After a while, the climb became quite tough, and it had become very cold. To add to that, it started drizzling and then snowing lightly.

On either side of the path, there were a few natural caves. Babaji had warned me that Himalayan bears could some times be found living in them. So when I heard a kind of humming, murmuring sound coming from one of the caves, I was gripped with fear and froze. Then I smelled incense that seemed to come from the same direction.

Cautiously, trembling with excitement, I crept towards the mouth and into the cave. In a minute, my eyes got accustomed to the dim light that was coming from a small fire, burning in a deep pit, at the far end of the cave. Facing the fire sat a bare-bodied figure who seemed to be throwing incense into the fire and chanting something that I could not understand, in a droning tone. I quietly sat down at a distance, waiting for him to acknowledge my presence, for I was sure he was aware of my entry.

After a while, he turned in my direction and gestured for me to come closer. I moved closer to the fire. Now I could see his face clearly. It was a wrinkled and weather-beaten old face of Mongolian origin. A few grey strands of hair formed his beard and thin moustache, and he was totally bald. I guessed that he was a Buddhist monk of some sort. Surprisingly, he spoke haltingly in English. His voice was rough and sounded more like a croak. 'Greetings,' he said with folded hands, 'May the Buddha, Avalokatishwara bestow his blessings on you.' I prostrated before him and explained who I was and why I was there.

'I know, I know,' he said, 'I know your Babaji. We meet often. I am a wandering Tibetan yogi belonging to the Kargyupa sect of the great yogi Milarepa. Milarepa means cotton clad. We wear only a small cotton loincloth even in the severest of winters.'

'What were you chanting, sir, and how do you know English?'

'I shall not answer your second question. You will come to know eventually. As for the first, I was chanting the Buddhist mantra *Om Mani Padme Hum*.'

'May I ask you, sir, how you manage to remain bare-bodied even in the height of winter? Even Babaji is like you.'

'I will explain, child. We, who belong to the lineage of Milarepa, practise a breathing technique combined with visualization, called Thummo. This builds up the heat of the inner fire at the navel centre, the Manipura, and spreads it throughout the body. If you will notice, I am sweating profusely. That is because of the internal heat. Some of our yogis can dry wet sheets of cloth wrapped around their backs in minutes, even in winter.

'The Manipura is the same centre where the fire touched you yesterday. If and when necessary, your Babaji will teach you a technique similar to Thummo, which he practises.'

'Wait a minute!' I said. 'How do you know about the fire touching my navel. Babaji has not left my side since that incident, unless of course he slipped off during the night while I slept, and discussed this matter with you. I don't think so myself...'

'Child, we possess means of communications which most people do not know of, and they are not mysterious. When the mind becomes tranquil and acquires the power of one-pointed attention, it is possible to exchange thoughts. Now, because I have said this, please do not get hoodwinked by advertisements in magazines and newspapers purporting to teach telepathy for a fee. It is all nonsense. The real thing is not so easy.'

'Two more questions, sir, if I may?' I said.

'Go ahead.'

'Some books say that hidden away in certain parts of Tibet, there are remains of old extraterrestrial civilizations, is that true? Secondly, does the yeti, the abominable snowman, really exist? Have you seen one?'

'To the first question,' said the Tibetan yogi, 'yes, there are such places, and I have myself seen such a cave in an almost inaccessible part of Tibet. There, I have seen, well-preserved bodies of small-built humanoids, with skulls larger than ours, and a dark-almost-grayish complexion. However, we believe that they are an ancient race from the earth itself, and not from some other planet or galaxy. Our teachers say that this particular race was destroyed by a war between two rival civilisations that had both evolved to great heights intellectually, and ignored the feelings of love and compassion totally. The way our present civilisation is progressing, one wonders what fate awaits us.

'Now, regarding the yeti—well, it exists, although many reported sightings may be false. On the ancient route to Kailash from Badrinath, across the Mana Pass which is now almost never used, there exists an old Buddhist monastery called Tholingmutt on the Tibetan side. In the caves not far from Tholingmutt, some lamas have sighted the yeti even recently. I have seen one myself. Ask Babaji if he could take you to Tholingmutt or even to Kailash. He is quite familiar with the route, and has been there many times. Maybe you will see a yeti too.'

'I'll try,' I said. 'One last question—are you a lama?'

'No, not in the way you think. Lama is a common word used for a holy man. He may be a formally ordained lama, married or unmarried, or he may even belong to a shaman like pre-Buddhist sect in Tibet called the Bon-pa. People like us who wander about without showing symbols of affiliation to any sect, are called jogis. Milarepa was one such jogi, although the Kargyupas who follow his teachings are now headed by an ordained monk called the Karmapa, who wears formal robes. A high-ranking lama, who wields temporal and religious authority, need not necessarily be spiritually advanced.'

'Where would you place the Dalai Lama, sir?'

The old man hesitated for a while, and then, with a faraway look in his eyes said, 'The late great Thirteenth Dalai Lama was acknowledged as a highly evolved spiritual person. The first Dalai Lama was a political appointee, ordained by Kublai Khan, the great-grandson of Chengiz Khan, the Mongolian conqueror. Dalai means "the ocean", and the post of the great Lama was created because Kublai Khan, who ruled China, wanted to play a greater role in Tibetan politics. The second Dalai Lama was in fact a relative of his. Politics has always remained intertwined with religion. I won't say anything more.

'Now you must be hungry.' He gave me some horrible tasting, gluey stuff called *tsampa*, made by mixing roasted barley flour with yak's fat. I swallowed it as fast as I could and after drinking black tea, which he poured out for me, I prostrated, bid him goodbye, and left the cave.

When I got back, I saw Babaji sitting outside the cave, looking closely at some old palm leaf manuscript. 'So how is the young explorer doing?' he said smiling. 'How did the meeting with the old Tibetan yogi go? You asked him so many questions.'

'Yes, Babaji,' I said, no longer surprised by his intimate knowledge of everything I did. 'I need to ask you...'

'Later,' said Babaji, 'Now you lie down and take a good nap. In the evening, we have an important session.' I stretched myself inside the cave and was fast asleep in no time.

24

Yoga, Vedanta, and the Nath Pant

IT WAS A COLD morning. Many of the surrounding peaks wore caps of snow. It had snowed lightly the whole night, but the dhuni was still burning.

'Today, we can begin with the Upanishads,' said Babaji. 'But Babaji, aren't the Upanishads too difficult to understand and meant only for monks and great scholars?'

'That is the idea spread among the masses, by priests who feared that the direct, no-nonsense teachings of the Upanishads would make people think rationally, and take them away from the irrational beliefs and superstitions propagated and popularized by them. They were afraid that they would lose control over the public if the public began to think for itself.

'The crafty priests, who controlled both kings and their subjects by acting as middlemen between them and their Gods, therefore discouraged the study of the Upanishads. Part of the reason for the decline of this great civilization is this neglect of pure wisdom.

'That the Upanishads are meant for only sanyasins, was another myth invented by the priests. You have only to look at the Upanishads and you will find that almost all of them were taught by great rishis who were married, and even had children. Some of them, like Janaka, were great kings, and the great rishi Viswamitra who gave us the Gayatri Mantra, was a Kshatriya, a warrior, before he became a rishi.

'One must not forget that the illustrious rishi Vyasa, compiler of the Vedas and author of the *Brahmasutra*, was born of a fisherwoman. It is merit that matters, not birth in a particular community or lineage. If you think you have a soul that is incorporeal, does it have parents? Great rishis, in those days, sent their children to other rishis to study the Upanishads. That was the enlightened age, the age of Upanishads, open to all sincere seekers, irrespective of caste or creed.

'The Namboodiri Brahmin Vedantin Adi Shankaracharya, was labelled a "prachhanna baudhika"—a Buddhist in disguise—by the priestly class when he taught that one had to go back to the Upanishads, and that the Supreme Brahman, "The Truth", cannot be found except through Viveka or reasoning. Ritualistic religion was dealt a heavy blow, and the priests were fearful of losing their hold over the public. How clever they were is proved by the fact that finally, they even managed to influence the Mutts established by the original Shankaracharya, so much so, that today, they have turned into mostly, ritual-oriented establishments.

'I concede that one needs certain qualities to qualify as a student of the Upanishads: a clear, unprejudiced mind, sufficient intellectual capacity, and a sound body. A sick person does not have the energy to persist with such deep enquiry as is required in this process of self-study. Nor does an ailing body have the quality of patience, a great deal of which is required in this search. Therefore, the practice of yoga, a proper and healthy diet, and a certain peaceful mode of being is essential.'

'But Babaji,' I said, 'One needs the right teacher too!'

'I agree, but no teacher is better than a wrong teacher. The job of a teacher is to guide, not make the student dependent on him eternally. A spiritual teacher should guide the student to attain that level of knowledge and realisation at which he can stand on his own feet. Independence, Swatantrya, is the soul of the Vedantic teaching.

'So now, when I say Upanishads, I mean the eleven principal Upanishads which are the earliest: the *Isavasya*, the *Kena*, the *Chandogya*, the *Brihadaranyaka*, the *Mundaka*, the *Mandukya*, the *Katha*, the *Prashna*, the *Svetashvatara*, the *Aitareya* and the *Taittiriya*. Many of the later

Upanishads do not exist in their pure form, and some were concocted to support sectarian beliefs. So we will leave them alone.

'The word Upanishad comes from the root "upa", which means "close". It implies that the Upanishad is understood by those who sit close to the teacher, or who are intimately involved with the teacher in understanding a multi-dimensional reality—an experience which often cannot even be put into words, or described to a mind which normally operates within limited dimensions.

'The ordinarily wandering mind should learn to "shad", sit—the last syllable of the word Upa-ni-shad, which means, all unnecessary movement of thought has to cease and in that restful moment of the otherwise constantly agitated mind, that which is beyond the confines of thought, is revealed.

'The *Kena Upanishad* which belongs to the *Sama Veda* says, "That, which the mind cannot conceive but to which the mind owes its very existence, know O! disciple, that alone is the Brahman, the Truth; nothing that you worship here."

'You will learn Sanskrit so that you can understand the originals. It is the neglect of the Sanskrit language that has resulted in the colossal ignorance of the wisdom of this country. Not knowing the originals, people are led astray by unscrupulous translators and interpreters, who usually twist the scriptures to suit their sectarian beliefs. We will study the *Kena*, the *Isavasya* and *Mandukya*, one by one as we proceed.[1]

'Babaji, were Buddha's teachings close to the Upanishads?'

'The very fact that the orthodox priests called Shankaracharya a Buddhist in disguise shows the similarity of the teachings. Even the grand guru of Shankara, Gaudapadacharya, who wrote the famous commentary on the *Mandukya Upanishad*, is considered by many to have been a Buddhist. This is because, in his "Ajaatha Vaadha" doctrine, he taught that the world was an illusion, a delusion rather, and that the Brahman is the only reality that ever existed. Substitute the word Brahman with the Buddhist term shunya (nothingness) and

---

[1] For a full discussion on the above Upanishads, see *Wisdom of the Rishis* by Sri M.

you have the central theme of the great Buddhist teacher Nagarjuna's *Prajna Paramitha*.'

'Please Babaji, this is getting too philosophical. Tell me something about yoga and yoga practice,' I said.

'Alright,' said Babaji with a smile. 'Listen carefully, Madhu. Yoga is an ancient science that was later codified by the rishi Patanjali. The *Ashtanga Yoga Sutras* of Patanjali are priceless gems. The aim of the eight-limbed yoga is *Chitta Vritti Nirodha* which means "eliminating the agitations of the mind." When the mind has been stilled by following the rules and regulations prescribed for the contemplative yogi and the practice of asanas, pranayama, bandha, mudras and kriya, it enters the state of samadhi.

'Now, there are many kinds of samadhi, and samadhi is the basic requirement. After that, the mind, which has understood the Upanishadic concepts, enters greater levels of consciousness and is freed of all conditioning. This is the state of freedom or *Kaivalya*, that is the final aim of yoga.'

'But Babaji,' I said, 'What about the yogic powers, the siddhis, the supernatural powers of Omnipresence, Omnipotence and Omniscience?'

Babaji laughed loudly and said, 'Everyone is interested in yogic powers. Any book with a title like *How to Develop Yogic Powers* will sell like hot idlis. The fact is that yogic powers exist but are quite rare. Most demonstrations of so-called miracles are however mere conjuring tricks[2]. It is true that in the process of yogic practice, the mind becomes so one-pointed that what an ordinary man may take years to achieve, the yogi who sets his mind on the same, may achieve in a short while.

'Also, by virtue of the mind becoming still and peaceful, and to a great extent free of self-centredness, a link is established with other minds, and what passes in other minds, may be sensed by the yogi, even a beginner. In reality, there is only one mind, and when this is understood, not in theory but actually, then the thoughts and actions of a yogi

---

[2] See *How to Levitate and Other Great Secrets of Magic* by James Talbot.

appear to those whose minds are still fragmented, as extraordinary, and even miraculous.

'But take this from me—no man or woman born of the physical union of male and female can ever be omniscient, omnipotent and omnipresent, no matter how highly advanced he or she is. A body that is born will die however long it might have lived due to proper diet and rejuvenation through yogic means. Even Sri Guru Babaji, my guru, who has lived many hundred years will die. I too shall die someday.

'What the common man calls miracles are the workings of certain laws of nature which he has not hitherto understood or discovered. The yogi who knows some of these laws also knows how to make them work.'

I then asked him about the Naths. 'Babaji, you said to me once that you belonged to the Nath tradition. Can you please tell me about it?'

'Yes,' said Babaji, 'I will tell you a little now. By and by you shall learn more. The Naths are an ancient order founded by Shiv Mahadev who is also known as Adinath. The next teacher was the great Matsyendranath, who was the teacher of the famous Goraknath. The yogi called Balaknath in the Nath tradition, because he always appeared like a teenager, is none other than my master Sri Guru Babaji who was also your personal teacher in the past.

'The Naths were yogis par excellence. All the important works on yoga like the *Goraksha Shataka*, the *Gheranda Samhita*, the *Hathayoga Pradipika* and so on were written by Nath yogis. The asanas, pranayama, Kriya Yoga, bandhas and mudras were practised and perfected by them. They were usually itinerant yogis and were popularly called "Kaanphatas" or torn-eared ones, because they punctured the cartilage of their ears and wore large earrings like I do.'

Babaji let me examine the rings. 'What about me, Babaji?' I asked. 'When should my cartilage be pierced?'

'Yours don't have to be,' said Babaji, 'because you have to go back into the world and live like an ordinary man. But I shall pierce your earlobes instead of the cartilage, and you can wear copper earrings while you live with me. Afterwards, before you go to the plains, you can take them off. The holes will heal after sometime.

'Also, the Naths light dhunis wherever they live. Sainath kept his dhuni constantly burning in Shirdi and it still is. You are given special permission. You need not keep a dhuni burning always because the nature of your work is such. You may light a dhuni on special occasions, if you wish to.'

'Babaji, you have taught me the Kriya Pranayam, the hot and cold one. Please tell me something more about Kriya Yoga.'

'That,' said Babaji, 'I shall tell you later when we make the first journey on foot to Tholingmutt in Tibet on the way to Kailash. There, I shall pierce your ear lobes and give you copper earrings. Aren't you eager to go to Tibet, to Tholingmutt?'

I marvelled at his capacity to read my mind. From the time the old Tibetan jogi had mentioned Tholingmutt, I had wanted to ask Babaji if we could travel there together, but had put it off for one reason or another. 'That would be great, Babaji!' I shouted in excitement. 'Kailash, the seat of Shiva, the Mahayogi.'

'Tholingmutt yes, but Kailash we shall see. Now it is time to get the noon meal ready, and get some firewood for the dhuni. Too much of learning at one time is like eating too much food at one sitting. It doesn't digest properly. Om Shanti Shanti Shanti.'

With that, the session came to a close.

25

Tholingmutt and the Mountain Man

I WAS ALL EXCITED when, one evening, Babaji suddenly declared, 'Madhu, the day after tomorrow, we start for Tholingmutt in Western Tibet.' This was going to be my first journey with Babaji.

The next morning, we set out to meet the Ravalji, and I wondered what the Ravalji's reaction would be when he saw me with Babaji. But a greater surprise awaited me. As soon as the Ravalji saw Babaji, he stood up and greeted him with folded hands saying, 'Namaste. Please come, Swami,' in Malayalam. After that, the conversation continued in pure, North Travancore Malayalam. I could not believe my ears. Babaji looked more like a Kashmiri than a Malayali, and had never spoken to me in Malayalam. Then I wondered, maybe he was from Kerala. After all, I saw him for the first time in Trivandrum.

'I warned this young man about the fraud gurus who abound in places of pilgrimage,' said the Ravalji, 'and advised him to go back and do some useful work. Thank God he found you, or is it that you found him, Swami?'

'We have an old link,' said Babaji, 'and I am glad you had that chat with him. Tomorrow morning, we are setting out for Tholingmutt and I need a little help from you.'

'At your service,' said the Ravalji.

We spent the night in the cave of Vyasa, and set out at daybreak towards the Mana Pass. With us was a Nepalese porter-cum-cook, Fateh

Bahadur, a tough young man a little older than me, and a pony provided by the Tibetan headman of Mana village. The pony was carrying a lovely tent—enough for three—provided by a Marwari trader, and bags containing warm clothing, provisions, a gas stove, some utensils and all other things necessary for the journey. I also carried a little money, which the Ravalji kindly gave us.

I was clad in a thick woollen Kashmiri robe and wore a sheepskin cap, socks and sheepskin moccasins. Babaji, as usual, wore nothing other than a cotton sheet around his body and brown canvas shoes. Fateh Bahadur wore a coat of some thick furry material and thick leather boots. He said he had accompanied Indian and Tibetan merchants previously and knew the route. Not to worry, said Babaji, he had himself travelled on that route a number of times.

As we set out, I asked Babaji how long we would take to reach Kailash. I was told that this was the ancient route to Kailash taken by Sri Rama, the Pandavas and the great rishis including Sukadev. Babaji said, 'We will first reach Tholingmutt, and then decide about Kailash.'

This was to prove ominously prophetic. We had to return from Tholingmutt because I fell seriously ill. It took me forty years to fulfill my desire to visit Kailash. After I turned sixty, I finally travelled to Kailash with a group of fifty-seven friends. The route was different—we travelled from Kathmandu.

From Kesava Prayag, the confluence of the Saraswati and the Alakananda, we travelled north along the bank of the Saraswati. The path was difficult and it was extremely cold. We could not walk more than ten kilometres a day. Food was no problem since our Nepalese porter Fateh Bahadur cooked chapatis and potatoes on his gas stove. A handful of soaked chickpeas and jaggery kept our energy levels high. Babaji's special pranayama helped to tackle the oxygen shortage in the air as we climbed higher. At night, the three of us slept in the fairly spacious tent.

The trek however was very tough. After Vyasa Guha, there was hardly any road. We had to make our way through boulders and heaps of snow. We just followed the Saraswati. All around, looking down at us, stood snow-covered mountains. Many of the tributaries of the Saraswati that we had to cross were freezing cold and we managed to cross them with great difficulty. Fifty or so kilometres from Badrinath, the landscape became grim. The way was covered with snow, and was slippery in the extreme. In some places, Fateh Bahadur had to clear the snow with a shovel.

We were headed towards the Mana Pass, 18,000 feet above sea level, which is usually attempted only by hardened mountaineers. The pass, well known since ancient times, stood before us, dazzling like pure, polished silver. A deep blue mountain soon appeared. The Neela Parvat, said Babaji, where the great sage Kakabhusundi lived once upon a time.

On the eleventh night, we pitched our tent, some twelve kilometres or so below the Mana Pass. Fateh Bahadur, with the little help that I could provide, managed to light a small dhuni outside the entrance of the tent. Babaji drew a protective circle around it with his right hand, and it remained lit for a few hours in spite of the cold winds that were blowing outside. That night, before I fell asleep out of sheer exhaustion, I asked Babaji if he was from Kerala.

'No,' he said, 'but I have travelled quite a bit in Kerala. That time I came to reestablish contact with you in Trivandrum, I was on my way back from Agastya Kuta near Kovalam Beach. I have also been to Guruvayoor, Sabarimalai...'

'That doesn't answer my question, Babaji,' I said. 'You spoke Malayalam like a native with the Ravalji, and you never spoke a word of that language with me.'

'I know what you are thinking,' said Babaji. 'Babaji must be omniscient. He knows everything.' Well the fact is, no human being with a physical brain can ever be omniscient. Yes, one can acquire the capacity to tune into someone else's mind when required and temporarily utilise the knowledge acquired by that mind to accomplish certain tasks. My speaking Malayalam was a demonstration of that.

'Now you should sleep. We have a tough journey tomorrow. Invoke the fire in your Manipura centre, with the Rang, Bijakshara, and the special Thummo Pranayama. Do vigorous Nabhi Kriya and you will feel warm enough.' I fell asleep with Babaji sitting beside me.

The next morning, we started the climb to the top of the pass. The whole scene was of glaciers and snow-covered rocks. I had a terrible headache and nausea. Babaji explained to me that it was because of the shortage of oxygen. Even the experienced Fateh Bahadur complained of severe headache. Babaji advised us to do the dog-breathing exercise—breathing in and out with the tongue hanging out like a dog. Soon, we passed the beautiful Neela Parvat, and in a few hours, were on top of the Mana Pass. Beside us was a frozen lake called the Devasaras, the lake of the gods. Babaji asked us to sit for a few minutes and meditate.

To me, the scene looked divine. The bare-chested, resplendent master of yoga, sitting steady and straight in padmasana, surrounded by the magnificent snow-clad peaks of the Himachala, the immovable snow-mountain. I closed my eyes and meditated on the godlike figure who sat before me. What other god had I seen with my mortal eyes?

Something strange happened. The headache disappeared. A peaceful mood wafted into my soul. The bitter cold was replaced by a soothing warmth, and for a brief moment it was as if we, Babaji and I, were not two, but one single being. I felt myself floating, and opened my eyes to see if I was really levitating, and found that I was not, but the deep meditation mood had vanished by then. Babaji smilingly said, 'Enough for now. Not to hurry, lad.'

Fateh Bahadur said, '*Chhota jogi*,' and laughed.

We began the descent to the other side, where the Indian boundary ends and Tibet begins. It was getting colder and there was nothing but snow all around. By evening, the three of us and the pony had reached the Tibetan plains. The earth was reddish and we no longer had to walk in snow and ice. That night, we pitched our tent in a small meadow. Wild horses were grazing nearby, unafraid of strangers.

After a gap of many days, a dhuni was lit, and after meditating for an hour or so, we had a lovely meal of chapati and potato curry prepared by Fateh Bahadur. He had found water in a nearby stream, and soon we were sipping black tea and chatting merrily. It was a starlit night. I woke up startled by fierce growls coming from close by. 'Sleep,' said Babaji. 'It is the snow leopard hunting the wild horses. You have nothing to fear.' The horses neighed piteously and then fell silent. We heard the satisfied grunts of the snow leopard as it enjoyed its meal. I went to sleep again.

The next morning we set out towards Tholingmutt. After six days of pleasant journeying we arrived. It had taken us twenty-one days to complete the journey from Badrinath. The first thing our eyes met with was a gigantic Buddha, whose head was as tall as the Buddhist monastery. We were allowed to set up our camp close by.

Babaji took us around the monastery. It had many Hindu deities, including Bhadrakali, the terrible manifestation of feminine divine energy. The lama who looked after the shrine, told us that they believed that Tholingmutt was the original Badrinath, and that the present Badrinath temple was built because Tholingmutt was inaccessible to most people.

We were taken to see the abbott, the High Lama called the Rinpoche. The Rinpoche showed great respect towards Babaji, and Babaji reciprocated the gesture. They began to talk in Tibetan and this time I was not so surprised. After the conversation, the Rinpoche blessed me as I kneeled in front of him with my tongue stretched out.

The monastery had more than ten monks in residence, and there was a large kitchen. But Babaji preferred to live in the tent and Fateh Bahadur cooked for us. After the meal, Babaji told me that in the night, he would formally initiate me into the Nath Pant. I did not have to puncture the cartilage of my ears. I would wear copper earrings as long as I remained in the Himalayas, and remove them when I went back to the plains.

In the night, sitting in front of the dhuni, I was initiated into the secret mantra of the Nath tradition. Babaji expertly punctured my ear lobes, and I wore the copper rings. My great desire to look like a yogi was fulfilled. Babaji said, 'All of us Naths light the dhuni wherever we go. But in your case, that condition does not apply. You need not keep the dhuni except for special occasions like Shiv Ratri or Gurupoornima—so my master has ordained. You may also remove your copper rings and wear ordinary clothes when you go down to the plains, for you have a special mission. Live on earth like anybody else, and keep your mind on the highest level of consciousness. From now on, you are a Nath, and in our lineage, you shall be known as Madhukarnath—M.'

I prostrated at Babaji's feet. Fateh Bahadur, tired after the long journey, fell asleep. We sat chatting in front of the fire. I asked Babaji what he thought of the lama's belief that the Buddha of Tholingmutt was the original Badrinath. 'The fact is,' said Babaji, 'in ancient times, there were Buddhist monks and Buddhist temples all over India. It is quite possible that the deity at Badrinath was that of a cross-legged Buddha which the great Shankaracharya turned into a cross-legged Narayana. Nowhere else does Narayana sit in padmasana. What does it matter really? Purity of life and devotion are more important than being Buddhist or Hindu. Did you observe what a spiritually advanced soul the Rinpoche is? So let's not get into such controversies.'

The next morning, I saw very tall Tibetans from the Kham district, who lived in small huts in the hills. Some of them, who were professional messengers, practised a skill which is the closest thing to levitation that I have seen. They had long sticks, like the poles used for pole vault, which they used to travel long distances, almost as if they were flying in the air. They would strike one end of the pole on the ground; practise a certain breathing technique and, holding on to the other side, fly quite a long distance.

After three days of rest, we proceeded east towards Kailash. In three days, we had reached the village of Daapa. There was a Buddhist shrine there and a large lamasery. A large number of monks lived there. Nearby was a big market where Indian merchants came to trade with Tibetans. We could not proceed further than Daapa because something unexpected and unfortunate happened. I fell ill. A terrible fever came upon me. In spite of the blankets and proximity to the fireplace, I was overcome by bouts of shivering and a severe headache. It felt as if someone was pounding my head with a hammer.

The physician in the lamasery gave me many doses of bitter herbal preparations, but the fever persisted. One night, I was lying alone in the tent running very high temperature, semi-conscious, when I heard a low whine, like that of a dog in pain. My face was turned towards the entrance of the tent and I saw the silhouette of a huge creature that looked like a gorilla. I wondered if I was hallucinating. I wanted to shout but no sound came out of my mouth. I trembled with fear.

As the creature came towards me, I saw by the light of a hurricane lamp that it had cream-coloured fur. Again making that funny whining sound, it moved close to me and suddenly pushed something into my mouth. In spite of the fever, I could taste the sweetness of the gooey stuff. Then, it quickly turned and ran out of the tent.

I heard a scream from outside and Fateh Bahadur ran into the tent. 'Mountain man!' he gasped. 'Are you alright?'

'Yes,' was all that I could say, before I drifted into a deep sleep.

The next morning I was cured sufficiently to be able to travel. 'No Kailash this time,' Babaji declared. 'You will go after many years with a big group and celebrate Gurupoornima on the way. Now, we should head back to Badrinath.' I had no option but to agree. We started back, with me sitting on the poor pony most of the time. On the way, I asked Babaji, 'Was that a yeti I saw last night?'

'Well,' Babaji said, 'Let's not speculate. In any case, keep it to yourself. Most people don't believe in the yeti, and they are likely to dismiss it as a fever-induced hallucination.'

It took us only sixteen days to reach Badrinath. On the way, perched mostly on the pony, I enjoyed the divine scenery: the snowy peaks, the beautiful streams, the frozen lakes and the magical moments created by the rising sun reflected on the icy peaks. In Badrinath, we returned the pony and the tent and bid farewell to Fateh Bahadur. Babaji paid him handsomely. Fateh Bahadur left us reluctantly. By then, I was almost normal.

Back in the cave at Charan Paduka, Babaji nursed me back to health, even bringing me special food at times. In almost two weeks, I felt I was fine and back in shape. 'Now,' Babaji said, 'get ready to travel to the Valley of the Flowers, Hemkund Sahib, and then to the five Kedars.'

26

The Valley of Flowers and Hemkund

ONE COLD MORNING, BABAJI and I set out for Govindghat near Pandukeshwar. This time, I found myself quite fit, and could easily follow Babaji as he walked briskly down the path. I no longer needed footwear, and both of us trekked barefoot—the master and the disciple. Compared to the tough climb to Mana Pass, this was child's play. I had also learnt to eat whenever food was available, and remain without food for long periods if necessary.

Staying at night in temples and wayside dharamshalas, we reached Govindghat in three days. That night we stayed at the gurdwara in Govindghat. One great thing about Sikh gurdwaras is that any traveller is allowed to stay for three nights, and free food and blankets are provided if necessary.

The next morning, we began the fourteen-kilometre trek to Ghangaria. The climb was quite steep, and the path went alongside the Laxman Ganga. On the way, we passed the small village of Bhyandar. Beyond the village, the path descended, and one could walk beside the river. Babaji was silently enjoying the beauty of the scenery. For a long time, no words were exchanged between us. Words were not required. It was a joyous silence.

Already, exotic flowers were visible. Babaji broke the silence. Like a botanist, he pointed to various flowers, saying, 'that is the cobra lily, and that sunflower-like flower is the imela.' After the last bit of steep climbing, we reached Ghangaria. We crossed the small bridge across the Laxman Ganga that originates from the Hemkund lake. From there, the path to the right goes to Hemkund Sahib, 15,000 feet above sea level, and the path to the left goes to the Valley of Flowers.

Further up, was a small iron bridge over the Puspawati River, which hurtles down and joins the Laxman Ganga. Already, 'blue poppies,' as Babaji pointed out, had begun to appear.

We crossed the bridge and climbed up the narrow path until we came to the remains of a glacier. We crossed the glacier, went up for around three kilometres, and entered the valley after crossing a small, wooden bridge. The beauty of the place stunned me. I never expected anything of such magnificence. As far as the eye could see, one saw vast meadows of flowers of different varieties, as if a divine being had sorted them out and farmed them expertly.

Babaji once again astonished me with his knowledge of flowers and other details of the valley. 'This is the Himalayan balsam,' said Babaji. 'And this white one is the Himalayan hogweed. This whirly white flower is the famous edelweiss, the symbol of the Alps. See there, on the other side, those are trailing blue flowers, the lovely forget-me-nots, blue poppies, blue geraniums, asters... Oh! So many varieties.'

'How did the public discover this hidden heaven, Babaji?'

'It was known for long by some yogis and the locals,' said Babaji. 'The locals believed it was inhabited by divine fairylike beings called apsaras and gandharvas. My master, Sri Guru Babaji, loved to bring me to this valley. Further up, is a little cave which he frequented. Let's go and meditate with open eyes. Such tremendously beautiful manifestations of nature are divine. The divine you seek within is right here before your eyes. Just relax, look, and breathe in the perfumed air.

'As to your question regarding how the world came to know of the existence of this paradise, Frank Smith, a mountaineer and botanist came upon the valley in the year 1931. He was stunned, and it was he who called it the "Valley of Flowers". Come, let's go to the cave.'

Walking through a narrow valley with abundant white flowers on either side, we came to a small cave, hidden under a rocky ledge. 'My master and I have sat in meditation here,' said Babaji. 'You and I shall sit now.'

We sat for a long time in that beautiful spot, absorbed by the myriad colours and the faintly intoxicating scent of some exotic flowers. Babaji was silent.

After a while, I broke the silence softly, 'I now understand the meaning of what the *Isavasya Upanishad* declares,' I said. '*Isa Vasyam Idam Sarvam*. For a long time, I had thought that it meant that Isa, the Supreme Being, resided hidden inside everything, but now I have realised that all that is: what we see, and smell, and touch, and taste, are no different from Isa. There is no need to search anywhere.'

'Ah!' said Babaji. 'Slowly and steadily, don't hurry. Now your brain is clearing up. Let's go see the Margaret Legge monument, and then we have to walk back to Ghangaria.'

We got up and walked a short distance. Margaret Legge, Babaji explained, was a botanist from the Botantical Gardens at Edinburgh who, while exploring the Valley of Flowers in 1939, slipped and had a fatal fall. The local people buried her, and later her sister came and erected a memorial. The epitaph inscribed on a stone slab read: 'I will lift my eyes unto the hills from whence cometh my help.'

We walked as quickly as possible and reached Ghangaria just before nightfall. The air was chill and crisp. That night, we stayed in a small stone hut belonging to a sadhu from Rajasthan known to Babaji. He seemed to be in awe of Babaj and took great care of us.

The next morning, we set out on the trek to Hemkund Sahib. The climb to Hemkund Sahib is quite steep. There were large crowds of devoted Sikhs chanting '*Wahe Guru*' at the top of their voices, sustaining their strength through faith, and winding their way up the path. There is a place midway where most travellers rest before completing the rest of the journey the next day, but we preferred to walk up after a few minutes of rest and a cup of tea. By late evening, we were at Hemkund Sahib. As expected the cold was severe.

The Sikhs believe that their last guru, Guru Gobind Singh, spent many days performing penance and meditating near the Hemkund lake in one of his past births. The oxygen content in the air was low, and Babaji advised me to change the rhythm of breathing. Soon the mild headache I had vanished.

The Hemkund, literally 'lake of ice,' was extremely beautiful. The water was crystal clear and part of the surface was frozen. The surrounding peaks were all snow-covered and the whole setting was magical. Some devout Sikhs were taking a quick dip in the freezing waters of the lake, braving the risk of pneumonia.

We went to the gurdwara and were served hot kichidi, chapatis and a sweet pudding known as *kada* prasad. Enough blankets were provided and I went to sleep early. I was tired.

The next morning, we began the trek to the old Laxman temple. This time we were alone. Very few travellers even knew of its existence. After an arduous trek, we arrived at the Laxman temple, a dilapidated stone structure. It was biting cold. There was no priest to fleece the public. Someone had installed a small human figure, supposed to represent Laxman, brother of the legendary hero, Rama. The idol was neither washed nor cleaned, and it stood leaning against the wall of the sanctum sanctorum.

'My master and I have sat here too, for a whole night,' said Babaji. 'You see wonderful lights coming down from the mountains and moving in the direction of the lake. But we cannot spend the night here this time. It gets freezing cold, and you have just recovered from high fever.' We sat for an hour or so, quietly admiring the divine panorama. The Brahma kamal, a rare bluish lotus, grew in and around this area. Babaji was in a spiritually exalted mood. His face shone as if lit by a powerful light. Peace reigned undisturbed. Suddenly, Babaji said, 'Now, let's go.'

We retraced our steps to the gurdwara, arriving just in time for a hot meal of chapatis and dal, and immediately afterwards began our descent to Ghangaria. By dusk, we were at Ghangaria, and stayed the night with the same Rajasthani sadhu who belonged to the Juna Akhada.

Babaji went out for a stroll in the night and I was left alone with the sadhu. We sat before the dhuni, and the sadhu lit his clay chillum, which was loaded with hashish and tobacco. 'Will you have a puff of the sacred smoke?' he asked me. I declined.

'Your Babaji doesn't either,' he said. 'You belong to the class called Raja Yogis. You probably don't need this to fix your attention on the great inner reality. You know, you are lucky, really fortunate. This Babaji is a greatly advanced yogi. He does not take disciples easily. I have seen him reject even those I thought were really sincere seekers. Perhaps, there is some past-birth connection between you two. I saw him glance at you with great affection, the other day, as if you were his own child. I am truly amazed.'

I meditated for a long time, sitting a little away from the smoke. It was a great and deep meditation. Certain doubts I had were spontaneously answered in a flash. Even when I finally rolled myself in the quilt provided by the sadhu and prepared to sleep, Babaji had not returned. I felt like a little child waiting for his mother. Sleep mothered me in her cozy arms, and I drifted off.

27

Meeting the Siddhar

EARLY THE NEXT MORNING, we set out for Kalpeshwar.

Among the five Kedars, Kedarnath is the best known and perhaps the most impressive. Every year, thousands of pilgrims brave the severe cold and climb the tough, steep fourteen kilometres to the Kedarnath temple, 12,500 feet above sea level, in the Kedar range.

The other four are mostly unknown, except to locals and a few wandering sadhus. Untouched and uncorrupted by the crowds that visit well-known centres of pilgrimage, they stand in splendid isolation amidst the most beautiful natural surroundings. Kalpeshwar was the first of these Kedars, if one started from Badri.

From Govindghat, we walked down the road that leads to Joshi Mutt. By noon, we had moved out of the main road and entered a mud track to the right called a pagdandi. To our left, flowed the Vishnu Ganga. Soon, the mud track also ended, but Babaji seemed to know the way. Walking through the jungle, sometimes over rocks, sometimes between them, we arrived in a short time at a tiny hamlet called Chaim Khal.

There, the small community of Garhwalis came out to welcome us, for they had recognised Babaji. The village head, a very old and wizened man wearing an old coat patched in several places, bent down to touch Babaji's feet. 'Pranam Babaji,' he said. 'So you have found a disciple.' Babaji just smiled and blessed him.

We were fed a sumptuous meal of rotis made of ramdana and hot pumpkin curry. A piece of sugar candy and a hot cup of black tea completed the meal. The whole village stood around us watching. Some women came forward with their children to be blessed by Babaji. They tried to persuade Babaji to stay, but Babaji was determined to leave.

We set out from Chaim Khal a short while after our lunch. Then began a climb that became steeper as we went along. We were headed for Barki, quite close to Kalpeshwar, and reached it in a few hours. There was a small, neglected Shiva temple which, Babaji said, got some attention from the hill folks once every year during the annual puja.

Two hours later, passing through a beautiful forest filled with marigolds, we entered the wondrous valley of Urgum. The sun had just begun to set and the scenery was a painter's paradise. In the distance, the snow-covered peaks reflected the golden light of the setting sun. Marigolds grew in abundance everywhere. A stream gushed on one side, its waters pure and crystal clear. Nearby was a waterfall whose white waters flowed over dark blue-black cliffs from which, Babaji said, the resin known as *shilajit* in Ayurveda oozed out.

Hidden away amongst these unspoilt manifestations of nature, in the centre of a natural cave, dwelt the Kalpeshwar Shiva in the form of a stone linga. One entered through a small arch with a brass bell suspended from it. Babaji and I rang the bell to announce our arrival and went into the cave temple. The priest, who came from the nearby village of Devagram in the Urgum Valley, greeted Babaji with great reverence, touching his feet and bowing down with folded hands.

Darkness was approaching and he sought permission to perform the evening aarti with a fairly big oil lamp. The aarti was performed by the priest and Babaji chanting the *Om Namah Shivaya* mantra. I rang a little silver bell. In the light of the lamp the priest swung around, I saw that the linga was one of many stone lingas scattered around the sanctum sanctorum. After the worship, we sat in silence. The silence was one of peace and love, and was all-pervasive.

The priest then offered us some consecrated honey that was very sweet and had a faint fragrance of marigold. He insisted that we accompany him to Devagram, but Babaji preferred to stay in the single-room rest house built for travellers. It had an open doorway and in front of the doorstep was a firepit. The priest said he would come back with firewood and food, and inform the village headman about Babaji's arrival. Soon, we were left alone. The moon came out of the clouds, and the sky was starlit. It was cold. We sat outside the room and Babaji reminded me to wrap the blanket and muffler properly around my body.

'For many years,' said Babaji, 'one of the senior-most disciples of my master lived here in Kalpeshwar. Now he has shifted to Rudranath. Hopefully, we shall meet him there.'

'Babaji,' I said, 'may I ask you something?'

'Go ahead.'

'Where were you born and how old are you?'

Babaji laughed. 'That's not important, but if you insist, I had Kashmiri parents. About my age, I can only say that I am much older than I look. When the great yogi Shyama Charan Lahiri first met my master Sri Guru Babaji, I was the one who led him to Babaji's seat inside the cave.'

'But that was over a hundred years ago!' I exclaimed. 'You do not look more than maybe thirty.'

'With proper diet and the practice of kayakalpa, one can live for long and retain one's youth,' said Babaji. 'You may also need to practise kayakalpa occasionally, to cope with the pressures of society later in life.'

'What pressures, Babaji?' I asked. 'It's so wonderful here. No pressures of any kind. I will live with you forever, wandering in the Himalayas. I don't want to go down to the plains.'

Babaji looked at me affectionately. 'You may not want to, but you have to,' he said. 'You have work to do, my master's work. Not immediately, so don't worry. We will wander in these beautiful regions for some time.'

'I have no problem,' I said. 'As long as you are around, and I can see you. Like your master, I am sure you'll keep your body young and intact, and always guide me.'

'No,' said Babaji. 'Only the great one, my master, whom we call Sri Guru Babaji can do that, because he is here for a special purpose. As for me, I have to go at some point in the future, although I can keep my body well preserved till then.'

I was shocked. Trembling with emotion, I said 'Babaji, don't ever go away, please.'

'Silly boy,' said Babaji. 'Guidance does not depend on the physical body. Also, don't get attached so much to this body. The aim of all your training is to make you independent. You should stand on your own feet. Even dependence on a guru is an obstacle. Be free.'

The priest arrived, accompanied by the headman of the village. They carried firewood and food. The headman was unhappy that Babaji had not come down to the village to rest.

'How's your health?' inquired Babaji.

'By your blessings, alright,' said the headman. 'So, you have a young yogi with you, Baba. Good, looks bright.' He turned to me. 'You are lucky,' he said, 'to have found a guru like Baba.'

They lit the dhuni, left the food inside and departed. 'Please grace the village tomorrow, Baba,' they said as they left.

We meditated, sitting in front of the dhuni. The flames danced with joy and bestowed warmth to our bodies and peace to our minds. We then ate the familiar ramdana roti and potato curry, but this time we had plenty of wild honey to dip our rotis in. Babaji told me to sleep as we had a long way to travel the next day.

The early morning was magical; the river, the mountains, the abundant marigolds. We had a dip in the river, and after drying ourselves, set out for perhaps the most fascinating valley in the Garhwal Himalayas. We soon reached the hamlet of Devagram. The entire village, led by the headman, had come out to welcome us. We were taken to the headman's humble dwelling. The women washed our feet; we were made to sit on cushions and fed sumptuously. Curious children pointed at us, giggling.

Babaji talked to some of the villagers. They seemed to know him. 'Frequent traveller,' I said to myself. After an hour or so, we were reluctantly allowed to proceed, but not before we were given two bags of food and a bottle of honey to eat on the way.

'When you meet Jogi Maharaj in Rudranath, please give him our prostrations,' said the headman as we walked away.

We walked through the green valley of Urgum. A light drizzle accompanied us, and a fully formed rainbow welcomed us. We walked for two hours, speaking very little. Babaji in front, as usual, nimble-footed as a mountain goat, and the disciple following behind, trying hard to imitate his master's movements.

Suddenly, the silence was broken by human voices. We had climbed down the pine-lined valley and entered the small village of Dumakh. Children came running out, shouting and laughing. The headman's eldest son welcomed Babaji and gave him the sad news that since Babaji's last visit, his father had passed away. Babaji and I were taken to the headman's house and fed rotis, dal and potatoes.

The little village of Dumakh was in a heavenly spot. Close by was a blue lake, and three or four rivulets sang their way down the sloping valley. I sipped the fresh water, which the villagers claimed had medicinal properties. Giant pine trees stood all around the village. Babaji took me to a raised spot in the hills and showed me the Dronagiri range, far away on the horizon. We bid farewell to the villagers and continued our trek.

By dusk, after a long vigorous climb, we reached Panar. 'The Kakabhusundi lake is not far from here,' said Babaji, 'but we can't go there now. In the morning, if the sky is clear, we shall see the Nanda Devi. We will have to spend tonight in a small natural cave close by. I have stopped here once with my master. These areas are the great one's favourite haunts.'

My heart lit up with expectancy—would he come and bless us, the great Sri Guru Babaji? Finding our way down a narrow valley, we soon reached the mouth of a large cave. By then, it was almost fully dark. I was surprised to see light coming from inside the cave. I trembled with excitement. Were my prayers going to be answered? Was the great guru going to… 'Come in quickly,' said Babaji. 'A storm is building up, and it will soon start snowing.'

Even the usually unruffled Babaji was taken by surprise as we entered the cave. 'Oh!' he exclaimed. A warm dhuni was lit in the middle of the fairly spacious cave, and facing us sat a dark-complexioned, short, chubby man, with long black hair falling to his shoulders, and a thick flowing beard. He too wore just a white loincloth like Babaji.

'Ah!' he shouted, and jumped up when he saw us, 'Aaha! I have caught the great Maheshwarnath, unawares. You thought I was in Rudranath. Well, here I am, in Panar.' Babaji tried to touch his feet, but he did not let him. 'Mahesh, you do not have to do that.' Then he rested his hands on my shoulders and looked at my eyes. 'So Sri Guru has plans for this young man. The great one told me about you, Madhu. Get ready for a tough life, my dear fellow. I am sure Mahesh is the best guide you can get.'

'This is my senior guru bhai, Tenkasi Siddhar,' said Babaji. 'He used to live near the Tenkasi waterfalls for many years, and Sri Guru Babaji instructed him to move to the Himalayas. He speaks Tamil and Malayalam.'

The Siddhar turned to me and said in Tamil, 'Of course, you know Tamil. Trivandrum is a border area. Many understand Tamil there, right?'

'Yes, Siddharae,' I replied in Tamil. 'I can speak Tamil well. I had many Tamil-speaking friends.'

'That's nice,' said the Siddhar. 'You must be longing to eat rice, right? See, I have made rice and your favourite sambhar for you—and that too piping hot—and some lovely milk payasam.' He pointed to some mud pots stacked near the dhuni. 'Enjoy yourself, come.'

After chanting Om, we enjoyed our dinner. At least I did, and after dinner, the Siddhar had a long conversation with me. Babaji preferred to listen. He told me that he had accompanied my master to the south when Babaji had come to Trivandrum, to re-establish contact with me. He had gone to Agastya Kuta near the Kovalam seashore to meditate while Babaji was busy with his work of finding me.

He also gave me a gist of the teachings of the Tamil Siddha lineage and suggested that I read the great *Thiru Mantiram* by the sage Thirumoolar, a disciple of Agastya. The link between the Tamil Siddhas, the Nath Pant, Kashmiri Shaivism and Sri Guru Babaji was explained. When I asked why some people referred to Sri Guru as Mahaavtar Babaji, he said the word Mahaavtar was coined much later by an enthusiastic writer who was not his direct disciple. 'To all of us,' he said, 'he is Sri Guru, and the mantra we use to invoke him is, "*Sri Gurubhyo Namah*." Anyone who chants that with attention and humility is immediately blessed by Sri Guru Babaji.'

'Now, you sleep. Tomorrow, you have a long climb to Rudranath. I am going to be here for a while. I am waiting for someone.'

I selected a corner closest to the fire, and rolled myself in my blankets. Babaji and Siddhar continued to discuss certain matters. I fell asleep chanting *Sri Gurubhyo Namah* and dreamt of Sri Guru Babaji carrying me in his arms.

In the morning, we set out for Rudranath. All around, the hills were covered with snow. The wind was cold and the blue sky was clear. The night's snowfall had left the hills covered with snow. As the sun rose from behind the distant peaks, the whiteness turned a dazzling golden yellow at the tips.

We reached Rudranath in the evening, after a vigorous walk, resting only for a few minutes at midday to eat a handful of channa and drink water from the nearby stream. From where we stood, the Nanda Devi range, fully clothed in snow, was clearly visible. A little to the right, stood the Dronagiri mountains.

Rudranath, like Kalpeshwar, has no temple; there is merely a tiny brick shrine which encloses the deity. It is on a mountain slope, at just over 8,200 feet above sea level, facing snow-capped mountains of the Nanda Devi range. We spent the night in a small shack adjoining the temple. The shack was meant for the priests, but thankfully, they had gone to Goreshwar. They would be back the next day said the priest's assistant. We decided to set out for Tunganath the next day.

28

Kedarnath: Opening the Channels

WE COMPLETED THE JOURNEY to Tunganath and Madmaheshwar and reached Kedarnath, through Guptakashi and Sonaprayag. Nothing significant happened, except two sightings of the musk deer—the 'kasturi mriga'.

My secret desire of running into Sri Guru Babaji remained unfulfilled. When I mentioned the hope that I might meet him at Kedarnath, the master admonished me, and told me that the aim of Kriya Yoga and spiritual practices was not to meet Babaji Maharaj but to gradually evolve and transform oneself into a spiritual being. If Sri Guru thought it was necessary, he would present himself unasked. I still hoped that the great guru would grant me an audience somewhere, sometime.

As you cross the bridge across the Mandakini and enter the narrow street that leads to the temple, you will see a few small kutirs to the left, built high up on the hills. These are mostly extensions and adaptations of existing natural caves, where yogis reside in solitude. One such kutir, was Babaji's favourite. A north Indian businessman who loved to frequent Kedarnath during the pilgrim season every year built it. He was one of the few disciples of Babaji that I knew of, and I met him a couple of times. He passed away in New Delhi in 1983.

When Babaji and I reached Kedarnath, we found the kutir clean and ready. Enough firewood for a week's dhuni had been stored in one corner. The gentleman had given instructions to his cook, to bring us two meals and boiled milk to the cave-kutir every day.

The view from the cave was fantastic. The snow-clad Kedar peaks, reddened by the setting sun, stood towering above the temple which housed the linga—a simple symbol of the immeasurable, brought down to worshipable proportions—like the emotionally aroused Rudra form of the great yogi Lord Shiva. All around stood Kedar's companions, also in icy white garments. In spite of the severe cold, I spent many happy days with Babaji here.

Every morning, we would go to the temple to view the linga. The senior South Indian priest of the temple always treated Babaji with great respect, and we were allowed to sit inside for as long as we liked. There was certainly a tangible energy pervading the sanctorum. I felt I could slip into deep meditation effortlessly.

After that, we would walk up the Bhairav Hills. The view from Bhairav Hills was breathtaking. We spent many hours sitting in meditation, mostly with open eyes. Adjacent to the hillock where Bhairavnath's image was installed, stood two little cottages. One was occupied by a matted-haired Udasi Sadhu, and the other, by a ganja-smoking Naga. Both bowed down to Babaji and took his blessings.

We would come back to the cave by noon and have the meal provided by the cook. Occasionally, the Delhi businessman came personally to take Babaji's blessings and to clear his doubts. In the evenings, we remained in the cave and Babaji taught me the Thokar Kriya and other advanced Kriya Yoga exercises. If I had any questions, he discussed them patiently.

In the night, after a light meal, we would meditate for a long time facing the dhuni. After that, I went to sleep, but Babaji, as usual, sat facing the dhuni, as motionless as a statue. Thus, six happy days went by.

On the seventh day, Babaji said to me, 'I have to go away for four days to be with my master. He is at not far from here at the moment, but I can't take you along. Tomorrow morning, three men sent by Sri Guru Babaji will come and take you to a secret place for a certain procedure that will help you open up and enhance your brain's access to the multi-dimensional. They will whisper the code word which only you and I know. You can go with them safely. I will be there. Meanwhile, relax and continue with your practices. Don't eat anything at night today, and drink plenty of water.'

With that he touched my head affectionately and left. I wanted to send a message through him that I very much longed to see Sri Guru Babaji, but I thought it wiser to keep quiet. He knew, and there was no need to say anything. Everything had its proper time.

They came the next morning; they were three of them, and they all looked alike—not a single hair on their bodies, fair complexioned. From the waist to the knees they wore a white cloth wrapped like a dhoti. They wore wooden sandals which made a clacking sound as they walked. They had long, brownish-black, shoulder-length hair, and their faces were hidden by green strips of cloth that looked like the surgical mask-like strips worn by Jain monks. The only visible facial features were their broad foreheads and brown eyes.

They spoke together in Hindi in one voice, soft and firm, 'Madhu, we have been sent to take you to the secret place for a certain procedure. Come with us.'

'Tell me the code word that Babaji gave me,' I said.

They whispered the code word in unison. I followed them without hesitation. We climbed down, past the temple and walked behind it. At one point, they said, 'This is the place from where Adi Shankara followed the secret path and met the great Sri Guru. After that, he disappeared from public view.'

After walking for another ten minutes or so, they said, 'Now, we have to blindfold you.' They blindfolded me with a black cloth and led me on. After a while I heard them opening some kind of door, and then, they led me down a steep staircase. From the quietness and the sudden absence of the chill breeze that was blowing, I guessed we were in an underground tunnel.

When we stopped, I smelled incense. The blindfold was removed and I found myself in a large underground cave, lit by oil lamps. Incense wafted from a fire pit in the middle of the cave. At the far end, I was relieved to see Babaji. 'Have no fear,' he said. "We have to activate certain centres of your brain, using means other than meditation, as there is not much time. We are in a hurry. Unless these centres are activated, your channels to the higher dimensions will take many lifetimes to open up. Now, drink the soma juice used by the ancients. We have prepared it especially for you.' He handed me a silver bowl filled with a light green liquid.

I drank the bittersweet concoction sitting in the vajrasana posture. The first change of mood I experienced was similar to what I felt when I had half a bottle of beer with my friend Ranjit while in college. Then it changed and became more intense. The three people who had brought me there were sitting cross-legged and chanting the *Sama Veda* hymns. My mind became one with the flow of chants, expanded and spilled out of my body. Intense multi-coloured lights appeared, and I remember thinking of the LSD experiences I had read about.

Babaji led me carefully to a stone slab on the left side, and made me lie on it full-length, in the shavasana posture. When he spoke, it was as if his voice was coming from far away. 'Close your eyes,' he said, 'and let your Self ease out of your body.' In a flash, I found myself standing near the left wall of the cave watching, in astonishment, my body stretched on the slab, like a corpse.

Under Babaji's directions, the three companions, who had stopped chanting, brought a black hemisphere and placed it near my head. From the hemisphere they pulled out two golden strings and connected them to either side of my head. Then they pressed hard on the top of the device. I saw from my safe corner, my body going into a seizure of sorts, similar to epileptic seizures. One minute I was safe but rather frightened at what I was seeing, and in the next I found myself back in my body, subjected to terrible convulsions.

A searing pain shot up my backbone, and such heat was generated that I felt that my whole body, especially my head, was on fire. I almost thought that this was the end, and that I might not come out of it. Suddenly, a roaring sound, that quickly transformed itself into a soothing hum entered into my consciousness. It was as if someone with a Jim Reeves voice was chanting a long drawn 'Om.'

The convulsions ceased, the heat subsided, and a warm glow, like the comforting warmth of a fireplace on a winter night, suffused my body and soul. From the crown of my head, a sweet elixir began to flow down my spine, and from head to toe, I experienced a wondrous, blissful ecstasy.

I opened my eyes and looked around. Everything was fresh, new, and pulsating with life energy. I was a new person, resurrected from the old one, who seemed to have vanished and died. I was no longer an isolated self. The centre of consciousness was everywhere from the humble dust to the Milky Way. All boundaries were broken. When I saw Babaji, it was as if I was him, looking at me.

Babaji said, 'Yes. Now, you are reborn. This is the real meaning of "dwija", born again. Rise slowly, for it will take some time to come to terms with your new self. Like a newborn babe, you'll have to crawl, then sit up, and finally walk with faltering steps until practice gives you the steady, confident stride of a full-grown being.

'Bless you. Sri Guru Babaji has promised to see his old disciple Madhu sometime soon at Rishikesh. Let's get back to our cave now. Just close your eyes once more, and sit in padmasana.' I obeyed his command and felt as if a powerful wind was blowing me away somewhere. In a few moments, I felt myself descending, and then the motion stopped. Babaji said, 'Open your eyes.'

I opened my eyes and saw that both of us were back in our residence—the cave on top of the cliff. 'This mode of transportation shall not be practised ever again,' said Babaji, 'except at the end of your tenure on this earth, for a specific reason. Now, go to Lalaji, and ask him to send up some food for yourself. Meanwhile, I will light the dhuni.'

We stayed for four more days in Kedar, during which I discussed certain matters relating to the *Brahmasutras* by Badarayana Vyasa, and the Gnostic work called the *Pistis Sophia*.

29

The Fireball from the Sky

ON THE FIFTH DAY, we began our descent towards Rishikesh, passing through Sonaprayag, Guptakashi and Rudraprayag, where we stayed for two days with a Vaishnav Bairagi Sadhu near the confluence of the two rivers. The next day, we reached Devaprayag. We spent two days there with an old yogi from Nepal who had had the good fortune of meeting Sri Guru Babaji briefly, a long time ago at Pashupathinath. I was thrilled to hear him describe his experience.

We set out from Devaprayag one morning, and in the evening reached the Vasishta Cave, where I had previously spent many days recuperating from a serious condition of bruised and battered feet, and had been looked after kindly by the brahmachari from Kerala. The brahmachari had not met Babaji before, although Babaji had met his guru Sri Purushottamananda, during the latter's early days at Vasishta Guha. However, he gave Babaji all the respect due to a saint.

Babaji however did not want to stay at Vasishta Guha. Close to the Vasishta Guha, as you walk along the rocky banks of the Ganga, if you look carefully up at the hills on your right, you will come across a little cave, nicely tucked away behind the hanging roots of a big banyan tree. It is known as the Arundhati Cave, and that was where Babaji decided to stay. He said he loved this cave, and had stayed there several times.

We climbed up to it from the rocky and slippery ledge. It was just enough for two, and had a large flat rock, like an open verandah, at the front end, which was just the right size for a dhuni. We had a dip in the green waters of the Ganga, and before night set in, collected enough dry firewood from the surrounding forest to light the fire. It was arranged that I would get food for both of us, once a day, from Vasishta Guha. We spent a beautiful week in the Arundhati Cave.

On the evening we arrived, I was, for some reason, very tired. While massaging Babaji's feet, something I enjoyed doing whenever Babaji allowed me to, I fell asleep. In the middle of the night, I woke up with a start. Something was holding my leg, and the first thought that occurred to me was that a wild animal was trying to tug me away. I was trying to sit up, when I heard Babaji's comforting voice, 'Sleep, son, you are too tired. Your muscles need to be relaxed.' I realised in that instant that my right leg was on his lap and he was massaging it.

'Babaji,' I protested and tried to pull my leg away but to no avail. 'Just keep quiet and sleep,' said Babaji. 'Why, are you afraid you'll go to hell because your feet are on my lap? There is no hell worse than a world gone wrong. Sleep, son, I'll wake you up early in the morning.' I wept silently in the darkness, overwhelmed by the kindness of this great being, and fell asleep again.

We spent that week in the Arundhati Cave in great joy. Babaji explained to me the technique of meditating with open eyes. 'For many people it is not easily possible to meditate with closed eyes. They might think they are meditating, but the mind, unable to remain disengaged from the outside world, conjures up an internal world, and is caught up again in the thought process. Instead, you can open your eyes, and watch the Ganga down below, flowing unceasingly like life itself—never stopping, never stagnating like the pool that has no movement, ever changing, ever new, clear as crystal, the ever-expanding Brahman, from the root "Brah", meaning to expand.

'As you watch, you will become one with the flow of universal life that has no limits. Don't imagine anything. Just observe with an open mind, and have no fixed goal. "Let go and rejoice," as the *Isa Upanishad* says. *Tena Tyaktena Bhunjitha.*'

Among the two unusual events at the Arundhati Cave, the first one was what I like to call the dosa incident. On the last day of our stay at the cave, I was practising kriya in the morning, and trying to fix my attention on the white, two petalled lotus centre between the eyebrows, called the ajna chakra. However, no matter how hard I tried, all I could see was the image of my favourite breakfast dish, the South Indian masala dosa. For the first time, I realised how fond I was of masala dosa. It was almost an obsession, and I fought hard against it, trying to get rid of the image.

Babaji walked up to me, tapped me on my shoulder and asked, 'So what are you meditating on?'

'The ajna chakra,' I replied.

'Yes? And it's shaped like a masala dosa?' he said, and started laughing.

'Please, Babaji,' I said. 'I know that you know all that is happening in my mind, but don't laugh. Please help me out.'

'Sorry,' said Babaji. 'I won't laugh. Tomorrow, we will go to Rishikesh and I will help you get rid of the obsession. The first step is to eat masala dosa to your heart's content. The Madras Café at Rishikesh has excellent masala dosas. I will get you as much as you want and then you shall be free of the obsession. The tantric dictum, "Yogo Bhoga Yathae" is based on the fact that sometimes you cannot get rid of an obsession without indulging it. So relax and try again.'

I was surprised that even the thought that I was going to have my fill of masala dosa the next day erased the image that had interrupted my kriya, and I could easily complete my exercise.

The other was a rather frightful experience to start with. On the third night at Arundhati Cave, I was woken up by what I at first thought was the rumbling of thunder. I opened my eyes and saw Babaji in his usual sitting posture, back towards me, silhouetted by the light of the dhuni. I looked beyond, and from between two parting clouds, emerged something that was roughly the size of a full moon, but could not be the moon.

Instead of the cool, silvery, white light shed by the moon, this object was a glowing ball of fire, and as it moved closer the rumbling became louder. Then it came towards the cave and landed right on the dhuni, with the sound of a thunderclap.

I was so scared that I could not even sit up, but Babaji sat upright like a statue, unaffected and unmoved. I wanted to call out to him, but my vocal chords refused to function. Somehow, I pulled myself up to a sitting position. My whole body trembled with fear.

A strange spectacle unfolded before my astounded eyes. The rumbling had stopped and there was utter silence. The fireball, which was about two feet in diameter, split vertically into two, and out of it emerged something that caused goose pimples all over my body. It was a large snake, with a hood like a cobra, glowing electric blue, as if made of a transparent, violet, glasslike material, with electric filaments lit inside. The snake-like creature's eyes glowed, and it hissed softly.

My fear vanished the moment I saw the creature bend down and touch Babaji's feet with its hood. Babaji blessed it by touching its head with his right hand, and then did something, which for a second made me wonder if what I was seeing was a silly dream, or reality. He hissed in reply.

The blue cobra straightened up and sat facing Babaji. A hissing conversation went on for quite some time. Then Babaji said, 'Madhu, come forward and see the deputy chief of the Sarpa Loka.' I moved forward and carefully sat behind Babaji. The snake hissed. Babaji said, 'Bow down to Nagaraj.' I bowed low before the snake. At close quarters, I could see that he was quite big and had intelligent sparkling eyes. The snake hissed and touched my head with his forked tongue. I found that I was not the least bit frightened, although I could feel a mild electric shock passing through my body.

Then abruptly, it slithered back into the globe, the two halves of which clicked shut, and with a rumbling sound, the globe took off and soon vanished in the clouds. I could not but ask Babaji to explain. 'Babaji,' I said, 'I deserve an explanation. If I said this to anybody, they would think I am utterly crazy, or that I am concocting some kind of fiction, so I shall keep this to myself. But please, explain to me.'

'Yes,' Babaji said. "You are right. Not many will believe this experience of yours but you will have to share it with the public, when you write your autobiography. It does not matter who believes or does not, but I will explain to you. Truth is often stranger than fiction.

'In the Milky Way, there exists a stellar system with seven planets and eighteen moons. One of these planets is called Sarpa Loka, and is entirely inhabited by highly evolved, hooded snakes. The serpents are called the Naga Devatas. The person you saw is the deputy chief of this realm and he is called Nagaraja. The supreme head of the Nagas is the five-hooded golden serpent, known in ancient Indian texts as Anantha.

'Thousands of years ago, when humanity was still in infant stages of mental evolution, there was regular contact with Sarpa Loka. The wise and evolved Nagas frequented the earth, and spent long periods here, teaching and educating human beings. The snake worship you come across in all ancient civilizations is a tribute to the advanced Nagas of yore. Their images were venerated for the deep wisdom that they possessed. They also taught the secret of the kundalini energy initially, again symbolized by a serpent.

'Patanjali, who gave the world the *Ashtanga Yoga Sutras*, was himself a Naga, and is depicted as half-man and half-snake. The snake on the pharaoh's head and the snake coiled around the yogi-god Shiva, are all symbolic representations of wisdom and power, imparted to certain human beings by the Naga teachers.

'But then, as always seems to happen, human beings, as they became more powerful, began to also become more self-centred and cunning. Humans, or at least a majority of them, were ready even to kill for personal gain. Some felt threatened by the intellectually and spiritually superior Nagas, and forgetting their indebtedness, began to use the powers that they had acquired from the Nagas against them.

'At one point, there were large scale massacres of the Nagas. The Supreme Naga Chief decided to recall the Nagas from earth and cut all connections, except with some human beings who were highly evolved spiritually. Overnight, they were transported back to Sarpa Loka. A small number of Nagas, who were either sick or too old, or in rare cases, rebels who defied the orders of the Supreme Chief thinking that they still could do something with the human beings, got left behind.

'The serpents and snakes that exist in the world today are the descendants of those who were left behind, and who, through years of in-breeding no longer possess the great qualities of their ancestors. However, as I told you, the channels of contact were kept open with highly evolved beings of the human race. When the great Sai Nath of Shirdi left his body for three days, and returned on the fourth day, to the great astonishment of the general public who had thought that he had died, he told his close circle of associates that he had gone to settle a dispute in some other world.

'The other world he spoke of was the Sarpa Loka. The dispute, which I cannot reveal to you, was not completely settled, and has come up again. Nagaraj here went to Sri Guru for help, and on his suggestion, came to me to discuss the matter.'

'Babaji,' I said, 'all this sounds so bizarre, that if I ever wrote an autobiography, which I might do, at some point, since you say so, the readers would either dismiss it as the ravings of an unbalanced mind, or as pure fiction. I don't care. So let it be.'

Babaji laughed. 'I repeat again,' he said, 'truth is stranger than fiction, and even if the story stimulates their imagination, there is hope that they might at some point realise that there are greater realms of consciousness which cannot be comprehended by dry logic, and currently available levels of intelligence.

'However, by the time you attempt your biography, even the scientific world would have expanded its knowledge of outer space and other planets. The suspicion that life exists, or existed on other planets or stellar systems, will be strengthened by the discovery of water, and other conditions suitable for the evolution and sustenance of life forms in hitherto unsuspected parts of the cosmos. Perhaps, some unprejudiced scientist might consider it worthwhile to at least give your story the attention it deserves. Beyond that, considering the stupid attitude of dismissing anything that does not fall under the category of "established norms" as unscientific, have no hope.

'Now, you must be tired. Go sleep.'

30

The Healing and Meeting the Grand Master

THE DAY AFTER THE masala dosa episode and the coming of Nagaraj, we set out in the morning for Rishikesh, walking along the narrow path on the right bank of the river Ganga. The scenery was very charming: the gushing river, the chirping birds, the mountains, and the humble hermitages where serious sadhus lived, untroubled by the city dwellers with their greedy ways. In one place, on a hillside close by, we saw peacocks. One of them, a male, danced with his tail spread out. Then there were the rhesus monkeys, and the black-faced langurs.

We halted for a while at Laxman Jhula, which in those days had a rickety and narrow rope bridge across the Ganga. Sadhus and monks of all kinds lived in Laxman Jhula. There were also many big ashrams belonging to different sects. The sound of devotional music, with drums and cymbals, could be heard as you walked along. It was a beautiful place.

We stopped at a bathing ghat further down and took a refreshing dip in the Ganga's cool waters. I procured some roti and dal from a nearby annakshetra, which we ate with pleasure, sitting on the banks. O! How wonderful life can be when you can walk so carefree and joyfully with a person like Babaji: my father, mother, teacher and dear friend.

We rested under the shade of a huge peepal tree for a short while, and then resumed our journey. By late afternoon, we were at Muni-ki-Reti. I loved Rishikesh. There was something wonderful about the place and I had felt this even on my first visit, when I had stayed at the Divine Life Society. I was happy to be back, and that too with dear Babaji. The heart was at peace, and rejoiced in his presence.

The busy road to Badrinath was on one side of the Ganga, and the Divine Life Society and the Yoga Niketan were on the other side of the road. Most of the other ashrams were on the opposite bank. The trekker's path we had taken took us straight to the other side. All along the banks of the Ganga were the dwellings of holy men. Some lived in little kutirs in solitude, while others were inmates of large ashrams.

Babaji took me straight to Mouni Baba's cave, which was on the way to the Neelkanth temple on the top of the Neelkanth Hill. Walking alongside the Ganga, one comes to a forest where elephants roam even today. Most of it is now part of the Rajaji National Park. Just before you enter the thickly wooded area are the air-conditioned caves, built by the famous Mahesh Yogi, who was perhaps the first one to franchise a yoga technique, and make what he called TM, known worldwide. One hour of trekking uphill from here will bring you to Mouni Baba's cave.

The arrangement between Babaji and Mouni Baba was that when Babaji went to Rishikesh, he would stay in the cave, and Mouni Baba would shift to his kutir to the top of Neelkant. The higher communication channels they used worked even more perfectly than a telephone.

When we arrived at the cave, a young disciple of Mouni Baba greeted us. Babaji addressed this tall, dark, well-built man with dreadlocks and a thick beard, as 'beta', or son. He touched Babaji's feet and Babaji told me to pay my respects to the young sadhu because he was a senior. He reciprocated and paid his respects to me, as I was Babaji's disciple.

The dhuni was all ready at the entrance of the rather spacious cave, and two wooden planks with blankets spread on them constituted our cots. 'I have filled the water pot with fresh water and have brought chapatis, dal and vegetables for the two of you,' said the young sadhu. 'Baba has also sent some sugar candy for the young man. I shall bring food in the morning and, at dusk, Baba's orders. He hopes to see you in a few days, and sends his pranams. If you need anything more, just let me know.' He prostrated at Babaji's feet and left.

'Oh! I forgot to tell you,' said Babaji. 'Mouni Baba has met Sri Guru Babaji once, at Neelkanth and has been blessed by him.' I wondered how even he could forget sometimes.

We spent twenty wonderful days in the cave, and I got a lot of instructions in practical yoga, as well as the essence of the sacred books. The Upanishads, the *Yoga Sutras*, the *Hatha Yoga Pradipika*, the *Sat Chakra Nirupana*, the *Goraksha Sataka*, the *Kularnava Tantra*, the *Mahanirvana Tantra* and the famous Buddhist text of Nagarjuna, *Prajna Paramita* were some of the great works that Babaji discussed with me. He needed no books of reference. Everything was inside his head. I won't go into the details of all that happened, for then I would go on writing endlessly. I shall instead tell you of three incidents which I think are important and relevant.

The first was my visit to the Madras Café in Rishikesh. Those days it was a very small place run by a South Indian who tried to be a monk, failed, and started a small restaurant to cater to the ever-increasing South Indian population. Many years later, he was murdered by unknown assailants, and the restaurant was taken over by locals.

On the second day after our arrival at the cave, Babaji gave me twenty rupees and told me to go to Madras Café, and eat masala dosa. 'Eat as much as you can,' he said, 'and satisfy yourself fully.'

I crossed the river by boat, and made my way to the Madras Café, which I had discovered during my last visit. I ordered a masala dosa, relished every bite, ordered another, and finished that as well, followed by a cup of coffee. I burped loudly and got out of the restaurant. Never again did I have any special attraction for masala dosa. The obsession was totally erased.

I do eat masala dosa occasionally even now, but am no longer obsessed with it.

The second incident was my meeting with a young American girl, who I shall call Jenny to protect her privacy.

Almost every day, after the learning session, and just before the midday meal, I came down alone from the cave, wandered around a bit, and sat on the banks of the Ganga, enjoying the cool breeze and the sound of the flowing waters, before having a dip in the river and heading back to the cave for my food. Babaji encouraged me to go out and wander all by myself, and I loved it.

One day, while sitting on my favourite rock, and doing nothing in particular, I noticed a young, golden-haired girl, in a light blue dress, sitting on another rock not far away. Her feet were immersed in the cool waters of the Ganga, and from where I sat, I could see her sad and serious face. From her complexion and colour of her hair, I guessed that she was either European or American.

As I watched, she suddenly started vomiting. She had turned away from the water and I could see that she was in great pain. She was vomiting, and clutching her abdomen tightly with her hands. After the vomiting stopped, she took a small sip from a flask that she was carrying. It was then that she saw me, and I thought she was embarrassed. Her face was pale and she looked down at her feet.

A feeling of great sympathy flooded my heart. I wanted to go and talk to her, hold her hands, console and comfort her, and find out if I could help her, but I found myself in a dilemma. I was a free man, and did not want to get entangled with the world. Was it mere sexual attraction posing as compassion? Then I remembered Babaji's words, 'If you can meditate perfectly for thirteen years, for thirteen hours a day, but cannot hear the cry of pain of a living being in distress, all your thirteen years of meditation have been wasted. If meditation has not softened your heart, throw it out of the window. It's of no use.'

Idiot, I said to myself, how self-centred can you get? I got up, went to her and said, 'Can I help you in any way?'

At first, she was startled. Then, she calmed down, looked at me and said, 'I wish someone could but it can't be done.'

'But, why?'

'Well, it's a long story but I don't want to burden you with my sorrow.'

'Please tell me. I would like to know,' I said and sat down on a nearby rock.

'Okay,' she said, 'if you want to.'

She told me her story. She was from Philadelphia, USA, and was a microbiologist. She loved to travel, and four years ago, she had come to India and visited Haridwar and Rishikesh among other places. For some strange reason, which she was not able to understand, she fell in love with the river Ganga and the pilgrim town of Rishikesh; so much so, that she continued to come every year and spend about a month. She confessed that she had no faith or interest in Hinduism or its gurus or ashrams, but just loved to wander around the hills, and be beside the river she loved.

Disaster had struck six months earlier. Troubled by severe indigestion and frequent abdominal pains, she had gone to the doctor who, after the necessary tests, had declared that she had cancer of the colon. After two months of being treated by an oncologist, the disease seemed to come down, but within two weeks had come back in an even more severe form. The doctor had continued the treatment for two more months, and then given up. He had said he would try his best but the disease was in a very advanced stage. He said that he wouldn't like to give her false hopes. According to the doctor, she would not survive for more than two months, and the only thing that could be done was to take analgesics to reduce her pain.

She could no longer hold any food in her stomach. Even the liquids she had were being vomited out, and traces of blood appeared in her stool. That was when she had made the crucial decision to come to Rishikesh. She had decided that she would be with the river she loved, and spend time in Rishikesh before the end came. The disease could destroy her body, but she felt her heart and soul would be at peace in Rishikesh, soothed by the cool waters of the river.

Her brother, her mother and her friends thought that she was taking a crazy decision, but she stuck to it, bought a ticket, obtained a tourist visa and came away. She had been in Rishikesh for about two weeks, and the disease was getting worse. She couldn't hold even water in her stomach anymore, and she felt she wouldn't last for long. Could I, she asked, inform her brother if she passed away? She was staying at the Swarg Ashram, and if I could walk to the ashram with her, she would give me her brother's telephone number, and enough money to make a call from the public telephone at the post office. She had a return ticket dated three days later but she doubted she would survive for so long.

She had to then stop speaking because she had another severe bout of vomiting. After she had washed her face and gargled, I said, 'Listen Jenny, I know you don't believe in gurus but will you please come and see my guru. He is quite different. I don't know what will happen, but I believe his blessings would prove beneficial in some way. Please, Jenny.'

'Okay,' she said, 'you seem to be a good fellow. I'll come, but when?'

'Just wait here for a while,' I said. 'I'll go to him and find out when he can see you. Please don't go away before I return.'

'Okay.'

I think I haven't ever run as fast as I did that day. When I came face to face with Babaji, who was standing in front of the cave, I was panting so heavily that I had to calm my breath down, with deep breathing. 'That was a swift sprint,' commented Babaji.

'Babaji,' I blurted out, 'there is this young American girl who I would like to bring to you.'

'Oh! So now the yogi sees a young American girl and …'

I had never done this before but I cut him short, 'Babaji, it's not that I am … no, no, she is very sick and …'

'Take her to a doctor. The Divine Life Society has a hospital. I am not a doctor, and in any case, I don't want to see any American girl right now.'

'But Babaji,' I pleaded with tears in my eyes, 'Don't be so hard on her. She needs your blessings. You don't need to talk to her. Just let your holy eyes rest on her. Please Babaji…'

Babaji put his hands on my shoulders lovingly, and smiled, 'Just testing you, son. Of course, I'll see her. Bring her up, or should I come down?'

'No no, I'll bring her up,' I said and shot off like an arrow, forgetting even to thank him. She was there all right, waiting for me.

'Come,' I said, 'and hurry. He'll see you.'

This time we had to go slowly because she was so weak, she could hardly walk. I had to hold her most of the time. When we reached the cave she was almost on the point of collapsing. 'Give her water from my kamandalu,' said Babaji in Hindi, 'and make her sit down on the rug.'

She sipped a little water carefully, perhaps afraid of vomiting again. When she was seated, Babaji sat facing her, and stretching forth his right hand, touched her head in blessing. She started off right away, telling him her story in her heavily accented American English. I thought she was going too fast, and intending to explain, interrupted her. Babaji said, 'No, no continue, I understand you perfectly. Go on.' His accent was exactly like hers. She completed her story with, 'and now the doctors have said that I have only a month and a half to live. I am going to die soon. So that's where I am, sir.'

A look of infinite kindness came into Babaji's eyes. 'Child, my dear girl,' he said, 'we are all going to die. You, I, he, all of us are going to die. Death is inescapable, and is our constant companion. So accept it, my child, in tranquility. Make peace with death and it turns into your friend. I shall teach you a simple meditation and breathing technique that will help you keep your pain under control. So, return to your country in peace, and may the blessings of all the Great Beings be with you.'

He then taught her a simple technique that she was to practise twice every day. Her face lost its troubled look, and she became, on the whole, calm and collected. Babaji told me to escort her to Swarg Ashram. As we walked down, Jenny marvelled at the fact that she hadn't vomited for more than two hours. She thanked me profusely. After leaving her at Swarg Ashram, I went back to the cave.

'Is she feeling better?' Babaji enquired. I said she was. 'You have now repaid a karmic debt you had in one of your past lives,' said Babaji. 'Many lives ago, she nursed you when you were very sick. Now, you helped when she was in distress. Now, no more questions about this, is that clear? And one more thing, I don't want to see her again.'

'Yes Babaji,' I said reluctantly, for I would have loved to go into the details of my past connection with Jenny— but he knew best what should be done, and what should not be done and I had learnt this through experience.

I sought Babaji's permission and went to say goodbye to her on the day she was to leave. She was already looking better, and she said she had vomited only twice in two days and could drink some tea and eat a biscuit. She told me to give a million thanks to Babaji and tell him that she will remember him always. 'He is my Jesus Christ,' she said.

She wanted to stay in touch with me but I had neither an address nor a telephone number. Just before we parted company, she surprised me by giving me a hug, and a kiss on my cheek. Embarrassed, I walked away from her and went back to the cave. 'Taken aback, yes?' was all that Babaji said, as he chuckled to himself.

The wheel of time turned. Soon, Jenny was relegated to the past. Once in a while, I did think of her and wondered what had happened to her, but that was it. Babaji said nothing.

Three years later, I was in Rishikesh on a special retreat. Babaji had gone to Mount Kailash, refusing to take me with him, and had given me specific instructions about my daily routine. I was to finish my retreat and wait for him to come back. One evening, I was sitting on the banks of the Ganga near the Swarg Ashram, when I saw a blonde walking towards the river. I could not believe my eyes. Was that Jenny? She looked a little fatter than when I had seen her last, but it certainly was Jenny. I decided to confirm and ran towards her. She was sitting on a rock with her feet in the water. I stopped behind her and called softly, 'Jenny?'

She turned and looked at me for a little while, then shouted, 'Oh my God! Madhu, I can't believe this.' She jumped up and hugged and kissed me on my cheek. 'What's happened to you? You are wearing decent clothes, pants and shirt, and you have snipped off your lovely locks. Sit down, let's talk. I have been looking for you here and there. Went twice to the cave and found a naked sadhu who couldn't speak English!'

She then told me how, after going back to Philadelphia, her health started improving. Her vomiting became less frequent and soon stopped altogether. Her abdominal spasms vanished and she could do without analgesics. The only therapy she did was to practise the technique given by Babaji. She discovered that she could eat normally. At the end of the two-month deadline given to her by the doctor, she was alive and healthier than ever before. She waited for another two weeks and then went to her doctor. He was surprised to see her alive and so healthy.

After a series of tests, he declared her cured. The cancer had disappeared. He said it was a rare case of spontaneous remission. It was truly a miracle, and there was no way she could contact me. Meanwhile, she had found a job in a laboratory and could not get leave for a long time. Finally, when she was granted leave for two weeks, she had lost no time in flying to India and coming to Rishikesh. She was to fly back to the States the next day, from Delhi.

'I was desperate to find you, and I have to personally meet the Master and thank him and hug him and…'

'Wait a moment,' I said, 'You can't find him now. He has gone to Mount Kailash in Tibet and is not expected for two months. When I see him I shall convey your thanks to him.

'As for me, after spending three-and-a-half years with him, Babaji asked me to go back home, and now, I am with him, once every year for about a month, at a place chosen by him. We are actually lucky to have run into each other. Maybe it has all been planned by the old man.'

'So, Mr Vagabond,' she said, 'can you now give me some address or telephone number, so that I can keep in touch?'

I gave her my real name, address and telephone number. We spent some time walking around and talking of old times. Rishikesh was getting busier and noisier day by day. We drank some coffee at the Madras Café, and I told her about myself and how Babaji came into

my life. We then returned to Swarg Ashram, where she too had rented
a room.

In the morning, I saw her off at the boat jetty. A taxi was waiting
for her on the other side. She had to go to Delhi, and from there she
would take the midnight flight.

She gave me her address but I didn't write to her. By nature, I dislike
writing letters, and kept postponing the act.

When I met Babaji after his return to Rishikesh, I mentioned all that
had happened and conveyed Jenny's thanks to him. 'Ummph, *theek hai*.
She is a good girl and my blessings are with her. I shall take care of her
and do what's good for her,' was all that he said.

I returned home at the end of the month. Two months later, I
received a letter from the United States. I thought it must be from
Jenny and opened it eagerly. It was, but with a covering note from her
brother. It said:

Dear Mr. M,

*I am Bernard, Jenny's brother. Jenny died in her sleep on the night of
October 16th. She was keeping well after returning from India. The medical
report says she died in her sleep of cardiac arrest. We found at her bedside,
an interesting, but to us, a quite puzzling letter written by her and placed
in an envelope addressed to you. We thought that since she intended to
mail it to you, perhaps the next day, and could not, it would only be fair
to mail it to you. You need not be compelled to reply but if you do, we,
especially my mother, would be very pleased for Jenny's sake.*

Thank You,

Bernard

I opened the letter from Jenny, which was in another envelope. It said:

Dear Madhu,

*It was wonderful seeing you again. I am sure you would have conveyed my
thanks to the Master. I am in the best of health and spirits but something
strange happened yesterday night and I must share it with you. I had a*

vivid dream. The Master appeared before me smiling most beautifully and asked, 'So my dear, you are perfectly well now, yeah?'

I said, 'Yes, master.'

'Then isn't it time to go back home, darling? To your real home? I shall be present to welcome you.'

Then he disappeared in a rainbow-coloured blaze of light. Madhu, do you know what it means? Is he calling me to the Himalayas? Anyway, ask him when you see him. Hope to see you sometime. Please reply and keep in touch.

Yours affectionately,

Jenny

I went into my bedroom and wept as I had never wept before. I had lost a good friend; and what did Babaji mean by what he said?

In the night, as I meditated, I addressed Babaji, visualising him in my heart lotus, 'Tell me Babaji, please. What happened to Jenny? I know you don't like to answer such questions. I know you don't want me to be dependent on you, but just this once, answer my question, please Babaji. Jenny was a dear friend, you loved her too.'

The answer came in a dream that night. Babaji appeared wearing a violet loincloth instead of the usual white one. 'Don't bother me with such questions again,' he said. 'And don't pester me when you meditate. Meditation is for higher development and helping others, not to keep calling me every now and then.

'Anyway, since you have asked; when I told Jenny to come home, I meant the resting place where every human being goes to after a hard life on earth. Yes, she is here and I was there to welcome her. After some rest, I'll help her find a womb in a suitable place in India and help her evolve spiritually. Now that's all I will tell you. No more questions on this matter.'

With that he disappeared behind a golden cloud. I woke up relieved and thankful to Babaji, my true friend and guide.

Now, the third incident, I consider to be the most important one in my life. I finally got to see the Grand Master, Sri Guru Babaji. It happened this way.

Babaji and I were walking in the forests surrounding the Neelkanth Hill. Far away we heard the trumpeting of an elephant, but we were too preoccupied to pay much attention. We were in the midst of a heated discussion. Babaji said that some time in the future, I would be ready to give Kriya Yoga initiation. Then he spelt out a list of twenty-one qualifications required of a person who wishes to be initiated into kriya.

I said with the qualifications he had listed out, it would be well-nigh impossible to find someone fit to receive kriya. He said that was not true, and that I seem to have a low opinion of the character of human beings in general. I said that an average human being would not be able to fulfill the qualifications he had listed, and pleaded with him to cut down the list a bit. For over an hour we argued, which was quite unusual. Finally, he cut it down to ten, and I still held on to my opinion that the first four qualifications on the list were sufficient. I begged him to do something out of compassion for humanity.

Then, he said that times had changed, and that disciples these days teach gurus the meaning of compassion. That was the last straw, and I burst into tears. While Babaji was trying to console me, something wonderful happened. A lovely scent filled the air. Babaji said to me, 'It's okay. I am sorry I hurt you. Now wipe your tears and stand up. Your wish is going to be granted.' He stood up beside me and we both turned in the direction of the path to Neelkanth. From behind the tall teak trees, emerged a figure so beautiful, so transcendental, that my hair stood on end. I knew by instinct that it was Sri Guru Babaji who had come to grant me *darshan* out of his love and compassion.

My beloved teacher fell prostrate at his blessed feet, and I followed suit. 'Get up,' said a melodious voice, 'I have urgent business with you. Now Mahesh,' he said addressing my master, 'I think you should listen to Madhu. Times have changed, and I think we will shorten the list.'

'As you wish,' said my teacher.

I could not take my eyes off from the golden complexioned being standing before me, bare-bodied, except for a shining white loin cloth that barely reached the knees, and flowing brown hair that fell to his shoulders. He looked divine. The lovely scent that emanated from him entered my soul. He turned to me, and as I gazed into those compassion-filled eyes, my mind went back to my past lives and my connection with him.

'Come here,' he said and put his arms around my shoulders. Then he touched my chin tenderly and said, 'Madhu, my boy, you needed to go through this life to further your evolution. However, you'll come back to me after doing your work. Mahesh is so kind. He is your special guide.' Tears streamed down my face and my whole being pulsated with bliss that I had never experienced before.

Then he turned to my teacher and said, 'I am grateful that you have taken this young fellow under your wings. Mahesh. There is an important matter I would like to talk to you about. Meet me Thursday night in the subtle body.'

He raised his hands in blessing. We once again prostrated at his feet. When we raised our faces from the ground, he was already gone. Only the fragrant scent lingered. We walked back quietly to the cave. My heart was still full of Sri Guru Babaji. After meditation, I went to sleep, and Babaji sat as usual in front of the dhuni, steady as a rock, tender as a flower.

31

A Truly Holy Man

OUR NEXT DESTINATION WAS Uttarkashi, the gateway to Gangotri and Gomukh, the source of the river Ganga. Travelling through Tehri, Narendra Nagar and other places, we arrived in Uttarkashi. While passing through Tehri, Babaji showed me the place where Yogi Ramtirth committed suicide in utter frustration by jumping into the river.

Uttarkashi in those days was a quiet little Himalayan town. As in Banaras, the Ganga—also known as Bhagirathi—flows from south to north for a certain distance. There is also an ancient and beautiful temple of Shiva; and, like the one at Banaras (otherwise known as Kashi), it is called the Kashi Viswanath temple. Shiva, the lord of the yogis, is also known as Viswanath, Lord of the Universe.

A small community of sadhus lived there peacefully, enjoying the fresh air and simple living conditions, going for walks, and meditating—uninvolved in politics and competition. There were two or three annakshetras, places where sadhus were given free food twice a day. These were run by the Kalikambliwala Ashram and the Punjab Sindh Ashram. Little cottages or kutirs were available for those who wished to live in solitude and engage themselves in spiritual practices. In short, it was an ideal place for contemplatives. Some ashrams in India, where the monks had busy schedules running educational institutions—hospitals and so on, sent their monks periodically to Uttarkashi to live in solitude and re-energise themselves.

Babaji arranged for two kutirs side by side: one for him and one for me. I went twice to the Punjab Sindh annakshetra to get simple food for both of us. Babaji rarely ate, and mostly fed stray dogs that gathered in the woods not far from the kutir. He loved the dogs and they loved him.

Babaji also arranged for me to take Sanskrit lessons from his disciple Krishnanand Sharma, who specialised in Vedic studies, especially the *Sama Veda*. Two weeks after we had arrived, Babaji went away to Gangotri, instructing me to remain in Uttarkashi for seven months, till the middle of April. When he returned, we would walk to Gomukh, the source of the Ganga, and from there, to Tapovan and to the Vasuki Lake.

My stay in Uttarkashi was one of the most wonderful experiences I have had in my life. Apart from practising the special yogic techniques that Babaji had taught me and attending Sanskrit classes, I got the opportunity to interact with sadhus of all kinds, and visit many ashrams. My favourite spot was the courtyard of the Kashi Viswanath Temple. I felt very special vibrations there, and occasionally met advanced spiritual practioners. I would enter into deep meditation from the moment I came out of the sanctum sanctorum, and would find a quiet corner in the courtyard to sit and meditate till it was time to go for the midday meal. Once or twice, one of the priests had to bring me back to the waking state.

On one occasion, after a really deep meditation, I opened my eyes and was startled to see a naked man with dreadlocks and bloodshot eyes, kneeling beside me and inspecting me as if I was some kind of a strange specimen. Seeing that my eyes had opened, he peered into them. I felt like I was in front of an X-ray machine. His face broke into a toothless grin and he started dancing, gesticulating like a madman and shouting, "*Siddao, siddao, bhalo, bhalo, hoyae gyaloo.*" Before I could stand up or communicate with him, he gave a low whistle, shot out of the courtyard like an arrow, and vanished from sight.

There was a senior monk of the Ramakrishna Order who was on a two-month solitary retreat at Uttarkashi. We became great friends and often went to the temple together to meditate in the courtyard. On that day, he was sitting not far from where I was, and had witnessed all that had happened. So, I went to him, and asked him what it meant. 'Well,' said the swami, speaking softly as he always did, 'I think he was a paramahamsa, a man gone mad with divine love. The words he uttered were in Bengali. *Siddao* means well-cooked, or it could mean one who is a Siddha, an accomplished yogi. *Bhalo* means great or good, and *hoyee gyaloo* means, it's over, it has happened.

'If he was referring to your spiritual state, I can only say that you are lucky, and the great Babaji you talked to me about the other day, your teacher, has indeed brought you to a highly advanced spiritual state. I have been watching you in samadhi, and it seems to me that you are undoubtedly in a high state of consciousness.

'The great master Sri Ramakrishna Paramahansa, the guru of Swami Vivekananda, who founded our order, used the same words. It is said that he would examine a spiritual aspirant carefully and if satisfied say, "Siddao, Siddao"—well-cooked, well-cooked. I am amazed that this person used the same words.'

Laxmanpuri, a monk belonging to the Dasanami Order, told me one day that a holy man who had reached a lofty level of spiritual advancement wandered about on the banks of the river. A monk who had known him before, and who belonged to one of the well-known monasteries, had visited Uttarkashi. When he saw this wandering sadhu, he prostrated at his feet, and later on, revealed the sadhu's antecedents to a few people.

According to him, the holy man originally belonged to a wealthy and well-known monastery of the Dasanami Order in western India, founded by the famous Shankaracharya. When it was time for him to become the head abbot of the monastery, he had vanished, leaving a note that he disliked the pomp and special status associated with the office of the abbot. He said that he was going away of his own accord to become a wandering monk, with only the Supreme Being as his support.

He had been a dandi swami, which means a Brahmin sanyasin (monk) who carried a staff called a dandi, to show his special status. Coming to Uttarkashi, he had thrown the dandi into the Ganga along with his water pot. Until the visit of the monk who had known him in earlier days, no one even knew his name. They simply referred to him as Swamiji, which means a holy monk.

I was told that he walked, or sat on the banks of the Ganga most of the time, and at night slept in the courtyard of the temple. Since he hardly spoke and did not visit the annakshetra for food, a young sadhu from South India had taken upon himself the responsibility of feeding him, and took food to him once a day. The holy man ate only as much food as he could hold with his palms cupped together, and drank water from the Ganga.

He wore an old, ochre cloth that almost reached his ankles, and carried a single blanket that served as his meditation mat during the day, and a protection from the cold at night.

'It will be good if you have his darshan,' said Laxmanpuri. So, one sunny Monday morning, I went to the banks of the Ganga hoping to see him. I did not have to wait for long. A tall, thin man in ochre was walking slowly beside the river, and he fit the description given by Swami Laxmanpuri perfectly. Heading towards a large flat rock not far away from where I stood, he climbed on to it, and sat cross-legged, looking at the river.

I plucked up enough courage to walk up to him, and stood silently near the rock. He turned in my direction. I prostrated with great devotion and remained silent. I had been told that he seldom spoke, and I did not want to disturb him. But, the unexpected happened. He actually spoke. He asked softly, 'What is your name?'

'Madhu,' I said.

'So what are you doing here? Learning something?'

'Seeking the Truth,' I said.

A kind expression came into his eyes. 'Poor boy,' he said. 'It's hard work, my son. I have worked hard for many years. I am seventy now. I have even thrown away my dandi, and eat only what chance brings, yet truth eludes me. I have studied every book available on Vedanta, and yet I haven't found the Brahman. Do you have a guru?'

'Yes,' I said proudly. 'He is wonderful. He is a direct disciple of the great Sri Guru Babaji. I am blessed.'

'I have heard of the legendary Babaji,' said the old monk, 'but then, there are so many stories, and these days one does not know what to believe and what not to believe. Gurus are fake, ashrams have become centres of political activity, and the true aspirant is confused. Anyway, have you seen this great Babaji?'

'Yes,' I said. 'Once. When my teacher, whom I call Babaji, returns, I shall request him to see you if it's all right with you.'

'A few weeks ago, I would have been too proud to admit that I needed help,' he said, 'but now, I am willing to seek it. Who knows how long this body is going to last. Please do ask him. I have talked too much today. Go your way, my son,' he said, and terminated the meeting abruptly. I prostrated and walked away. When Babaji returned to Uttarkashi, I took him to meet the holy man.

But before I come to that, I must mention my Sanskrit teacher Krishnananda Sharma's astonishment when he started my first lesson in the chanting of the *Taithiriya Upanishad*. After the very first lesson, he found that I could chant perfectly, with the right stress and intonation, if I heard him just once. When he asked me if I had attended chanting classes before and I said no, he thought I was lying. I said that there was no reason for me to lie to him, and that it seemed to come to me quite naturally. Finally, he shrugged his shoulders and said, 'Perhaps you learned chanting in your past life. I can find no other explanation, or it might be Babaji's magic.'

It was also in Uttarkashi that I realised how important an incentive food could be, even when it came to learning the Bhagawad Gita by heart. I loved chanting the Gita, and Babaji had taught me a beautiful way of doing it, which he said he had learnt from his master. But I always used a text. Learning by heart was a nightmare, as far as I was concerned. Reading something to understand what it conveyed, I enjoyed, but memorising, I thought, was a waste of time and energy. At Uttarkashi, I had to overcome my aversion to memorise, and was soon chanting the Gita by heart. This is how it happened.

Many of the ashrams there periodically held sumptuous feasts, to which all the sadhus and brahmacharis were invited. Before they begin to eat, the sadhu guests were expected to chant the fifteenth chapter of the Gita, 'Purushottama Yoga'. Most of the sadhus, young and old, knew the fifteenth chapter by heart, and the few who did not were looked down upon. So after two feasts, I decided to memorise it. At the third feast, I could manage somewhat, and by the fourth I was fluent. Memorising the fifteenth chapter was too small a price to pay for such sumptuous food.

At one of those feasts, I met Swami Venkateshananda. He invited me to go to his kutir in the evening. He was a prominent disciple of Swami Shivananda Saraswati of Rishikesh and was widely respected for his deep Vedantic knowledge and insight. After the first visit, we spent many evenings together, and I derived great benefit from the discussions I had with him.

Many years later, I happened to listen to a lively discussion between Swami Venkateshananda and J. Krishnamurti, in which Swami Venkateshananda's contention was that one needed a guru, and J. Krishnamurti's contention, as usual, was that a guru was not only unnecessary, but also, would prove to be an obstacle in one's search for the Truth. The discussion ended without any firm conclusion.

Babaji returned in May, and we spent five days together in Uttarkashi. On the second day after Babaji's arrival, I told him of my meeting with the venerable, old, holy man. 'I know,' he said, 'and you think I should see him?'

'I feel that only you could help him,' I said.

The next day, Babaji took me along and we went to meet the holy man. He was sitting on his favourite rock when we arrived. He saw us, stood up, and climbed down to the ground. When we were close, he put his palms together and greeted Babaji. I did the same while greeting him. Babaji said, 'Greetings Swamiji, do you want me to send Madhu away while we have a chat?'

'Pranams Yogiji Maharaj,' said the old monk, 'Let him stay. Perhaps he will benefit from the discussion. I have no problem.' So I was privileged to be present during the discussions. We sat down right there, and Babaji started off straight away in his direct style. 'Swamiji,' he said,

'I have great respect for your learning, and more so for the courageous way in which you declined to succeed as the head of your Mutt. You have thrown away your dandi and crown, and today, live like a simple itinerant sanyasin. Great! But you are still far away from the Brahman you seek because the burden of knowledge and scholarship that you carry on your head acts as an effective barrier to your understanding of "Reality". Shall I continue?'

'Yes, please do. I am beginning to grasp what you are saying.'

'You are so full of the knowledge that you have acquired, that there is no space to receive the "Truth" which is waiting to enter. Unburden yourself. Throw away all that and embrace emptiness, so that you can receive in abundance.'

'I have often wondered what the sloka "he who worships knowledge enters into greater darkness", from the *Isavasya Upanishad*, really means,' said the monk, 'and have never accepted the conventional explanation that "knowledge" here means the *Apara Vidya* or non-essential knowledge and so on. The rishis were very direct and would have used the word Apara, if that was what they intended to convey. Now, I am beginning to understand. Pray continue, Sir.'

Babaji said, 'You are right. The word Apara was not used because it was not necessary to qualify Vidya. The fact is knowledge, by itself, is an obstacle to understanding the Absolute Truth. I'll explain. You see, when I set out to acquire knowledge of something, what is the process involved? First, I observe, then understand it, and then, store it in my memory, right?'

'Yes, Sir.'

'When I say that I have knowledge of x or y, what I actually mean is that having understood something, it is now stored in my memory, and I can recall it instantly. This is what constitutes knowledge, any knowledge. So, all knowledge is memory, and memory, the very word, means, it is a thing of the past. In the present, there is no memory. Memory is stored information, and is always in the past. Can you, with your keen intelligence, follow what I am saying?'

'Yes.'

'Now, "Truth" cannot be something in the past. It is the "eternal present", and therefore, cannot be stored in the memory, which is a thing of the past, the dead past. "Truth", on the other hand is in the present, the now, eternally flowing, pulsating with life, and therefore, cannot be touched by knowledge.

'The mind, like the *Keno Upanishad* says, "cannot comprehend it". It is only when the mind is empty of all the garbage which we carry around in our knowledgeable brains, and when it is quiet and still as it is no longer becoming anything or struggling to acquire, that there is space for the Truth, the ever present, to manifest.

"The doors and the window panes, thick with the dark tint of pride and secondhand knowledge, have to be left open for the sweet, divine breeze to enter. I hope I am clear."

After a long silence, the old man spoke.

'Ah! Great silence,' he said 'I haven't sat in such stillness all my life. Although, I must confess that once or twice, I was at its threshold when doing nothing in particular, just watching the river or looking up at the clear sky.'

Babaji said, 'When that silence comes upon you spontaneously, don't interfere. Just be still. May Sri Guru Babaji bestow his blessings on you so that you discover the "Truth".

'I will not see you again. We leave for Gomukh in a few days.' With that, Babaji stood up and we bid farewell to the old man. With tears in his eyes, he attempted to prostrate at Babaji's feet, but Babaji held him by his shoulders, and did not allow him to do that.

'You belong to the order of renunciants and wear ochre,' he said. 'Moreover, you are a sincere man and as far as the outside world is concerned, you are older than me. So, I cannot let you prostrate at my feet. I can see your love for me in your eyes, and that is sufficient.'

We left him standing on the banks of the Ganga, his eyes following us till we were out of sight. 'Babaji,' I said, 'guide me also to the "Truth". Today, I learnt something profound. You are so kind.'

Babaji laughed and put his right arm around my shoulders, 'Everything at the proper time,' he said. 'On Thursday morning, we shall travel to Gomukh.'

32

Sri Vidya Initiation

THE FOLLOWING THURSDAY WE set out for Gomukh, the source of the Bhagirathi, or Ganga. In the ancient Indian epics, the river Bhagirathi is named after Bhagirath, scion of the Sagar royal family, who was instrumental in bringing the river down to the earth from her celestial abode. The story goes like this:

Thousands of years ago, when the Himalayas were still young, the mighty King Sagara fought many wars and won many kingdoms. Then he performed the Ashwamedha Yagna—the horse sacrifice in which a horse was allowed to roam free through the surrounding kingdoms, and if anyone captured the horse, they would have to fight the king's army to claim the horse as their own.

Indra, the king of the celestials, thought that if Sagara's yagna was a success, he might become too powerful, and who knows, might even capture the celestial regions and dethrone him. So using his magical powers, he stole the horse, and hid it near the great sage Kapila's hermitage.

The 60,000 strong sons of Sagara who were searching for the horse reached Kapila's hermitage and found him there. Holding the sage responsible for stealing the horse, they threatened to teach him a lesson. The sage was in deep meditation. Disturbed by the commotion, he opened his eyes, and in a rare show of anger, reduced all except one to ashes by his very look. One of the sons was saved since he repented.

His son, Anshuman, performed severe penance to gain salvation for his uncles, but the sage Kapila, while letting him take the horse, declared that his uncles' souls would attain salvation only if the celestial river Ganga descended to earth, and their ashes came in contact with its waters.

Anshuman tried very hard, but could not convince Ganga to come to earth. His son, Dilip, also tried but failed. However, his grandson, Bhagirath, won over the heart of the celestial river Ganga by his severe penance, and she agreed to descend to earth. But there was a problem; the mighty impact of the Ganga, as she hit the earth, would wreak havoc, and even puncture the earth.

There was only one who could save the earth when the Ganga descended. That was the great yogi god Shiva, whose seat was on Mount Kailash. So, Bhagirath persuaded Shiva who, pleased by his devotion, agreed to receive the turbulent and powerful waters of the Ganga on his head, and release her gently on to the earth through his matted hair. Because Bhagirath persuaded her to descend, she was named Bhagirathi, and Gomukh is considered the spot where she descended.

The way to Gomukh lay through Bhairavghati, and the village of Gangotri, in which there is a temple dedicated to the goddess Ganga. It has a number of ashrams and many sadhus live in Gangotri throughout the summer. The Ganga flows into Gangotri with full force before descending to Uttarkashi. From Gangotri, one can see the shining Sudarshan peak.

We spent two days at Gangotri, and stayed at a kutir that belonged to the Juna Akhada of the Udasin sect of the sadhus. The roar of the river as it came down the hills fascinated me. It had taken us four days to reach Gangotri. The day before we started the trek to Gomukh, while sitting before the dhuni fire at night, Babaji suddenly said, 'The old monk has left his body in peace and stillness.' When I started to ask him for a more explicit explanation, he said, 'No more questions on the topic for the present.'

Later, when we returned from Gomukh to Uttarkashi, I was told by Swami Laxmanpuri, that four days after we had left for Gomukh, the old, holy man passed away, sitting on his favourite rock, facing the Ganga, and smiling in ecstasy. According to the medical officer of the government hospital at Uttarkashi, he had died of a cardiac arrest.

The next morning we started the trek from Gangotri to Gomukh and Tapovan. Once the holy village of Gangotri is left behind, everything becomes quiet. On the other side of Bhagirathi, there are many natural caves. In four hours, we reached Chirbasa, the pine grove named after the abundant pine trees in the region. From here, one could see the glistening Gangotri glacier far ahead.

After relaxing for half an hour, eating soaked channa, and drinking water, we continued on our way and reached Bhoj Basa, meaning the Birch Grove. At Bhoj Basa, we were guests of a Tantric sadhu who wore red clothes. He seemed to know Babaji well, and after serving us a sumptuous meal of rotis, dal and vegetables, kept persuading Babaji to stay on for a few days. Babaji was intent on staying at Gomukh, and so after lunch, we began to walk again.

From Bhoj Basa, the Bhagirathi peaks began to appear. After some time, we saw the pyramidal summit of the Shivling peak that is almost 21,000 feet above sea level. In an hour or so we reached Gomukh. To me, the sight was mindboggling. From a snow covered snout, shaped like a cow's mouth, emerged the waters of the Ganga. Beyond the snout was the Gangotri glacier, which is about twenty-five kilometres of sheer ice. Icebergs floated on the gushing waters. Everywhere you turned, there was only white ice and snow. In a fit of ecstasy, I jumped around and rolled on the ground. 'Calm down,' said Babaji with a smile. 'Let's have a quick dip.' We did, and immediately after, wiped ourselves dry. The sun came out briefly, to warm our bodies and dry our wet clothes.

Between Gomukh and Tapovan, there were a few caves. In one of them lived an old associate of Babaji, whom he simply called Dada (brother). He was from Bengal and spent every summer in the cave. We climbed the steep slope on the left side of the glacier, and in half an hour, reached the cave. Dada was waiting for us. Even in such a remote, snowbound place, he had managed to light a dhuni. The cave was quite large, and most of the entrance was walled in with boulders.

Wooden planks on the floor served as beds. He even provided us with extra blankets.

We had rice and potatoes for dinner, and spent the night in the cave. Dadaji told me I was lucky to have found Babaji. 'He is very reluctant to take disciples,' he said. 'Every time I ask him to accept me as a disciple, he says "let's be friends, Dada."'

The next morning, we walked up to Tapovan. It took us about two hours. The Shivling peak was now visible. The reflection of the sun's light on the vast array of pure, silvery, snow-capped peaks was kaleidoscopic. On the right, were the Bhrigupanth peak and the Meru. To the Shivling's left, was the Bhagirathi peak, and beyond was the top of Satopant. In the north were Mana Parbat and the towering Sri Kailash. Towards the south, was the Sudarshan Peak.

In another half hour, we had walked to the top of the ridge. The Gangotri glacier spread out below us. We walked further and came to the confluence of the Gangotri glacier and the Kirti glacier. On the right, we could see Kedarnath at a distance, and on the left, Satopant. Then we climbed down and returned to the cave. We spent five days in the cave. Dadaji had kindly stocked enough provisions and firewood for a week.

One day, Babaji said to Dadaji, 'Dada, you initiate Madhu into Sri Vidya tomorrow.'

'But Babaji,' protested Dada, 'with you here, how can I do it? You could do it yourself.'

'No, you do it. I have special reasons to ask you to do it.'

Dadaji agreed and I was given the sixteen letter (*shoda-sakshari*) Sri Vidya mantra belonging to the lopamudra category with the starting sound 'ka'. 'While Kriya Yoga clears up the central spinal pathway for the kundalini energy,' said Dadaji, 'the sound vibrations of the Sri Vidya help activate the cerebrospinal centres, and prepare them to receive the serpent power as it begins to ascend.

'Babaji is himself an expert on the Sri Vidya, and I am giving this technique of *chakra dharana* (contemplating the chakras) at his command.'

The next day I asked Babaji, 'Babaji, with you as my teacher, and from what I have learnt so far, I wonder if it is necessary to learn all this, especially from someone else. I am sorry, if I am wrong in saying this.'

Babaji said, 'Son, you will meet different kinds of spiritual aspirants and so-called spiritual teachers. I want you to learn everything possible on the subject, so that, one: you don't get intimidated by someone who says, I know all this, you are ignorant; and two: certain spiritual aspirants may require the Sri Vidya to speed up their growth, and unless you know it, how will you help?

'All the different theories and practices are moulds into which the shapeless, pliable, virgin material needs to be put in to bring about some order. But remember, you cannot take the product out until you break the mould.'

'So, the mould is necessary, and so also, the breaking of it ultimately. Get it?'

'Yes, Babaji, I am beginning to understand,' I said with humility.

From Gomukh we returned to Rishikesh.

33

Lessons from the German

IN THE THREE-AND-A-HALF years I was with Babaji, we travelled to Gomukh once, Gangotri twice, Jamunotri once, and Badrinath and Kedarnath twice. On our second visit to Gangotri, I met a German neurologist, a student of Babaji's, whom Babaji simply called the German. This German neurologist, whose real name I cannot reveal at his request, came to see us in the kutir at Gangotri.

Babaji introduced him saying, 'The German doctor is from Stuttgart. He is a neurologist and has been my student for ten years. He is going to be in Gangotri for one month, and I want you to learn the basics of anatomy and physiology of the brain, and the cerebrospinal system.

'To know your Self also means to know how the brain works. What we normally call the mind is the brain. If you understand it properly, it is easier to explore the higher levels of consciousness that transcend ordinary thought.

'We keep in touch non-verbally, and the German knows a great deal about you.'

The doctor had the typically German characteristic of being very thorough in his approach, and was armed with charts and pictures. I studied the cerebellum; the mid-brain called the limbic system or 'reptilian brain'; the cerebrum with its two hemispheres connected by the corpus callosum; the spinal cord; the autonomous nervous system;

the sympathetic nervous system; the plexus; and everything else about the cerebrospinal system—short of an actual autopsy or dissection.

For the first time, I heard that as early as the 1700s and 1800s, neurologists suspected that the two hemispheres of the brain, though linked together, and complementing each other's functions, actually have distinct and unique personalities. At his laboratory back home, the German was engaged in comparing the information available in the old text books on yoga, like the *Hathayoga Pradipika* and the *Satchakra Nirupana*, with modern neurology, and investigating the possibility of explaining what he called 'breakthroughs in expanding consciousness' in neurological terms.

Now, as I read books by Oliver Sacks, *Descartes' Error* by Antonio R. Damasio, *Phantoms in the Brain* by my friend, Dr V.S. Ramachandran and other books, I find that his ideas contained the seeds of what modern neurologists now elaborate upon. Unfortunately, none of the modern writers have a firm grounding in the ancient teachings regarding yoga, and even more unfortunate is the fact that the German doctor died in a road accident three years after I met him, aborting the research he was engaged in.

Babaji said that he would be reborn under circumstances conducive to his research. I have no idea how, when or where, but I would like to tell you the fascinating story of how the German first met Babaji, as narrated by him.

'I travelled to the Himalayas for two reasons. One was sheer fascination for the snow-capped mountains. Glowing accounts from a couple of German travellers who had visited the Himalayas attracted me irresistibly. The other was my interest in Hindu philosophy, tantra and yoga. Having read *The Serpent Power* by Sir John Woodroffe, I was intrigued by the close resemblance that the pathways of the kundalini energy had to the cerebrospinal system. The crown chakra, the *brahmarandhra* (gateway to Brahman), and so on could not have been described unless the ancient yogis had a sound understanding of the anatomy and physiology of the brain.

'That prompted me to go to the Himalayas and seek real yogis, if they still existed. I was by then a full-fledged neurologist, working at a hospital in Stuttgart. With great difficulty, I managed a month's vacation without explaining the real reason for my trip. In those days, the scientific community in general considered any interest shown by a scientist in yoga and allied phenomenon as highly unorthodox and downright unscientific.

'It was also not so easy to travel to the Himalayas in those days. I flew into Delhi, and then took a whole day to reach Haridwar by train. From there I got into a rickety old bus that took almost half a day to reach Rishikesh. Having found a place in the Divine Life Society in Rishikesh, I sought the help of the late Swami Sivananda, the head of the ashram. The Swami said I did not have to wander, for he could teach me what I wanted to learn, but I was not satisfied. My eyes were on the upper Himalayas, and so, after a few days, I found a bus that went up to Uttarkashi. Those days it took a whole day, and the roads were dangerous. The Garhwali driver of the bus was even more dangerous.

'From Uttarkashi, I took another bus and reached Gangotri the next day. At Gangotri, I found accommodation at an old ashram, and planned my trek to Gomukh. One day, as I was walking near the Gangotri temple, wondering when or how I was going to find a knowledgeable yogi, I saw a tall, fair complexioned man with long hair, wearing a white loincloth, coming from the opposite direction. He walked straight towards me and said in German, *"Guten Taag."*

'I could not believe my ears. *"Guten Taag,"* I stammered. '"Well, my German is not so good. So can we talk in English?" asked the stranger. "Sure," I said. He surprised me again by saying, "Ok, doctor, let's sit somewhere and talk. Come to my kutir." That's how we met.'

The German then told me that he was initiated into Kriya Yoga on the same day, and that for the last seven years, had been practising and learning yoga and Vedanta under Babaji's guidance. He considered him his guru.

34

Going Back to Trivandrum

ROUGHLY THREE YEARS HAD passed since I had met Babaji, and I took it for granted that this wonderful phase of my life would continue forever. I loved the Himalayas, I loved Babaji, and I loved the total freedom of wandering about with no possessions whatsoever. I was glad that I was spared the complications and travails of living in the midst of so-called civilised society, with its utter selfishness and greed. To me, Babaji was God, and living with him in this magic world of mountains and rivers, was heaven. The thought that I would have to leave this ideal situation, never once crossed my mind. And then, Babaji did something that shattered my dream.

Already a few times, especially that year, he had sent me away to live by myself for short periods. But what he did that morning was completely unexpected, and shocked me to the core. After the morning meditation when I went to prostrate at his feet, he said with a serious expression on his face, 'Madhu, I have noticed that you are becoming too dependent upon me psychologically. The whole idea of the spiritual teachings is to make you truly independent, and therefore, free. The yogi whose consciousness has broken free from the cage of the limited self, needs no crutches, not even that of a guru.'

I was surprised to find that, after the initial shock, a great wave of anger exploded inside me. 'So what do you want me to do?' I asked, looking him straight in the eye. 'I have broken away from all that belonged to me, even my mother, and burnt my bridges. I thought you were my anchor, but it seems it is not so. Tell me what I am expected to do, and I'll do it.'

'Go,' said Babaji, 'you must go away from here and live independently by yourself henceforth.' I did not cry, complain or look for an excuse. 'Alright, Babaji,' I said. 'What you wish shall be done right now,' and burning with anger and resentment, I picked up my meagre belongings, which consisted of a cloth bag, a blanket, a walking staff and a water pot, and walked out after touching his feet. He silently laid his hands on my head, and stood looking at me, until I disappeared from sight.

Once out of sight and hearing, I sat down on the banks of the Ganga and wept loudly. My whole body shook as I broke down. The tears wiped away the anger and fear. I composed myself, as befits a yogi, and that too a disciple of the great Maheshwarnath and Sri Guru Babaji, and turned in the direction of Uttarkashi.

I had walked for over half an hour on the road that goes to Tehri when it started to rain. I was soaked thoroughly. I kept walking. The rain stopped and the sun came out, and I said to myself, 'Well, this is how the wandering yogi lives. The rain soaks him and the sun dries him. He begs for food and sleeps wherever he can find shelter.' Joy filled my heart. Indeed, this was the sweet taste of freedom.

On the banks of the Chandrabaaga, I saw peacocks dancing in ecstasy. The ecstasy entered my heart, and I too became one of them, and danced in the bliss of freedom. We were one, the peacocks and I. And then I heard footsteps. I came back to myself, no more a peacock. Someone was walking behind me. I resisted the temptation to turn and look. Looking straight ahead, I kept walking. A hand was placed lightly on my right shoulder. It was so familiar, the touch. No, I said to myself, it can't be—and then the affection-laden voice calling, 'Madhu.'

'Babaji!' I turned and saw him. He was looking at me fondly. I fought back my tears and assumed a serious expression. 'So,' he said, 'you are going away?'

'Yes, Babaji, I am going away. You told me to get out.'

'Oh! I told you to get out and so you walked away; and if I ask you to come back, you would come back?'

Say no, said one part of my mind—be firm, but the other part won without much struggle. I said, 'Yes.'

'Then come,' said Babaji. 'Let's go back, I was just testing you. Alright, now come.'

Quietly, I followed him back to Rishikesh. We walked silently. My heart was overflowing with love and gratitude.

Six months later, when I thought everything was fine and I would live forever in the magical Himalayan atmosphere, Babaji shook me out of my complacency.

One evening, sitting beside the dhuni, he dropped the bombshell. 'Madhu,' he said, 'you have learnt all that you had to, and the lotus of your heart has bloomed. Now, it is time to go back to the plains, to the outside world. Soon, you'll have to say goodbye to me, and go back to your parents.'

'But, Babaji,' I protested, 'you want to send me back to the world of cunning and deceit, where everyone is after money, and greed is the reigning monarch? Why can't I wander forever in this divine region, free of all care? I promise, I won't bother you very often. I'll stay away and come to you only when you call me.' I broke down and wailed shamelessly.

'Pull yourself together,' Babaji said. 'You know that I rarely accept disciples. I took you on at Sri Guru's express command. I certainly love you and will protect you, but I cannot go against his wishes. It was his wish that after three-and-a-half years of training, you will be sent back to the plains. He has planned a teaching mission for you.

'Moreover, how can you be so selfish and narrow-minded? You are actually afraid of the pain and sorrow that is part of living in the so-called civilised world. There are also good and sincere people in the world who will benefit from your knowledge. Even those that the arrogant and egotistic, self-appointed teachers of wisdom call "the downfallen" have great hope of rising to the higher levels of consciousness, if provided with the right inputs.

'If you consider them sick, well, it is the sick who need a doctor. So be kind and merge your identity with the rest of mankind. You know the great Bodhisattva oath: "Until I lead every living being to Nirvana, may I be born again and again"—how lofty an ideal. What do you think my boy?'

By then, I had composed myself, 'I don't like it much,' I said. 'But whatever you and Sri Guru wish will be done.'

'Good boy,' said Babaji. 'Your emotional outburst was expected, and it is perfectly all right. I see that you have now managed to deal with it. Good.'

'But I have a question, Babaji, does this mean that I'll never see you again, or...'

'No, no, son, of course you'll see me. Whenever I think it is necessary I shall meet you. The contact shall be made in a dream, or during meditation, and I'll tell you where to come and when.

'You are required to familiarise yourself with the teachings of as many different streams of religion as possible, and spend time in already established ashrams. You should also meet different gurus, well-known or otherwise. Choose for yourself who you want to meet or where you want to go, but one place you must spend some time in is the Ramakrishna Mutt; and one person you must meet towards the end of your learning period is J. Krishnamurti.

'When you go back, wear normal clothes and live like anybody else. Make no attempt to project yourself as someone with special capabilities or special knowledge. Let all that be kept secret. If someone discovers that you possess special capacities, ask them to keep quiet and not advertise it.

'For several years, you are not to take up any teaching work. But the time will come when you'll get a green signal. You'll understand it yourself. And then, will begin the teaching phase. Even after that, go about it quietly. Teach only those who seriously seek, and without propaganda or any attempt to attract a large following. A few good seeds sown are more important than thousands wasted on barren soil.'

'Babaji, I have a serious problem. My parents might find a girl and try to get me married. What shall I do?'

'Don't worry, nothing will work out—but I was just going to tell you, that it is Sri Guru's wish that you eventually marry, have children and live like a householder. Set an example. There are people who think that to reach the highest level of consciousness, one has to become a monk. Disprove it. Shyama Charan Lahiri did it many years ago. Now, you have to do it. Moreover, the person who you will marry has a role in maturing your mind, and she will come into your life after your association with J. Krishnamurti.'

I discussed several other matters in detail and took the train from Rishikesh the next day. Babaji handed me some money and a Mr Agarwal's address and said, 'Go to Delhi and meet Agarwal. I have instructed him to give you the *taalabya kriya*. Then, proceed to Trivandrum. Agarwal will provide you with tickets and some more money.'

For the first time, Babaji hugged me. I left with my eyes brimming with tears.

In Delhi, Mr Agarwal was waiting at the exit gate of the railway station. 'Babaji informed me that you were coming,' he said. He took me in his car to his house in Greater Kailash. The next morning, he taught me the taalabya kriya. In the evening, the tailor arrived with two pairs of trousers and shirts for me. 'Babaji's instructions,' said Mr Agarwal. 'You are to discard the brahmachari's clothes you are wearing and wear these. I have also got a pair of sandals for you and a bag.'

On the third day, Mr Agarwal handed me a sleeper ticket on the train to Madras, and some more money. 'After reaching Madras, buy a ticket to Trivandrum,' he said. 'And remember what Babaji said. Act perfectly normal. Keep all your spiritual inclinations under wraps and your spiritual practices secret.'

Mr Agarwal put me on the Madras Mail and bid goodbye by whispering, 'Glory be to Sri Guru.'

35

Preparations for the Mission

THE TRAIN REACHED TRIVANDRUM in the evening. The railway station looked as sleepy as ever. I got off the train and went to the nearest salon outside the station and got myself a 'decent haircut' as my father would say. The barber snipped off my shoulder-length locks, and gave me a clean shave. It was already dark and I was spared the embarrassment of explaining my absence to acquaintances one was likely to meet on the road. I decided to walk, and within forty-five minutes had arrived home. I hoped my parents had not shifted their residence.

Carefully, I opened the door and entered the garden. Everything was as it had been. I entered the sitting room and the first person I saw was my father. He was sitting in his favourite armchair, reading Paul Brunton's *Search in Secret India*. As soon as he saw me enter, he put down the book and looked at me. He was surprisingly calm and cool. 'Where were you? We thought you had died in an accident or something,' he said. 'Next time, keep in touch wherever you are. Now go and see your mother.'

I went inside the dining area and then into the kitchen. My mother, as usual, was cooking. As soon as she saw me, the big ladle she was holding fell from her hand. She hugged me and started to cry uncontrollably. 'Where did you go leaving us here?' she cried. 'Why didn't you even write a letter? Your sisters were feeling so sad.'

'I was in the Himalayas,' I said, 'for a special purpose. I can't tell you anything more. But rest assured, I was engaged in a good activity, nothing bad.'

'Next time you want to go, tell us where you are,' said my mother. 'We won't stop you. Now go and see your sisters.' I went to their room and they were taken aback. My little sister, who was fourteen years younger than me, came running to me saying, 'Dada, dada!'

It was an emotional reunion. That night, my mother made my favourite egg curry and rice for dinner.

Now, at sixty, as I sit in a log cabin overlooking the beautiful Lake Fanny Hoe in Copper Harbour, close to Lake Superior in the Keeneewow County of Michigan in the United States, I am unable to lay my finger on the exact dates when the events that I am about to relate took place. I will try to stick to a general chronological sequence.

During the first year after my return to Trivandrum, I visited Mai Ma, the naked woman ascetic at Kanyakumari twice, and the second time, was embraced by her. On the way to Kanyakumari, I went to the Marutwa Malai hills near Suchindrum, and spent some time in the cave there. I loved Marutwa Malai so much that I subsequently made many weekend trips. Sometimes, my close friends accompanied me. Ranjit came along twice, my friend Thomas Kurien, who I lovingly called Thomaachen, came once, and so did Sivananda, one of the Tamil brothers.

On one occasion, I spent two nights in the cave, all alone. On the second night, my meditation was disrupted by someone loudly saying, what sounded like 'naina naina.' Opening my eyes, I found a thin and short man, with bulging eyes, wearing torn, old khaki shorts, standing close to me and shouting 'naina naina!' When he saw my eyes open, he became quite excited and said in Tamil, 'I have come to teach you Shiva Raja Yoga, Thirumoolar's teaching, seven more centres in the brain. Sri Guru's orders. You learn now.'

I got up and paid my respects to him. He sat down and gestured to me to sit in front of him. As the cool light of the full moon came in through the mouth of the cave, he taught me the essentials of Shiva Raja Yoga, in simple language. Then, he made me go through the exercises he taught, and apparently satisfied, he clapped his hands in glee, jumped up and ran away into the darkness. Many years later, on a trip to Marutwa Malai hills with my friend Madana Gopal, I met him again. My friend thought he was talking utter gibberish, but I could understand that he was trying to convey something important.

I also met Swami Abhedananda a couple of times and met Swami Chinmayananda, who was giving his Gita lectures in Trivandrum.

The Trivandrum Public Library, the British Council Library and the American Library were my favourite haunts. I read all the books on philosophy, religion, psychology, anatomy and physiology that were listed by Babaji for me, and some which were not, like the novels of P.G. Wodehouse—which even now are my favourite bedtime reading, Arthur Conan Doyle, Charles Dickens, James Joyce, and others. Of the books on Babaji's list, the ones I loved were the works of Helena Blavatsky, and of course J. Krishnamurti, whose book, *Commentaries on Living*, is my all-time favourite. Every time I read it, I find something new.

I also developed new friendships. Some of my friends, like Prem Kukillaya and Govindan Nair, came from distinguished families, and some from quite ordinary backgrounds; but to me, they were all equal.

A few of the latter were notified offenders too, and being friendly with them meant occasionally getting embroiled in gang warfare, or a drinking bout—but I did not care. All I wanted was to sow the seeds of transformation, which would mature perhaps in future lives. Babaji had opened my eyes, and I saw potential saints in the worst of criminals. As Babaji always said, 'It is the sick who need a doctor.'

Meanwhile, I assisted my father by supervising the roadwork he was engaged in. At the end of the day, I took long walks all alone. I visited temples, mosques and churches, wrote poems which were never published, and tried my hand at writing articles for the newspapers.

One year thus passed with no contact signals from Babaji. I thought he was teaching me to become independent.

One night before sleeping, I sent him a message, using the technique he had taught me: 'If you don't contact me soon, I am going to the Himalayas to look for you again. Pranams.' That night, Babaji appeared in my dream. I was surprised to see him wearing a long green robe and a white turban. 'Come to Ajmer,' he said, 'I'll wait for you there.'

36

Lessons from a Sufi Master

THERE WASN'T MUCH OF a protest when I told my parents that I wanted to go to Ajmer. I even got a little money from my mother, and with that plus my pocket money, I had enough to finance the trip. Those days it was quite a long journey. I had to go to Madras, then Delhi, from there to Jaipur, and finally take the local train to Ajmer.

Eventually I reached the Ajmer Sharif complex, where the great Sufi saint Khwaja Moinuddin Chisti is buried. He is much venerated by both Muslims and non-Muslims, and there is a steady flow of visitors filing in to pay their respects and pray for intercession.

Like most pilgrimage centres, Ajmer too had its share of clever confidence tricksters who grabbed at you from all sides promising their intercession with the saint for granting special favours—of course, for a fee. Many of them claimed to be direct descendants of the saint, and wore special and colourful robes to proclaim their importance.

There were also innumerable shops selling flowers, shawls, incense and other offerings to be made at the tomb. It was a weekend, and in the midst of the surging crowds, I was looking out for the familiar, bare bodied, loincloth-clad, matted-haired figure, and wondering how strange and out of place, he would look in contrast with the long-robed, turbaned, Muslim fakirs.

On the right side of the compound was an old mosque that, according to legend, had been used by the saint. It was close to the mausoleum that housed the tomb. I turned in that direction and made my way into the mosque.

It was not yet prayer time, and just a few people sat inside, either counting their rosary, reading the Quran, or engaging in silent contemplation. Imagine my surprise, when I saw that one of the long robed and turbaned figures, sitting in the prayer posture practised by Muslims, and which yogis call Vajrasana, was none other than Babaji. He was dressed exactly as I saw him in the dream, in a long green robe and white turban.

He beckoned me to come close. Before I could prostrate, he stood up, and pulling me towards him, hugged me three times in true Muslim fashion. While hugging, he whispered, 'No prostrations. Don't you know the Muslim law? Prostrate only to the Supreme Being, not even to Mohammad. Adapt your behaviour to suit circumstances, as long as it does not hurt anybody. "Each according to his capacity, each according to his needs" is a fine Sufi dictum. When in Rome, do as the Romans do.'

I then held his hands and kissed his fingers. 'Sit beside me in Vajrasana,' Babaji said, 'turn towards the tomb and sit in silent contemplation.' My heart was filled with a blissful sensation that travelled to my head. Beautiful green and violet lights appeared to me. I wished to remain forever in that blissful state, free of the bustling outside world, but Babaji shook me out of my trance. 'Come, let's go,' he said, and took me on a guided tour of the complex.

First, we visited the tomb, and although the rush was heavy, the caretakers took one look at Babaji's face and ushered us in with great respect. Inside, it was beautiful. The feeling of devotion palpably permeated the mausoleum. The tomb was draped in red and green velvet. In spite of the surging crowd, the chief Kadhim let us stay in one corner for quite some time. Everyone was praying and chanting in Arabic. My hair stood on end and tears rolled down my face. Babaji seemed to be having a whispered conversation with someone invisible. After sometime, he bowed low, and signaled to me that it was time to go. The chief Kadhim kissed Babaji's hands before he showed us out.

We circumambulated the mausoleum and then went out of the shrine complex. A ten-minute walk brought us to the Usmani Chilla, the place where Khwaja Moinuddin Chisti had sat for forty days in solitude. In Sufi terminology, this kind of forty-day, intensive contemplation in solitude is called 'Chilla'. It was a peaceful and calm place, overlooking a lake, which in the otherwise parched state of Rajasthan was indeed a welcome sight. There, Babaji gave me a brief account of Khwaja Moinuddin Chisti's life, the order that he founded, and his teachings.

Born in 1135 in Sanjar, near Asfahan, he was named Moinuddin Hasan. His father, Ghayas Uddin Hasan, himself belonged to a Sufi group in Khorassan. His mother, Bibi Mah Noor, belonged to the family of the great Sufi master Sheikh Mohiuddin Abdul Qadri of Jilan, who founded the Sufi order known as Qadriya. At fifteen he became an orphan, and shortly afterwards came in contact with the Sufi master, Ibrahim Qandoozi in his garden. Accepting a bunch of grapes from the young man, Ibrahim Qandoozi gave him a piece of sweetmeat, which he had already chewed for some time. After eating it, Moinuddin suddenly became fed up with the world and its ways and began to seek the higher reality.

He left home and travelled far and wide in Baghdad, Samarkhand and Bukhara, which were centres of Sufi influence and Islamic learning. It is said that in Baghdad, he met the great Sufi teacher Abdul Qadir Jilani. After that he travelled to Mecca and Medina, and then to Harun in Iran. There, he found his teacher, who was actually looking for him.

Khwaja Usman of Haroun was a teacher belonging to the Chisti order, founded by Khwaja Abu Ishaque of Syria. Hence, he became Khwaja Moinuddin Chisti (and was not the founder of the Chisti order, as some think).

After three years in the company of his master, during which time he practised severe austerities; Moinuddin Chisti began to travel again, meeting saints and dervishes, including the great Sheikh Abu Najeeb Suharwady of the Suharwady order. He visited the tombs of many a Sufi saint and came in contact with a number of living Sufis of a high caliber like Abu Said of Tabriz, Nasiruddin of Astrabad, and Hasan Khirqani. Many fascinating stories are told about these encounters.

At the age of fifty-four, his Sheikh, Usman Haroun declared him his successor, gave him his own prayer rug and walking stick, and bade him to go away and do his work. Khwaja Moinuddin Chisti then went on a Haj pilgrimage, circumambulated the Kaaba and reached Medina, where the tomb of Prophet Mohammad lies. It is said that he received the mandate to go to Ajmer in India and settle there, in a vivid vision.

In 1191, he reached Ajmer for the first time, and then in 1200 travelled to Balk and Baghdad. After some time, he returned to Ajmer via Multan and Delhi. In Delhi, he visited the Sufi saint from Khorassan, Qutub Shah, who became his disciple, and then the great ascetic, Baba Farid Ganj-e-Shakar. The well-known Sufi saint Hazrat Nizamuddin Aulia of Delhi belonged to the line of succession of the same Ganj-e-Shakar.

Qutub Shah of Khorassan was with Khwaja Moinuddin Chisti in Ajmer during the last year of the Khwaja's life. One day, he gave him his robe, turban and the divine scepter of his teacher Khwaja Usman Harouni, and said that in a few days, he would leave the world. He then told him to go to Delhi and settle there. His last words to Qutub Shah: 'Go wherever you may; live like a perfect man.'

Twenty days after Qutub Shah was sent away to Delhi, sometime in May 1229, Khwaja Moinuddin Chisti entered his bedroom after the night prayers, issuing instructions that no one was to disturb him till morning. It is said that a musical sound, like that of a softly played sarangi, was heard coming from the room throughout the night. In the morning, when they opened the door, wondering why he had not come for the morning prayers, they found him lying dead on his couch, with an ecstatic smile on his face.

Babaji said that Khwaja Moinuddin Chisti wrote many books. Those that have been traced are the *Anis-ul-Arwah, Hadis-ul-Maarif, Kanjul Israr* and *Kashful Israr*.

Khwaja Moinuddin Chisti was the pioneer of what could be called the Sufi wave of devotion, the 'Bhakti Marga' of Sufism in India.

Orthodox Islam bans music of any kind other than the chanting of the Quran with no musical accompaniments. The Chisti Order of Sufis, however, makes use of music and considers the playing of musical instruments and singing a major component of their spiritual practice. The music thus used is called Sama, and when properly done, plunges the singer and listener into ecstatic states that result in the expansion of consciousness.

The Chisti order is primarily based on the concept of all-sacrificing love. The Supreme Being is the veiled beloved, and the singer is the lover whose soul yearns to catch a glimpse of the beloved's sweet face. The Sufi falls in love, head-over-heels, and pines for at least a single moment alone with his beloved, looking into the eyes of the beloved, embracing the beloved, drunk with the heady wine of love called Ishq, and abandoning his limited individuality. The annihilation of the self in the love of the eternal divine Self is called *fana*.

Qawwali and ghazal singers owe much to the Chisti order and Khwaja Moinuddin Chisti. In the Sufi shrines in India, notably Ajmer and Nizamuddin in Delhi, at certain hours of the day and night, the most heart-melting ghazals and qawwalis are sung to the accompaniment of harmoniums and tablas.

It was evening. As the sun began to set, the call for prayer went up from half-a-dozen mosques in the vicinity. Babaji said, 'Now, I am going to take you to a living Sufi, Syed Gudri Shah Sahib, who lives close by. Do you remember the Muslim prayer postures that you were taught in your childhood?'

'No Babaji, not fully.'

'Okay, doesn't matter. Just follow what others do. Gudri Shah Sahib will surely invite us to join the evening congregation in the small mosque beside his house. Don't forget to say salaam and kiss his hands when we meet.'

We got down the steps and walked across the hallway. A young man wearing a white skullcap greeted us near the door. Before Babaji could speak, a wizened old man with a grey beard and turban walked out. When he saw Babaji, his face broke into an ecstatic, toothless grin. He literally ran towards him and embraced him and kissed his hands. There were tears in his eyes as he held Babaji by his shoulders and looked fondly at his face. 'Bawaji,' he said, speaking in Urdu, 'A thousand salaams. What a privilege—and who is this fortunate young man?' Babaji introduced me using the name I was born with. 'Aha!' he exclaimed, 'won't you join us for prayer? Then, we'll go to the dargah and enjoy the qawwali singer's mehfil. After that, some good biryani, or will you stick to vegetarian food?'

'No problem, come; let's go for prayer.'

After the customary ablutions, we went for prayers. There were only a few people who had congregated. After going through the ritual prayers led by Syed Gudri Shah, we sat for a while in silent contemplation and then were led by him to the dargah. From the fact that many people saluted him on the way and inside the complex, I gathered that he was a well-respected person in that locality.

The qawwali singers sat outside the tomb with a harmonium and tabla for accompaniment and sang with deep feeling and total abandon. They were basically love songs, the expression of deep longing for the beloved, for union with the beloved, for the beloved to shed the veil so that the lover could perchance catch a momentary glimpse of the beautiful countenance. The songs touched my heart.

After the concert, Gudri Shah Sahib took us to his house. One of the two rooms that served as the guest rooms was given to us. 'After the night prayers, please join us for dinner,' said the old man and left the room.

Babaji said, 'There is a purpose to your coming here. I have informed Shah Sahib that you will be his student for a short period of three weeks. You will get a crash course in Sufism and he has agreed to initiate you into its practices. After that, you can go back home and wait for my next call. Tomorrow, I need to go to Maharashtra to meet one of the Nath yogis, belonging to the lineage of the great saint Jnaneshwar, whose samadhi is at Alandi, near Pune. I have been watching you. You are doing fine, but I suggest that you don't get involved in gang fights even to save your new friends.'

After the night's prayer, Shah Sahib came personally to usher us to his house for dinner. There were about six or seven of his disciples. We sat cross-legged on mats and ate from ceramic plates. Two disciples served the food. 'Vegetarian food is also cooked specially for Bawaji,' said Shah Sahib. 'Young man, if you are also vegetarian, you can have the special food.'

Babaji surprised me by saying, 'Today, we shall eat mutton biryani and kebab.' He winked at me. 'This young man used to like biryani, except that he thinks his mother makes the best biryani in the world.'

Everyone laughed, and after a silent prayer, we enjoyed one of the best biryanis I have eaten in my life. After the meal, Shah Sahib announced to the group that I would be joining their *halqa* (circle) for three weeks. I was welcomed with hugs and exclamations of 'Allah be praised.'

The next morning, Babaji left, leaving me with Shah Sahib. I did not feel too bad when I said goodbye to him. I was beginning to learn the art of remaining calm under all circumstances. For the next three weeks, I was Shah Sahib's disciple.

The first few days, I was taught the philosophy and theory of Sufism, and also about the different Sufi orders. And the rest of the time, I was taught the techniques practised by the Sufis. I learnt, for instance, that the founder of Islam, among other things, said, '*Man arafa nafshu, fa khad arafa rabbu*,' which could be translated as 'he who knoweth his self, knoweth his Lord.' I learnt what *khalb*, or the spiritual heart, meant, and how to awaken it in myself. I was taught about the whirling dervishes of the Mevlavi founded by Jalaluddin Rumi, and how and why they whirled. A brief introduction to his poetic work, the *Masnavi*, was provided, and so also to his prose work *Fihi Ma Fihi*, which roughly means, 'It is, and yet it is not.'

I learnt the works of Abdul Khadir Jilani, the founder of the Qadiriya order, and the mystical meanings of the *Rubaiyat of Omar Khayyam*. I listened to the Chisti qawwali singers and learnt to sing a little myself.

The works of the great teachers of the Naqshabandi, Rifayee and Suharwady orders, and the stories of Mullah Nasruddin, opened up wondrous dimensions which I never thought could have existed within the framework of Islam. My favourite book however was the *Mantiq-ut-Tair* (*Conference of the Birds*) by Fariduddin Attar.

I was put through a grinding routine of study, contemplation and fasting during the day, until my *Nephsh*, the controlling self, was dissected and laid naked before my eyes. At the end of the training, after having prescribed further titles I had to read, which included the classic textbook *Kasf-ul-Mehjoob* (*Revelation of the Veiled*) by Ali Hujviri, Shah Sahib said to me, 'Your Bawa is a great soul. He is an aulia, a pir. By divine mercy, you have found him. You don't need anything else. Much of the journey has been covered. Go your way son, and may Allah be with you.'

After saluting him with great respect, and embracing him, I left for the railway station and, in a few days, was back home.

37

The Ramakrishna Mission

THE YEAR AFTER I returned from Ajmer, I found myself enrolled as a student of pharmacy. My parents thought that my vagabond instincts would be curbed if I was engaged in doing what they thought was a meaningful occupation. My first cousin's wife was a doctor at Cannanore in northern Kerala, and it was she who suggested that I could get admission in the Calicut Medical College for a diploma in pharmacy. She was, and still is, a good friend, and I accepted the suggestion, since my parents were keen. My father was planning to set up a pharmaceutical concern at Madras, and he thought it would be useful if I did the course.

On my part, I sort of enjoyed the course. I had to study a good deal of anatomy and physiology, which included dissections and visits to the hospital morgue. Organic chemistry and pharmacology were also part of the curriculum. I did well in the first year. During the second half of the second year, the restlessness and desire to move, which visited me periodically, possessed me again, and I began to make plans for a quiet exit. One night, I dreamt of Babaji chatting with Sri Ramakrishna Paramahansa on the banks of the Ganga. Taking that as a cue, I left Calicut one morning without informing anybody.

For some reason, after reaching Chennai, I took a train to Mumbai, and realised that I did not have enough money to go to Calcutta where the headquarters of the Ramakrishna Mission are located. A fellow traveller told me that there was a beautiful Ramakrishna Mission centre at Khar in Mumbai. He lived in Khar, and he would be happy to drop me off there if I was interested. I said yes.

It was indeed an oasis in the midst of noisy Mumbai. First, I went to the exquisite temple of Sri Ramakrishna and sat for a while in meditation. At my request, I was granted an appointment with Swami Hiranmayananda, the president, a senior monk and disciple of Mahapurusha Maharaj, a direct disciple of Sri Ramakrishna. He heard me out patiently and agreed to take me in as a brahmachari. Only, he thought it was a good idea to keep my non-Hindu name secret, for various reasons, and named me Shivprasad. From then on, for one-and-a-half years, I was brahmachari Shivprasad.

The Ramakrishna Mission, started by the illustrious Swami Vivekananda, believes that service to humanity is the best form of worship. Unlike some ashrams I have seen, where the residents study, eat and sleep, and usually don't get involved in any social service, the monks of the Ramakrishna Mission are always kept busy in social service activities. Hospitals, orphanages, schools, colleges and the large publication division are handled mostly by monks and acolytes. These activities also keep them from turning lazy and complacent.

When I was asked what kind of service I would prefer, being educated and so on, I volunteered to work in the temple, cleaning, and in general looking after the space. After consultation with Bhatuk Maharaj, the orthodox and aloof monk priest, I was given the job. From there, I graduated to working in the inner shrine, cutting fruits and vegetables, and collecting flowers for the offerings, and finally being allowed to wipe and clean the inner sanctorum, and look after the marble image of Sri Ramakrishna, as if he lived there in flesh and blood.

At other times, I learnt to chant the Vedas, and sing, from a wonderful monk Swami Gautamananda, a disciple of the great Swami Yatiswarananda. He later on became the head of the Ramakrishna Mutt at Madras, one of the oldest centres of the mission. Swami Vivekananda was himself associated with its origins. A direct disciple of Sri Ramakrishna, Swami Ramakrishnananda was the first head of this centre.

I learnt a lot during those one-and-a-half years. I cultivated qualities that would stand me in good stead in the journey of my life. Their library was well stocked and I read almost all the literature available on Sri Ramakrishna and his direct disciples. *The Gospel of Ramakrishna* by 'M,' *Ramakrishna the Great Master* by Swami Saradananda, the *Complete Works of Swami Vivekananda*, and the lives of some of the direct disciples of Sri Ramakrishna, were my favourites.

I was also able to meet some exemplary monks of the Ramakrishna order like Swami Vireshwarananda, the president of the Ramakrishna Mission and a direct disciple of Sharada Devi; the illustrious Swami Ranganathananda, by whose efforts, the Ramakrishna Institute of Culture was established in Calcutta, and so many others. When Durga Puja was celebrated that year, I got the opportunity to interact with other senior monks of a different category who visited the Khar centre. These monks were experts in the tantras, and some of them were highly advanced in the spiritual levels associated with it.

If I had wanted to become a monk, there was no better place for me than the Mutt, but I was destined to be a householder. In any case, Babaji's plans for me were different. After one-and-a-half years, I quietly left the Ramakrishna Mission at Khar, and was free to wander once again.

After reading most of the books about Sri Ramakrishna and Swami Vivekananda, I had a strong desire to visit two places: the Dakshineshwar Kali temple in Calcutta, on the banks of the Hoogly river, where Ramakrishna had spent most of his life; and the Belur Mutt, the headquarters of the Ramakrishna Mission that stood on the other side of the river.

I waited for a signal from Babaji, but since none came, I just went to the Mumbai Central Railway Station and bought a ticket to Calcutta. I had just enough money to reach there and had to walk all the way to Dakshineshwar from the Howrah Station. Accustomed to timely meals and good food by now, I was very tired and hungry by the time I reached Dakshineshwar. Imagine my joy and excitement when I saw a familiar figure standing outside the main entrance to the temple—my beloved Babaji. Hunger and fatigue forgotten, I ran to touch his feet. He gave me a warm hug and said, 'First, some food for the hungry brahmachari Maharaj?'

After a delicious meal of luchis, potato curry and sandesh, we entered the temple complex. Built by Rani Rasmoni 150 years ago, it consists of a small temple of Gopal Krishna on one side, and the main temple of Bhadrakali, the ferocious, wrathful, female deity and a symbol of pure energy in its explosive, volatile form. As you enter, on the right are the twelve lingas that represent the twelve sacred Jyothir lingas, phallic symbols of Shiva. Kali is said to be his consort.

As soon as I entered the gate, my hair stood on end, and I experienced a certain change of mood. Babaji's face looked unusually serious and was turned towards the main temple of Bhadrakali. It was a weekday and the darshan line was not too long. In just a few minutes, we had climbed the stairs and were face to face with the turbulent goddess, the mother of the universe.

The idol in Dakshineshwar, Bhadrakali, is the most wrathful aspect of the ten great energies of tantra called *Dasa Maha Vidyas*. She is black in colour and her eyes look ferocious and angry. Her tongue hangs out of her mouth dripping blood and her thick hair is loose and unruly, blown by the wind. She is naked except for a garland of severed human heads and a skirt made of human hands. She is four armed. One palm is pointed downwards, the other is raised in blessing, a third holds a sword dripping with blood, and the fourth a freshly severed, bleeding, human head.

She dances in wild ecstasy that verges on fury, one leg resting on the chest of her Lord Shiva who lies prostrate and passive, while the other is raised in a dancing pose—on the whole, a gory picture. The moment my eyes fell on her, something extraordinary happened. The fiery energy that lies dormant at the bottom of the spine, which Babaji had taught me to activate and coax to travel upwards to the head, now unwound itself spontaneously. I felt a tangible tremor as the fire rushed up my spine, breaking into rainbow colours as it reached the crown of my head. I uttered a moan and fell down.

When I woke up, I found myself in a corner of the dance hall in front of the temple with my head on Babaji's lap. He was stroking my head gently and saying, 'Too much for you, yes? The body could not bear the impact. Lucky I was here, or you would have gone crazy.'

'My whole body is pulsating with a bliss I never experienced before,' I said in a feeble voice.

'You will be alright. Stand up now. Let me show you around.'

Soon, we were walking around the complex. My bliss had abated a little, and I was tottering around like a drunk. We visited the famous Gopal Krishna temple, which houses a small image of Krishna. The idol had once fallen from a priest's hand, while being bathed, and its leg had broken. Experts in the scriptures were called to decide if a broken idol could be worshipped. The verdict, in general, was that it was inauspicious to worship a broken image.

Rani Rasmoni, the founder of the temple thought that the saintly young priest of the Kali temple, Gadadhar Chattopadhyaya (Sri Ramakrishna Paramahansa was the name given to him later by his devotees) should also be consulted. She considered him divinely inspired. The young Ramakrishna merely said, 'I am not an erudite scholar like the distinguished pundits here but I have a question. If the Rani's son-in-law fell down and broke his leg, would she throw him in the Ganga and get a new one? As far as the broken leg is concerned, I can repair it perfectly and no one will be able to see the crack. However, it is left for you all to decide.' The idol, repaired personally by Ramakrishna, was reinstalled, and continues to be worshipped even today.

We also visited and circumambulated the twelve lingas, symbols of the one Supreme Being Sadashiva, which means, eternally auspicious. We then came out of the complex and went into the little room beside the river where Sri Ramakrishna spent a major part of his life. This was the room where all the future stalwarts of the Ramakrishna Mission, including Swami Vivekananda, whose real name was Narendranath Dutta, and other great *sadhaks* and spiritual teachers like Bhairavi Brahmani, Gopal Ma, Totapuri and others, spent significant periods of time with Sri Ramakrishna. My body again went into tremors, and tears flowed incessantly from my eyes as I sat with Babaji near the cot, where Ramakrishna used to sleep. With my eyes closed, I saw a film-like vision of the guru and his disciples having great fun, laughing, talking and eating sandesh. After a long time, I heard Babaji's voice, 'Let's go now.' We came out and stood near the verandah where Ramakrishna had prostrated at a prostitute's feet saying, 'O mother Kali, how beautiful you are, and in what myriad forms you appear.'

Then we visited the Nahabat, where the holy mother Sharada Devi, wife of Sri Ramakrishna, used to live and cook for her dear saintly husband, who, left to himself, was likely to ignore his bodily needs.

From the Nahabat, we walked to the banks of the Ganga. Babaji showed me the Panchavati grove, where Ramakrishna practised intense tantric rites under the guidance of Bhairavi Brahmani, the woman teacher who initiated him into the mysteries of the Kundalini. Babaji said that he had seen Bhairavi Brahmani coaxing Gadadhar, when he was in a trance, to eat a little food. A few years ago, I would have questioned how Babaji could have seen all that, when he himself did not look more than thirty or so, but by then, I had learnt to suspend all the conventional ideas of time and space when dealing with him.

He said that Bhairavi Brahmani, a disciple of the naked Trailanga Swami of Banaras, was a highly evolved yogini, and believed that Sri Ramakrishna was not an ordinary sadhak but some kind of an incarnation of divinity. Then, he told me this interesting story.

Wanting to officially declare Sri Ramakrishna an incarnation, she invited a lot of learned religious scholars and experts on the subject to Dakshineshwar to deliberate on her theory. The majority of the scholars agreed that the young priest of the Kali temple did possess certain extraordinary qualities and features that would qualify him to be declared an avatar. Finally, they decided to consult the young priest himself to know what he thought about the matter.

Sri Ramakrishna had, a few days before this, slipped and fallen near the temple while in a semi-trance, and broken his arm. He appeared before the committee, with his broken arm in a sling. When asked for his opinion, he laughed and said, 'I don't know what the scriptures say or what you think, but if you really think I am an avatar, I must say that this will be the first avatar with a broken arm in a sling.'

Bhairavi Brahmani, however, was convinced beyond a doubt that he was a special divine manifestation.

'What do you think?' I asked Babaji.

'Yes, he was,' he said.

From Dakshineshwar, we took a boat across the Ganga to Belur Mutt, the headquarters of the Ramakrishna Mission. Running into several wooded acres, the Belur Mutt monastery houses about 200 monks and acolytes at any given time, and consists of many blocks. But the most impressive structure is the temple dedicated to Sri Ramakrishna. Made of brown stone and granite, with its exquisite cupolas and marbled floors, it's a marvel of architectural excellence.

The deity in the sanctum sanctorum is a life-size, white marble image of Sri Ramakrishna, sitting cross-legged, absorbed in a trance. Under the platform on which the deity is seated lie Sri Ramakrishna's physical remains: bones and ashes, carried personally by Swami Vivekananda on his head, and installed by him. We then visited the small shrines built along the banks of the river which contain the remains of some of the disciples of Sri Ramakrishna including Swami Vivekananda, and the holy mother Sharada Devi.

Then Babaji took me to the first floor of a building near the dining hall with the balcony overlooking the Ganga. From the windows which opened into the balcony, I could see a beautiful, well-appointed bedroom, with a rosewood four-poster bed, a classic dressing table with an oval mirror, a period sofa, a roll-top writing table with a cushioned chair, and a Turkish rug on the floor.

I looked to see where the door was. It was on the left but locked. Just above the door frame was a plaque which said 'Swami Vivekananda's room.' The musical instruments he played were in one corner of the room, and in the other corner, his stylish walking stick, leather boots and calf-skin briefcase. I wondered how a great monk like Swami Vivekananda could have lived in such luxurious settings.

Babaji broke his silence, 'Swamiji was a Raja Yogi inside and outside. He was a king of all that he surveyed. Where great yogis live, and how they conduct themselves, depends upon their life's mission. The external really does not matter, it is the attitude that counts. Swamiji's life became comfortable outwardly only after he became famous, and the Belur Mutt was built. In his youth, he suffered incalculably, sometimes going without a proper meal. Even afterwards, he was ready to pick up his kamandalu, and become a wandering monk once more, with no possessions whatsoever at short notice. This is borne out by many incidents in his life.

'Remember, Janaka was the king of Videha and yet, a rishi, a raja rishi. You too will live like a raja rishi."

'I, Babaji!' I protested. 'If you would have allowed me to wander in the Himalayas without a care, I would have preferred it. But I admit, I love driving good cars.'

Babaji said, 'That's fine as long as you practise moderation. You tend to drive too fast. Watch out.'

We had a good meal in the dining hall of Belur Mutt and walked to the front gate. Once outside, Babaji gave me some money and said, 'Now, you go back home, and wait for the wanderer's bug to bite you again. You will come again to Belur Mutt and spend a longer period here.' Babaji then walked away. His prediction about my coming back to Belur Mutt was fulfilled some years later.

On the way back, I visited Bhubaneswar and Puri. In the temple of Jagannath, I felt overwhelmed by spiritual emotions. My heart was filled with bliss, and sitting on the floor in the courtyard, I saw scene after scene of Chaitanya Mahaprabhu's life: two glowing, young men, Nitai and Gouranga, dancing in ecstasy in front of Jagannath, to the accompaniment of drums and cymbals.

I also visited Chaitanya Mahaprabhu's seat, and the little place near the sea where Chaitanya's close friend and disciple Haridas Prabhu lived. Haridas was a Muslim by birth and was denied entry into the Jagannath temple. Chaitanya Mahaprabhu therefore made it a point to go straight to his residence every time he came out of the temple. It is said that Haridas Prabhu passed away uttering, 'Hari Hari', placing Chaitanya Mahaprabhu's feet on his chest.

38

Sri Devi and Neem Karoli Baba

EIGHT MONTHS AFTER COMING back home, I was back on the road. This time, I went to Delhi and worked with my good friend Balachandran Nair, who I had met and befriended on a train some time ago. He was much older than me, and was editing and publishing a spiritual and cultural magazine, *Accent*. I learnt the rudiments of editing from him and also drew diagrams for the magazine. Balachandran Nair, whom I called Chettan, or elder brother, now lives in a quiet coastal town called Kanjankad in Kerala, and publishes excellent books on spiritual subjects, writing under the pen name Srikant.

After some time, I quit and went away to the Himalayas. This time, I travelled in a different direction. Passing through Haldwani and visiting the cave of Herakund Baba, a great Siddha who lived many years ago and who is believed to be a disciple of Sri Guru Babaji, I proceeded to Ranikhet and Dwarahat, and from there to Kukurchina. My intention was to go to the cave where the great yogi Shyama Charan Lahiri met Sri Guru, and was initiated by him.

Trekking through Pandukhali, which is where locals believe the exiled Pandavas lived for a while, I scrambled down a rocky hill and reached the cave. There was no one there. It was absolutely still and serene inside. Sitting in the cave and doing my kriya, I effortlessly passed into a deep state of altered consciousness. I could feel Sri Guru's presence tangibly in my heart centre. I came out of the trance and decided to explore the labyrinth of tunnels which could be accessed through the single entry on the right side of the cave's interior.

I was feeling sad that Babaji, who I had thought would surely meet me, was nowhere to be seen. I entered the tunnel, and in spite of the darkness inside, kept going, finding my way mostly by feeling the sides, and roof of the tunnel, with my hands. The fear that snakes or Himalayan bears might be lurking in the dark, prompted me to return to the entrance. But just then, I saw a glimmer of light at the far end. Gathering courage, I walked forward. The light increased, and I found that the tunnel opened into another large cave, with its entrance on the eastern side.

A dhuni was blazing, and my heart leapt with joy. There was Babaji sitting in the lotus posture, ramrod straight, gazing into the fire. He did not turn around, but simply said, 'Come, come Madhuji, long time yes?' I prostrated at his feet, and we sat and talked for a long time. As usual, he had kindly got food for me: chapatis, dal and vegetable curry. After a long meditation session and dinner, he told me to sleep.

'This place, Panchkuli has been the final resting place of many great yogis and siddhas,' said Babaji. 'You will find many graves scattered throughout the hills. At one time, it was Sri Guru's and also my favourite haunt. We don't come here so frequently these days.' I unrolled my sleeping bag, causing Babaji to chuckle, and lay down. I was in that peculiar state between sleep and wakefulness when I sensed a sweet fragrance wafting into the cave. I did not sit up, but shook off my sleep, and became alert.

A glowing human form, swathed in translucent white raiment, floated into the cave. As it descended and stood before the dhuni, I could make out that it was a female being, extremely beautiful, with thick, long black hair. Babaji stood up and then prostrated at her feet. I too got out of my sleeping bag and prostrated. 'So, this is the young soul who knew us long, long ago,' she said in a melodious voice. 'Come close, my dear.'

I moved towards her. She ran her fingers through my hair, stroked my cheek and held me close to her bosom. The sweet fragrance saturated my soul and pulsated through every cell. I felt like a long lost infant reunited with its mother. 'Sri Guru said you were here,' she said to Babaji. 'Thought I will see the young man. I have to go now.' She floated out just as she had come and both of us prostrated.

'That was indeed a rare occurrence,' said Babaji. 'That was Sri Devi, Sri Guru Babaji's sister, a highly evolved being who normally leads a completely private life. You are lucky!'

'All your blessings, Babaji,' I said and went back to sleep. I fell asleep musing over the unusual experience, and wondering if anyone would ever believe me back home, if I related the incident.

The next day, we left the cave and came to Dwarahat. Before leaving, Babaji suggested that I go to the Advaita Ashram established by Swami Vivekananda at Mayavati, Pithorgarh district, and then visit Uttara Brindavan Ashram in Mihirtola and meet Sri Madhav Ashish, the head of the ashram. I was also to go to Kayanchi, between Ranikhet and Almora and see the Avadhoota Maharaj Neem Karoli Baba, and then go to Banaras and stay at the Ramakrishna Seva Ashram, before going to Belur Mutt in Calcutta.

I took a bus from Dwarahat to Lohaghat, and hitch-hiked on a jeep that was going to Mayavati. At Mayavati, I met the head swamiji, whose name I now forget. He was also the editor of the *Prabuddha Bharata*. The swami explained to me that normally, no one is allowed to stay without prior intimation but as a special case he would let me stay for two days.

It was one of the most beautiful Himalayan ashrams I have ever stayed at. The Advaita Ashram was specially set up by Swami Vivekananda for those who love the Vedantic way of life and were not inclined to idol worship. Here, there is no temple dedicated to Sri Ramakrishna, and therefore no daily service or puja. I was thrilled to see the room used by Swamiji. In the Advaita Ashram at Mayavati, I met Swami Devatmananda, an Iraqi doctor who had become a monk of the Ramakrishna order. We became good friends, and when I told him I was going to Banaras, he gave me a letter to the head of the Ramakrishna Seva Ashram there and said that he would also be there in a few days.

From Mayavati, I travelled to Mihirtola, to the Uttara Brindavan Ashram of Sri Krishnaprem, known to his close associates as Gopal Da. Gopal Da passed away in 1965 and I was to meet his disciple and successor Sri Madhav Ashish.

The ashram at Mihirtola, thirty-five kilometre away from Almora, with its lovely little Krishna temple, was established by the saintly Bengali lady Yashoda Mai. She was the daughter of Justice Chakravarthy of the Calcutta High Court, and had had the distinction of being worshipped as a symbol of the divine mother, a practice called Kumari Puja, by none other than the great Swami Vivekananda, when she was barely seven years old. Justice Chakravarthy was a close associate of Annie Besant of the Theosophical Society, and being a Theosophist himself, believed in the existence of ageless Himalayan masters. Yashoda Mai, however, was an orthodox Vaishnava sadhak, and the God Krishna was everything for her.

Krishnaprem's name, before he renounced the world, was Professor Ronald Nixon. He was British, a brilliant Cambridge graduate, and taught English Literature at the University of Lucknow and Banaras. He had been a scholar of Sanskrit and Pali, and was fluent in Bengali and Hindi. All this I learnt from Sri Madhav Ashish, who was British himself.

The ashram was set in a secluded spot, surrounded by pine-covered mountains and deep valleys. Once inside the gate, I felt I was in an enchanted garden. There were bright flowers everywhere and abundant greenery, and above all, there was silence. I could see the grey dome of the temple amidst the greenery. Climbing the steps, I discarded my chappals outside the temple's doorstep and entered. It was a traditional Vaishnava temple with beautiful images of Radha and Krishna, and everything was done in the Vaishnava style.

All the rituals, like regular aarti with the showing of lights, ringing of bells and sounding of the gong, were conducted diligently. The afternoon *bhog*, or offering of food, with the blowing of the conch, was also practiced. In fact, the entire ashram revolved around the

temple, and like in the Gauda Vaishnava cult, the deities Radha and
Rasbihari Krishna were treated like living beings: put to sleep, woken
up, etc.

It was evening aarti time, and as I stood inside the temple, a
westerner in typical Vaishnava attire, complete with the Vaishnava caste
mark on the forehead, tuft, and saffron dhoti, entered. He just looked at
me, and walked straight to the sanctum sanctorum. An elaborate puja
was expertly performed by this tall westerner. No detail was missed.
There were just two or three people in the temple including me. At
the end of the puja, he stepped out and came over to me. I did my
pranams and touched his feet. 'Madhav Ashish,' he said in the Queen's
English, 'a humble disciple of Yashoda Mai and Sri Krishnaprem. Did
you just come in?'

'Yes, Maharaj,' I said. 'I have been travelling in the Himalayas and was
told by my guru that I should visit this ashram. May I stay for a day?'

'Make yourself at home, young man,' he said. 'I'll show you a room.
Fortunately, there are only a few visitors at the moment.'

Later in the night, after a delicious vegetarian dinner,
Sri Madhav Ashish invited me to his residence for a chat. 'Please don't
mind, I have a habit of smoking,' he said and lit his briar pipe. With
the rich smell of good tobacco filling the room, we talked till late
that night.

'Good,' he said. 'To each his own, and as I said, we are orthodox
Vaishnavaites here. Follow your Baba's instructions. That may be best
for you. I can see something wonderful in your eyes. Did your Babaji
by any chance give you a Vaishnav mantra?'

'Yes,' I said, 'In Thokar Kriya, we have to chant "Om Namo Bhagavathe
Vasudevaya."'

'Hari! Hari!' he said with great emotion, 'Jai Sri Krishna. We have
reason to believe in the existence of great masters who live in the
Himalayas. Perhaps you have a link with us. Now, it is late. You should
be turning in!' With that, I was dismissed.

Many years later, I heard from Dr Karan Singh of Kashmir that
Ashish Da, as he called Sri Madhav Ashish, passed away after a protracted

illness. Cancer had not spared even this saintly soul. I also read the two wonderful books written by Gopal Da: *The Yoga of the Bhagawad Gita* and *The Yoga of the Kathopanishad*. They are truly insightful and useful for serious spiritual seekers.

The next day, I took leave of Sri Madhav Ashish and travelled towards Kayanchi, to see if I could catch a glimpse of the great Neem Karoli Baba.

I was lucky. When I reached Kayanchi, I was informed that Neem Karoli Baba had arrived the day before, and was going to be there for a few days. In the ashram, as in most places where Neem Karoli Baba spent time, a giant idol of Hanuman, the monkey-faced god, was installed. Hanuman, also known as the son of the Wind God, and known for his extraordinary strength and prowess, was very dear to Rama, the Prince of Ayodhya. Nearby was a temple of the mother goddess.

The baba was holding audience. He sat on a raised verandah, and there were more than a hundred people sitting on the floor in neat rows. I noticed that the front rows were mostly occupied by westerners. Neem Karoli Baba looked the perfect picture of what one might call the mad sage. He was big built and quite fat, with closely cropped grey hair. A grey walrus moustache adorned the upper lip of his chubby face. He was bare-chested, and wrapped around his fat belly, was a blanket with red, white and black checks. I was to learn later that come rain or summer, this was his standard attire.

He was laughing loudly, gesturing wildly with his hands, and sometimes swinging his body to and fro as if indulging in some secret joy. He answered questions usually in a few broken sentences, but was mostly loudly saying 'Ram! Ram!' Someone bowed to him and he hit him hard on his back and said in Hindi, 'Where are you looking for him? He is everywhere. Say Ram Ram.' Then in English, 'Very good, Ram Ram.'

Watching the scene from a distance, I wondered if he would even notice an insignificant new arrival like me. I was wrong. Suddenly, he craned his neck and looked at me. His eyes widened. I felt something like an electric shock going up my neck and towards my head. '*Babaji ka baccha'* he shouted, greeting me as Babaji's child. He pointed at me and called me forward.

I went. *'Upar aao'*—climb up—he ordered. I climbed up the steps and stood near him. I could smell incense. He reached over and gave me a tug, and I fell on his lap in a sitting position. 'Good, good,' he said, and then reaching into the folds of his blanket, produced a rotten apple. 'Eat,' he said putting it in my hands. Sitting on his lap, I debated what I should do with the apple. It looked rotten and dirty too, and then I realised that I actually had no choice. I bit into it and quickly finished the apple. Strangely, it did not have a rotten taste.

'Give my greetings to Babaji. Say Ram Ram to him,' he said. 'Now you can go.' He pushed me out of his lap, and gave me a whack on my bum. I prostrated and walked back to where I was sitting, somewhere in the last row. That night, I stayed at the ashram. Someone kindly provided me with food and accommodation. However, I could not sleep the whole night. I was in deep meditation. In the morning, I left the ashram after bowing down to Neem Karoli Baba from a distance. The blissful meditation lingered.

Before dinner the previous night, I had heard many wonderful stories about Baba, but the one that truly impressed and amused me was the LSD story. Those were the days of the hippies and flower children and a lot of them had been attracted to Neem Karoli Baba, thanks to Richard Alpert, who later changed his name to Ram Dass.

One day it seems, Baba saw a westerner pushing a small bottle surreptitiously into his pocket, 'What's that?' he asked.

'Bottle,' said the hippie.

'What's inside?'

'Medicine,' said the hippie.

'What medicine?'

'LSD, Baba.'

'Give it to me.'

'But, Baba this is strong medicine...'

'Give it to me, now.'

Trembling with fear and apprehension, the hippie handed over the bottle. Baba opened the lid and popped all ten or so LSD tablets into his mouth at one go. All the Westerners who knew about the fatal consequences of an LSD overdose, gaped at Baba helplessly. In a minute or two, Baba suddenly began to behave strangely. He roared, screamed, rolled his eyes, put out his tongue and swung his body in circles. The hippies thought that the drug had begun to take effect, and expected the worst. Instead, the Baba's strange behaviour ceased as suddenly as it started. He gave a big laugh and said 'Nothing happened. No LSD. Say Ram Naam, chant Ram Ram.'

To the Westerners, what happened was indeed unimaginable; a true demonstration of 'mind over matter', a miracle.

39

The Aghori from Banaras

FROM ALMORA, I WENT to Delhi, and then to Banaras. In Banaras, I went directly to the Ramakrishna Mission's Seva Ashram. Sure enough, Swami Devatmananda, the Iraqi doctor, was there as promised. He introduced me to the senior swami there, whose name I forget. This swami was himself a doctor, a very kind man. Together, both the doctor swamis were of the opinion that I should write to Swami Hiranmayananda, who was then one of the General Secretaries of the Ramakrishna Mission and was in Belur Mutt, and seek permission to join Belur Mutt as an acolyte. Till then, I could stay in the Ramakrishna Seva Ashram.

So, I wrote to Swami Hiranmayananda, and stayed for about a month in Banaras, waiting for a reply. It was a wonderful opportunity to explore the ancient city of Banaras.

Known as Kashi, which means 'light,' from ancient times, this sacred city has been the centre of learning, culture and hoary traditions of religious thought. Fa-Hien in the fifth century, mentions how, following the river Heng (Ganga), he came to the town of Banaras in the kingdom of Kashi. Hiuen Tsang in the seventh century calls it Varanasi. Some Muslim rulers tried to change its name to Muhammadabad, but Kashi continued to be Kashi or Varanasi. The Puranas also called this the sacred city, Avimukta Kshetra, Mahasmasana and Anandavanam. But by far, the popular name was and still is Kashi to the majority of Hindus.

In spite of the crowds of pilgrims, stinking lanes, dangerous horned bulls roaming free, the insidious monkeys, the dust, the flies and the rapacious pandas (priests), I found a certain tangible peace and tranquility in Varanasi.

I made it a habit of going daily to the Dasashwamedha Ghat not far from the ashram, trying to weave my way through the crazy cycle-rickshaws, ochre-robed sanyasins, naked nagas and beggars. The ghat had innumerable akhadas or monasteries belonging to various orders of ascetics. Hippies and flower people from the west mingled with the sadhus. At the Sri Yogiraja Sri 108 Bhagwan Dasjika Akhada Khak Chanka, the Ramavat sadhus smoked charas and ganja.

I also visited the Manikarnika and Harishchandra Ghats, where a large number of dead bodies are cremated every day. Although, the Dasanami sanyasins of the Shankara school are in the majority in Kashi, Vaishnavite sects also have their centres. I made it a point to visit as many centres as I could: Buddhist, Jain, Sikh, Nirmal, Udasin, Kabir Panthi, Nanak Panthi, Ramanandi, Ramanuji, Vallabh, Madhav, Nimbark, Gaudiya, Veera Shaiva, and of course the panth to which Babaji belonged, the Nath or the Gorakhpanth. I met many scholars and holy men, including the well-known dandi sanyasin and learned sadhu Swami Karpatriji, who explained to me that 'Kashi' meant light, and one can really get the full merit of living in Kashi only when the light of Brahma (*Brahma Prakash*) is attained. I had several Vedantic discussions with this scholarly and saintly soul, and learnt many new angles to the Vedanta philosophy.

Three days before the letter from Swami Hiranmayananda came, I ventured out one evening to get the darshan of the linga at the Kashi Viswanath (Lord of the Universe) temple. After viewing and touching the Shiva linga, I came out and walked to Manikarnika Ghat. Many bodies were being burnt. I descended the steps of the ghat, found myself a comparatively quiet spot, and sat down facing the Ganga. Sitting there my thoughts turned to Babaji. Where could he be at the moment? Would he be wandering somewhere in the Himalayas? How wonderful it would have been if he was here sitting beside me. Babaji had said once that he had lived for many years in Banaras. Was he by some chance in Banaras? Surely, he would not hide from me if he was here...

The sun was setting, and the gongs and the bells rang in all temples. At some ghats, aarti was being performed to the sacred river Ganga. 'Madhu!'

I was startled by the familiar voice. No one but Babaji could say 'Madhu' with such affection. He was standing three steps away from me. 'Babaji,' I exclaimed with joy and touched his feet.

'So, how is brahmachari Maharaj?' he said smilingly, and placed his hands on my shoulder.

'Great, Babaji,' I said, 'except that I was missing you.' '*Theek hai*, now I am going to be with you only for an hour or two. This strange city of contrasts called Kashi, the city of lights, is the abode of a number of greatly evolved beings who mostly live incognito. Some great souls like Trailanga Swami became well-known for a purpose, and so also Shyama Charan Lahiri, but most remain unknown. The unknowns are usually greater than the known ones.

'I want you to meet one such great one who lives in the Manikarnika burning ghats. He is an Aghori, and the general public shuns him because they believe that he eats the flesh of half-burnt corpses, and behaves like a completely madman. He never bathes, and his naked body is covered with dust. He lives in a dilapidated shed in the cremation grounds, amidst heaps of human and animal bones. But mind you, all these are screens, an effective camouflage that leaves him undisturbed, and free to enjoy the bliss of spiritual solitude, and share it with the deserving. Come, let's go.'

Walking through the cremation grounds in semi darkness, we reached an isolated corner of the Manikarnika Ghat. From the general direction of a tiny tin-roofed structure, came the loud voice of someone using the choicest abuses in the Hindi language. As we neared the shed, I could see a big fat man, naked and bearded, with dreadlocks wrapped around his head like a turban, sitting in a corner, and a man and woman standing before him. In the light of a single kerosene oil lamp that was lit in the middle of the shed, I could see the bones that lay scattered around. Babaji stopped me from going further, 'Wait,' he whispered, 'let him finish whatever he is doing.'

The Aghori was shouting at the top of his voice, 'So you think you can fool me, you loan shark. You lend money and charge such high interest. You blood sucker. How many people have you cheated out of their small pieces of land because they can't pay such high interest, or repay your loan? Didn't that woman commit suicide because she lost everything to you? You scoundrel, and then, you bring sweets for me. Will that wash off your sins, you bastard. Get out! I won't eat your sweets. They are poison for me. Go, before I kick you out.'

The moneylender in a silk shirt, muttered something which I could not clearly make out, and the Aghori reacted by throwing away the sweet boxes. One box of sweets came flying near me, almost hitting my head, and the silk-shirted man ran out of the shed in panic, escaping the wrath of the Aghori who was ready to manhandle him. He passed us and went his way.

Now, the woman was alone with him, and I marveled at her guts. After all that she had witnessed, she still remained there. The Aghori turned to her, 'Why are you here, woman? I am crazy, don't you see. Get out before I hurt you.'

The woman stood her ground, 'I am not afraid, Baba,' she said. 'I have heard that great saints behave like madmen. I have seen the world in all its aspects and I am fed up. I only want the "Truth". I will do anything you want me to. I surrender.'

The Aghori broke into a guffaw. 'Ha! What a great sadhak. You have lived in the make-believe world of cinema all your life, and you think that you can fool everyone by your acting talents. "Surrender" my foot. You will do anything? Alright, take off all your clothes, now, right now, I want to suck your teats and lick your breasts.'

The woman stood silent for a while, shocked. Then she screamed, 'You vile creature, you dirty fellow. I thought you were a saint. You should be put behind bars!' and ran out of the shed still cursing him at the top of her voice.

We waited for a while. The Aghori clapped his hands with glee and declared, 'The idiots. God knows where they come from. Talk nonsense. I have driven them away. Ho! Jogi Maharaj, don't hide in the darkness, please come. Sorry to keep you waiting.' We entered the shed and the Aghori stood up and welcomed us. 'Please be seated,' he said and waited for us to sit down before he did. I was surprised, that in spite of the dirt and garbage around, there wasn't any bad odour. Instead, I smelt a mild scent of roses.

'Jogi Maharaj, haven't seen you for so long. Hope you enjoyed my drama. So, this is the young fellow you found. Uumph! Are you afraid of me?'

'No,' I said.

'I brought him to see you,' said Babaji. 'We don't have much time. Sri Guru has asked us to see you. I want this young man to witness your transformation. He has not seen anything like that till now.'

'As you say, Jogi Maharaj, but you could have showed him greater things. Anyway, here you go!'

In front of my astonished eyes, the Aghori's body faded away, and in its place appeared an exceedingly handsome young man, clad in a red silk loincloth, and wearing a crystal rosary around his neck. I have never in my life seen such an attractive person with the exception of Sri Guru.

As we turned to leave, Babaji said to me, 'This is his real form. What you saw before was a cover. Now, return to the ashram and not a word about what you witnessed today to anyone. The letter from Belur Mutt will come soon. Go to Belur Mutt and spend some time there. I will get in touch sometime.' I prostrated and by the time I straightened up, they were gone.

I returned to the ashram late and went directly to the little room given to me, meditated for a while and went to sleep.

The letter from Swami Hiranmayananda arrived. I was given permission to go to Belur Mutt and join the Pre-probationers Training Centre. I was to report to the Assistant General Secretary, Swami Atmastananda.

I caught a train to Calcutta and reached Belur Mutt. After interviewing me, the Assistant General Secretary admitted me to the PPTC. In my interactions with him, I found the swami to be a wonderful human being.

At Belur Mutt, I had the opportunity to meet senior swamis of the Ramakrishna Order, including the president and general secretary of the order, and take their blessings.

Two months later, I was introduced to Chandan Maharaj who headed the Ramakrishna Vidyapeeth, a boarding school for boys in Deoghar in the neighbouring state of Bihar. On his request, I was transferred to the Vidyapeeth. Life at the Vidyapeeth was different. I taught English for the seniors, was made the warden of the senior hostel, and taught magic and karate in my spare time to those boys who evinced interest. The unruly seniors soon became good friends and I was nicknamed 'Karate Maharaj' and 'Magic Maharaj.'

I also got the opportunity to travel all over the Hooghly district with the head of the centre, and visit the places associated with Sri Ramakrishna like Kamarpukur, Jayrambhatti and so on. Rural Bengal fascinated me.

The famous Vaidyanath temple of Shiva, considered one of the twelve Jyotir Lingas (symbols of light) was not far away from the Vidyapeeth. I visited the temple twice. It is probably the only place in the world, other than Amsterdam, where a shop is licensed to sell ganja to pilgrims, who make an offering of it to Vaidyanath Shiva, and take home the consecrated prasad, to be relished with great devotion. Nearby were the meditation caves constructed by the well-known late Balananda Brahmachari, who had learnt kriya yoga from Sri Shyama Charan Lahiri.

I spent almost a year at Deoghar before I got the signal to move. Babaji appeared in a dream one night and said, 'Enough of the schoolteacher role. Move on. Go home for now.' This was repeated thrice distinctly.

The next day, I packed up and left Deoghar. In a few days, I was back home. By then, my parents had shifted to Chennai, and I appeared at their Chennai home one afternoon. My disappearing frequently for long periods, and coming back again suddenly had become such a routine occurrence that there was hardly any reaction. Of course, my parents were relieved that I was still alive.

Soon, I settled down, helping my father with the pharmacy business he had started, and visiting the Ramakrishna Mission centre or other places of spiritual importance whenever I got time. I frequented the beach, because our new house was not far from the sea. I had read J. Krishnamurti's writings, but for the first time I heard him live at the Krishnamurti Foundation Headquarters, Vasant Vihar. I was impressed by the man's personality, and the contents of his talks, which were direct and to the point, but did not have the desire to meet him personally.

Swami Tapasyananda, whom I had known quite well during my school days when he was the head of the Ramakrishna Mission at Trivandrum, was the head of the Ramakrishna Mission, Chennai, at that time. He was also the vice-president of the Ramakrishna Mission worldwide, and I came to know that, apart from the President of the Mission who lived in Belur Mutt, he was also authorized to initiate those he thought fit into the Ramakrishna *moola mantra*.

For some reason, I was filled with a great desire to receive the mantra from him. One Sunday, I went to the Mutt, met him and expressed my desire. Without the least hesitation, he said, 'The day after tomorrow is Gurupoornima, come prepared for the initiation. Have a bath before you come and bring a new dhoti, some flowers and some money to offer to Sri Ramakrishna as dakshina.'

And so, I was initiated into the mantra of Sri Ramakrishna that Gurupoornima day. Swami Tapasyananda's face was flushed, and he looked quite different for a few minutes as he gave me the mantra. My heart was full of joy as I clearly visualised Thakur sitting in the lotus of my heart chakra.

I spent eight months with my parents in Chennai waiting for yet another signal from Babaji.

40

Alandi, Shirdi, and Walking Through Doors

BABAJI'S CALL CAME ONE evening, as I sat quietly watching the waves at Eliot's Beach, a private beach, attached to the Theosophical Society's headquarters in Chennai. It was so tranquil that, in spite of the hot Chennai summer, I fell asleep. I was woken up by Babaji's familiar voice, 'Go to Jnaneshwar's samadhi at Alandi. Start in three days.'

I spent half an hour in the library at the Ramakrishna Mutt the next day trying to figure out the location. Reading a short biography of the great Maharashtrian saint Jnaneshwar, I found out that Alandi was just eighteen kilometres from Pune. So, two days later, I boarded a train to Pune, and catching a bus from there, reached Alandi.

It was indeed a quiet and lovely little hamlet. I walked to the samadhi of Jnaneshwar. There were a number of people sitting around the shrine. Some were reading the *Jnaneshwari*, a great translation and commentary on the Bhagawad Gita, written by Sant Jnaneshwar. Others were meditating with closed eyes. Most were elderly persons, probably Maharashtrian. Babaji was nowhere in sight. I sat down under a peepal tree, not too far from the samadhi, and fell into deep contemplation.

At this point, I think, a brief note on Sant Jnaneshwar is very much in order.

Jnaneshwar's father Vithalpant is said to have renounced the world, and gone off to Kashi to become a sanyasin without informing his wife Rukminibai. In Kashi, he became a disciple of Sri Ramananda Swami. When Ramananda Swami visited Alandi and met Rukminibai by chance, he blessed her saying, 'May you lead a happy married life.' With tears in her eyes, Rukmini said that it was not possible since her husband had gone away to Kashi and become a sanyasin. On finding out that her husband was none other than his disciple Vithalpant, Ramananda Swami, on returning to Kashi, reprimanded Vithalpant and sent him back to Alandi. At Alandi, he rejoined his wife and again became a householder.

Four saintly children were born to them. Of course, the local orthodoxy excommunicated them, as the general rule was that one who became a sanyasin and later reverted to a householder's life was to be considered an outcast. They had to live on the outskirts of the city with those considered to be lower than even the lowest caste.

The first son became a disciple of Gahininath and was named Nivrithinath. The second one, Jnaneshwar became his brother's disciple, and by virtue of his great spiritual attainment was considered greater than his brother. Their sister Muktabai was also a greatly advanced yogini. There are many stories prevalent in Maharashtra about the miraculous life of the siblings.

I love the story of the buffalo who chanted the Vedas which goes like this:

The orthodox priests of that locality had announced a marathon competition of Vedic chanting. The person who was judged the best, was to be conferred a title of excellence. Many pundits gathered, and among them was the young Jnaneshwar. The pundits were incensed. How could an outcast, the son of a former sanyasin, be allowed to take part in a conference of orthodox Brahmins? They therefore, abused him and told him to leave. He was an outcast, they said, and therefore was prohibited from chanting the Vedas. In any case, how much of the Vedas could a little boy chant? Did he even know what the Vedas were, they taunted him.

'No big deal,' said Jnaneshwar, 'even a buffalo could chant the Vedas.' He is then said to have called a passing buffalo, blessed it by placing his hand on its head, and commanded it to chant the *Vedas*. The buffalo complied by chanting the Vedas with perfect clarity. After having proved his point, he is said to have walked out of the gathering.

At a young age, having finished writing the *Jnaneshwari*, which is more popular in Maharashtra, than the Gita itself, Jnaneshwar declared that his work was done, and that it was time to leave the external world. He got a grave dug, big enough for him to sit inside in the lotus posture, and after entering it, practiced the breathing technique which is called the last kriya, and became still. As per his instructions, the grave was closed with a slab, and a mausoleum built over it.

This structure is called the Jnaneshwar's Jeeva Samadhi because it is believed that he still exists in a subtle form. While the populace considers him a great saint, the Nath sect to which he belonged, consider him as one of their most illustrious yogis.

As I sat there in front of the samadhi, the serpent power from the bottom of my spine uncoiled and moved upwards with a hissing sound, and reached first the heart centre, and then the crown centre—without any effort. Bathed in overwhelming bliss and a bright silvery light, I sat unaware of the outside world for hours. When I came back to earth, it was quite dark. Somehow, I managed to find accommodation in a choultry, which also provided simple food. For four days, I spent a blissful time absorbed in meditation. There was no sign of Babaji, but I loved it there.

On the fifth morning, at 4 a.m., I went to the samadhi to meditate. There was no one there except an old man with a grey walrus moustache, reading the *Jnaneshwari*. I was planning to sit a little away from him, when I saw a young lad with long hair, perhaps in his teens, dressed in a simple white loincloth, walking towards me. He smiled and hugged me. My body and mind were filled with blissful ambrosia. The thought occurred to me that this was probably Jnaneshwar.

He spoke to me softly in Hindi and said, 'Maheshwarnath, my brother, is waiting for you at Shirdi in the aasthan of Sainath. Go there today.'

He then walked up to the samadhi and went behind the banyan tree. I went towards the tree myself but could not find him anywhere. It was then that I realised that it was a vision, for the old man reading the Jnaneshwari showed no signs of having seen anything extraordinary. He continued to read.

From Pune, I took a bus to Shirdi and reached late at night. At the entrance of the samadhi complex stood Babaji. 'So you met the young yogi,' he said. 'Here everything is closed now but we shall go to the chavadi, where Sainath used to sleep.'

We walked past the samadhi, gurusthan and Dwarkamai, where the dhuni fire burns, and reached the small structure called the chavadi. There was no one around except a few stray dogs. The wooden door was closed. I wondered what we were going to do. Babaji said, 'Let's enter.'

'The door is locked,' I pointed out.

'I know,' he said. 'Now close your eyes and act as if you were entering the door.'

'But Babaji...'

'Just do it and don't open your eyes.'

With my eyes closed, I put my right foot forward with my knee bent. It felt like I was pushing against a cloth screen. It was the same feeling when the rest of my body came in contact with the door. In a flash, the feeling disappeared, and I heard Babaji saying, 'Okay, open your eyes.'

I opened my eyes and found myself inside the chavadi. The door was still locked. Babaji was standing beside me. I had hardly recovered from the astonishment of somehow walking through a closed and locked door, when I was taken aback by something even more astonishing and unbelievable.

On a narrow wooden plank, suspended from the roof by torn pieces of old cloth, twisted together like a rope, reclined the Sai Baba of Shirdi—who was supposed to have passed away in 1918! As I stared at him with wonderment and awe, my hair stood on end and my whole body trembled. He sat up on the plank, and as I wondered how he could come down from his peculiar bed, hanging six feet above the ground, he quietly slid off the plank and floated down effortlessly to the floor.

I noticed that the cloth that he is normally seen with, wrapped around his head was missing. His head was clean shaven, and when he stood beside us, I realised that he was a six-footer, and built like a wrestler.

He hugged Babaji, Muslim style, and they kissed each other's noses lightly. I prostrated at his feet. He lifted me back to standing position and said, 'Salaam boy, you have got a great guru, murshid. I also had a great guru, my Venkusha, and all I did, was stare at him. *Allah malik hai, Ram Ram.*'

Babaji said, 'Please bless him, Baba.'

'*Allah malik hai*, you have to do the kind of work I do, in a different way. Not easy, lad. This world is crazy and they think I am mad. Hu Allah, Ram, Ram, Ram. Do Kabir's work. Take guru's blessings.' He reached under the sheet that covered his plank bed, and took out a wad of currency. 'Here,' he said, '*Allah bhala karega* [God will take care]. Take this money and travel to Ganagapur, Pithapur and Akkalkot. Go, go.'

I hesitated to take the money. Babaji whispered, 'Take it.' I took the money and again prostrated. Babaji and Sainath hugged each other, and we exited in the same fashion as we had come in. Babaji said jokingly, 'Don't try passing through closed doors next time, you might end up with a flattened nose.' It was still dark outside, but dawn would soon be upon us.

Babaji told me to keep the money safe and begin my journey the next day. 'I will see you when it is necessary,' he said, before giving me directions to the places mentioned by Sainath, and walking away.

At dawn, I visited the Gurusthan, the *Samadhi*, the Dwarakamai, where the dhuni burns and once again the chavadi. Standing in the chavadi, looking at the large picture of Sai Baba, I marveled at the extraordinary experience of the night. After breakfast, I took a bus to Kopergaon railway station and waited for the train.

Before I wind up this chapter, I shall give you a very brief biography of the Sai Baba of Shirdi.

In the then little-known sleepy hamlet of Shirdi, sometime in the late 1800s, there appeared an itinerant young holy man who, to all appearances, seemed to be a Muslim fakir. No one knew his name or where he came from, but Mahalashapathi, the priest of the Khandoba temple that stands across the road from where Sai Baba's samadhi is today, welcomed him with the words, 'Ya Sai' (come, saint). The name stuck, and he was called Sai Baba.

For a year or so, he lived in Shirdi, slept under the neem tree, which he called his gurusthan (guru's place). Much later, under the instructions of a visiting holy man, someone dug up a plot adjoining the neem tree, and found a tunnel that led to a cave. In the cave were three oil lamps, still burning brightly.

After a short period, Sai Baba went away, but came back again with the marriage party of Chand Patil, a Muslim from neighbouring Rahata. After that he never left Shirdi, and lived in a dilapidated old mosque which was renamed Dwarkamai. (Dwarka is the name of the city where Lord Krishna of the Mahabharat had lived.)

Sai Baba, also known as Sainath, lit a sacred dhuni, as is the practice with the Nath sect, and spent most of the day there. In the evenings, he lit an oil lamp and danced and sang, wearing anklets. Later the chavadi was built, and he spent the night there. His bed consisted of a narrow plank, suspended six feet above the floor, from the middle of the roof of the chavadi, with ropes made of twisted old rags which looked quite worn out. No one knew how he ascended his bed without visible support of any kind. His pillow was a brick wrapped in rags.

He wore a long white robe that reached his ankles, and wrapped a cloth around his head. His clothes often looked soiled and torn. He shaved his head, and kept a well-trimmed beard and moustache, like a Muslim fakir. He kept repeating 'Ram Ram', and 'Allah malik hai', and at times behaved like a madman, flying into a rage, and threatening to beat people up—but at other times he was so kind and compassionate that everyone loved him.

He lived in Shirdi for many years, working innumerable miracles and wiping out the sorrows of all who came to him. It is said that in 1886, he remained clinically dead for three days and came back to life again. He died on 15 October 1918. Before he died, he said that he would be in Shirdi even after his body died, and would speak to those who came with sincerity and devotion. My acutely skeptical mind would never have accepted that statement if he hadn't played that little drama at the chavadi that night. I am eternally thankful to him for having been so kind, even to a skeptic like me with very little faith, and bow down to him, and to my beloved Babaji who took me to Shirdi, with utter humility and affection.[1]

---

[1] See *Sai Sat Charita* for an authentic biography of Shirdi Sai Baba.

41

More Travels: New Insights

FROM SHIRDI, I TRAVELLED to Ganagapur and Narsowadi, where the great Swami Narasimha Saraswati, believed to be an incarnation of Dattatreya[1], spent most of his life. From there, I went to Akkalkot, to the samadhi of the Akkalkotkar Maharaj, also known as Swami Samarth, and also believed to be a manifestation of Dattatreya.

He was a contemporary of Shirdi Sai Baba, and passed away in 1878. Akkalkotkar Maharaj was also called Vata Vriksha Maharaj because he lived under a banyan tree at Akkalkot. Widely regarded as a powerful godman, he worked numerous miracles and was greatly respected in Maharashtra and North Karnataka. Akkalkotkar Maharaj is believed to have appeared in far off places to his devotees even while he held court in Akkalkot. Many of the rulers of the princely kingdoms of Maharashtra, and the Scindias of Gwalior were his followers.

I stayed at a small choultry at Akkalkot for three days. On the third day, I had a vivid dream in which Akkalkotkar Maharaj appeared, wearing

---

[1] Dattatreya is considered to be a divine manifestation of the creator god Brahma, the sustainer god Vishnu and the yogi god Shiva, all put together. He is the patron deity of those holy men who break all the rules, even those imposed by religion, and wander free as the wind. They are known as Avadhootas. The naked among them are called the Digambaras. The *Avadhoota Gita* contains the teachings and practices of the Avadhootas.

a red loincloth and said, 'I am no different from the one at Shirdi. Now, you go to Pitapur and pay your respects to Sri Pada Vallabha.'

I headed to Pitapur near Kakinada in Andhra Pradesh and visited the shrine of Sri Pada Vallabha, also considered a manifestation of Dattatreya. Then, I proceeded to Maniknagar in Gulbarga, a district in Karnataka, to the samadhi of Sri Manik Prabhu—again considered a manifestation of Dattatreya. At the samadhi of Sri Manik Prabhu, while in a deep trance, Babaji appeared to me and said, 'Go to Chennai, to your friend Balachandra Menon's house. From there, dress like a sadhu, and go to the Hill of the Holy Beacon, Tiruvannamalai, the abode of Shiva Arunachala. Spend some time at the samadhi of Ramana Maharishi.'

Off I went to Chennai and did as I was told.

One morning, at dawn, I wore the mendicant's robes, and walked out of my friend Menon's house. Travelling by bus, train, and at times walking, I first visited the temple of Ranganathaswamy (meaning 'Lord of Drama') at Srirangam. This is a temple of Vishnu, in a reclining posture, resting on the five-hooded serpent Anantha. Srirangam is considered one of the most important temples of the Visishta Advaita school of Vedanta, founded by Sri Ramanujacharya.

Not far from Srirangam, was the well-known church of Virgin Mary, called, the Vellankani Matha church. I went into the church, which is visited by thousands of people every year, and sat in silence for a few minutes. Inside the church, it was quiet and peaceful.

Then I walked to the tomb and dargah of a sufi saint at a place called Nagore. The saint, whose name was Abdul Khader, is popularly known as Nagore Aandavar, meaning the Lord of Nagore. Many miraculous stories are told about him. He would often disappear into an underground cellar for days, and would distribute huge quantities of sweets to little children as soon as he emerged. The story is that he once lifted a little boy onto his back, asked him to close his eyes for a minute, and then open them. When the boy opened his eyes, he was in the holy city of Mecca. Using the same procedure he was brought back to Nagore. His astonished and awestruck parents named him Haji, or one who has performed the Hajj pilgrimage at Mecca.

From Nagore, I set out for Tiruvannamalai, taking a rather circuitous route, as I was longing to see the old and highly venerated Shankaracharya of the Kanchi Mutt, Sri Chandrasekharendra Sarasvati, at Kanchipuram.

The chances of meeting him were slim, I was told, because he had not been interacting with the public for some time. At best I might have had a glimpse of him from a distance, when he appeared briefly to bless the visitors. I was warned not to talk or ask questions, because the Acharya was in *mouna* (silence). By evening, word spread that he had broken his silence and might speak a few words. People were to form a line and file past him as he squatted on the ground in front of a small thatched hut.

He was a frail old man, very thin, bare-bodied except for an ochre cloth wrapped around his waist, and another covering his head. He held a dandi, which identified him as belonging to the Dasanami order of renunciants founded by Adi Shankaracharya. He wore thick glasses, and his forehead was painted with holy ash, the insignia of the followers of Shiva. As the devotees went past, prostrating from a short distance, he raised his right hand in blessing, and sometimes exchanged a few words. Sturdy Brahmins, wearing their sacred threads across their chests, controlled the crowds.

I joined the queue. When I was right in front of him, he looked keenly at me and asked in Tamil, 'What's your name?'

'Madhu,' I said holding my hand in front of my mouth, as instructed by the burly Brahmin standing beside the Acharya. Your breath is not supposed to fall on the saint.

He smiled faintly and said, 'The name given by your guru, right? Have you heard of Justice Ismail?'

'No,' I confessed.

'He is like you, but he is an expert on the Kamba Ramayana. Umph! A lot of work to do. Satsang is important.'

With that he raised his right hand in blessing, and I was shooed away by his attendants. Many years later, when my friends wanted to form a trust to help me with my work and were looking for a suitable name, the word satsang sprang to my mind and it was named the Satsang Foundation. The word 'sat' means the Truth and sanga means gathering, or a group. It can be translated as a group of people, intent upon finding the Truth or a group of good and truthful people. It could also mean, coming together in the interests of Truth. I wondered if the Acharya's parting words had anything to do with it.

Reaching Tiruvannamalai, I decided to first look for a holy man called Pankha Baba, also called Ram Surat Kumar. I had heard from a retired professor at Kanchi that Pankha Baba was childlike, and often behaved like a madman. He was, at one time, a schoolteacher somewhere in North India, and spoke good English and Hindi.

I found him in a small hut, beside the temple chariot. There were a few people, standing around him. He was fair, chubby, had long grey hair and a flowing grey beard, and was dressed in a dhoti and an old western style cream-coloured coat, that probably had not been washed for months.

He peered at me from inside and waved his hand, 'Come, come. Sit here,' he said in a voice, clear and affectionate. I entered the hut and sat down. 'Closer, closer,' he said and I moved forward till I was very close. 'Umph, what name?' he asked.

'Madhu, Baba' I said.

'Madhu, Madhu,' he said, as if he was enjoying the name, 'Madhu! So do you know namaz?'

'Yes,' I said. 'I know, but I don't do. I meditate.'

'Meditation, namaz, all same,' he said. 'Meditation, Madhu, all M, M, M, M, yum yum you are M, ha ha ha!' he laughed. The laughter came from deep down his belly, and exploded into loud guffaws. 'M, M, ha ha!'

As he shook with laughter, he landed such a hard slap with his right hand on my shoulder that the cloth bag I was holding flew out of my hands and landed at his feet. Some peanuts rolled out of the bag.

'Peanuts,' he said. 'This beggar loves peanuts,' and ate a few with great gusto. 'Good, good,' he said. 'And where are you going now?'

'To the Ramana Ashram,' I said.

He burst out laughing, again, 'Ramana is there?' he said between peals of laughter. 'Only samadhi is there. Ramana cannot be kept in one place. Here, there, everywhere. Okay okay. Go and enjoy.' He gave me one more slap on my shoulder.

I got up to leave. Someone said, 'Swami, I don't want anything, only peace of mind.'

'Peace of mind,' shouted Pankha Baba, and his whole body shook with loud laughter again. 'Peace of mind he wants, and this beggar's mind has gone to pieces. Ha ha!'

I picked up my bag, prostrated and walked out.

'M, M!' he shouted after me, 'Mind is gone to pieces. No mind left. Tell Ramana.'

I walked to the Ramana Ashram's office and asked for accommodation. I was allowed to stay in a dormitory, where there were a couple of other sadhus. The ashram was a very peaceful place, and the Arunachala Hill, the Hill of the Holy Beacon, known since ancient times as one of the most sacred abodes of Shiva, is not far from it. The *Skanda Purana* declares Arunachala to be the sacred heart centre of Shiva. Devout pilgrims circumambulate the mountain, especially on full moon nights.

Ramana Maharishi, after whom the ashram is named, considered Arunachala a great spiritual centre, and was irresistibly drawn towards it in his youth. Although many people in India and abroad are familiar with Sri Ramana Maharishi, I shall briefly introduce the great soul for the benefit of those who are not.

Born in a Brahmin family in Tiruchuli, a small and remote village in Tamil Nadu on 30 December 1879, Venkatramana (later shortened to Ramana), was a charming and intelligent child who loved outdoor activities and was given to sleeping so soundly that it took a great deal of effort to wake him up. When Venkatramana was twelve, his father died, and he went to live in Madurai with his uncle. It was here, when he was around sixteen years of age, that he had an unusual and spontaneous experience.

In his own words:

It was about six weeks before I left Madurai for good that the great change in my life took place. It was quite sudden. I was sitting alone in a room on the first floor of my uncle's house. I seldom had any sickness, and on that day, there was nothing wrong with my health. But a sudden and violent fear of death overtook me. There was nothing in my state of health to account for it, and I did not try to account for it, or to find out whether there was any reason for the fear. I just felt I am going to die, and began thinking what to do about it. It did not occur to me to consult a doctor or my elders or friends; I felt that I had to solve the problem myself, then and there.

The shock of the fear of death drove my mind inwards and I said to myself without actually framing the words: Now death has come, what does it mean? What is it that is dying? This body dies, and at once, dramatized the occurrence of death. I lay with my limbs stretched out stiff as though rigor mortis had set in, and imitated a corpse so as to give greater reality to the enquiry. I held my breath and kept my lips tightly closed so that no sound could escape, so that neither the word 'I,' nor any other word could be uttered. Well then, I said to myself, this body is dead. It will be carried stiff to the burning ground, and there burnt and reduced to ashes. But with the death of this body, am I dead?

Is the body I? It is silent and inert but I feel the full force of my personality and even the voice of 'I' within me is apart from it.

So I am spirit transcending the body. The body dies but the spirit that transcends it cannot be touched by death. That means, I am the deathless spirit.

All this was not dull thought; it flashed through me vividly as living truth which I perceived directly, almost without the thought process. 'I' was something very real, the only real thing about my present state, and all the conscious activity connected with my body was centred on that 'I.' From that moment onwards, the 'I' or 'Self' focused attention on itself by a powerful fascination. Fear of death had vanished once and for all. Absorption in the Self continued unbroken from that time on.

Other thoughts might come and go like the various notes of music, but the 'I' continued like the fundamental *sruti* note that underlies and blends with all the other notes. Whether the body was engaged in talking, reading or anything else, I was still centred on 'I.' Before this crisis; I had no clear perception of my Self and was not consciously attracted to it. I felt no perceptible or direct interest in it, much less any inclination to dwell permanently in it.

As a result of this, Ramana soon left Madurai, leaving a note saying that he was embarking on the virtuous enterprise of seeking the Truth, and that there was no need to search for him. The word 'Arunachala' had always fascinated him, and now, filled with an irresistible urge to remain uninterruptedly absorbed in the inner Self that had spontaneously revealed itself, he took the train to Tiruvannamalai, arriving sometime in September 1896. He had reached the abode of his beloved Arunachala Shiva—the Supreme Being symbolised as a light, represented by the Hill of the Holy Beacon.

Sri Ramana himself has said that as he hastened to the great temple of Arunachala Shiva, his heart was throbbing with joy.

Entering the sanctum sanctorum, he embraced the Arunachaleshwara linga in utter ecstasy. The burning sensation that had begun in Madurai vanished and merged with the light. The journey ended for he had found the Truth, the Supreme blissful Self in the core of his heart. After that, he only sought solitude in order to remain absorbed in that exalted state.

First, he lived in an underground cellar of the temple, and was discovered by a local holy man called Sheshadri Swami, who announced, 'here was a diamond unrecognised by anyone.' His body, bitten by scorpions, was tended to by this kind soul. Soon, he walked away to another isolated temple, then to another and so on. He never spoke and began to be known as the Silent Brahmin Swami. To avoid publicity, he shifted to the hill, and after spending time in various caves and isolated temples, settled down in the Virupaksha cave for seventeen years.

Soon, a small group of attendants and devotees gathered around him. The great scholar and spiritual seeker Kavya Kanta Ganapathy Sastri came here. He was the person initially responsible for spreading the word that there indeed lived a great sage who was established in the highest Truth, which the ancient Upanishads had talked about.

F. H. Humphreys, a British police officer, who can be called his first Western follower, also met him here. Ramana's mother also came and settled down there. She remained with her son till her last day. By then, Sri Ramana was called Maharishi or great sage, a title conferred on him by Kavya Kanta Ganapathy Sastri. Some even called him Bhagwan (God), but the man remained as simple as he was when he first arrived at Tiruvannamalai.

From the Virupaksha cave, Maharishi shifted to the Skanda Ashram, built by a devotee on the slopes of the hill. When his mother died, she was buried a little away from the Skanda Ashram. Later, Maharishi shifted to the simple ashram that grew around the tomb of his mother, and lived there quietly till he passed away in 1950. To the English-speaking Indian public, and to the world at large, Sri Ramana Maharishi became well known thanks to the writings of Paul Brunton, a British journalist who had met him.

Ramana Maharishi did not travel. He remained in Tiruvannamalai, always available to the crowds that in later years travelled to have his darshan, and to be taught in silence. Very few words were uttered by him, but in his presence many found an inexplicable peace and tranquility, with disturbing thoughts subsiding spontaneously.

I spent three days in Tiruvannamalai, meditating at the samadhi of Sri Ramana Maharishi, at the Skanda Ashram, at the Virupaksha cave and other places on the Arunchala Hill. On the last day, as I sat all alone on the tortoise rock enjoying the solitude, I suddenly realised that I no longer missed the physical presence of Babaji as I used to. I had thought he would meet me at Tiruvannamalai, but he did not—and that didn't upset me at all.

The sun was hot and even the breeze that blew was hot, but my heart was absorbed in a pleasant warmth that began somewhere in the chest area and spread to my head. The wind brought a torn piece of paper and laid it near my feet. I picked it up. It was part of a printed page from some book. As I read it, I knew that the words were that of Sri Ramana Maharishi. It read:

The deeper the humility with which we conduct ourselves, the better it is for us. Everything that is offered to others is really an offering to the One Self. Not to desire anything extraneous to one's self is *Vairagya* or dispassion. To hold on to one's true Self is *Jnana* or Enlightenment. *Vairagya* and *Jnana* are the same. Everyone must dive deep into himself and realise the precious *Atman*. God and *Guru* are one. He that has earned the grace of the *Guru* shall never be forsaken but the disciple should...

It struck me instantly that Babaji was an integral part of my psyche. How could one lose what is one's own self? That was it.

From Tiruvannamalai, I returned to Chennai and remained at home for ten months. I spent the days helping my father in his pharmaceutical business, and in the evenings went for walks on the beach. Twice, I went to the headquarters of the Krishnamurti Foundation and listened to J. Krishnamurti talk. Although Babaji had said that I should meet Krishnamurti, at that moment I had no inclination to do so. Sundays, I usually spent in the Theosophical Society's library or went to the ancient Kapaleshwar temple. Sometimes, I would go to the Shirdi Sai Baba temple or to the dargah of a Sufi saint, Moti Baba, near the Egmore Railway Station.

Meanwhile, I had started writing articles on South Indian temples and the Himalayan shrines in a magazine called *Probe*. One day, I read about a small newspaper called *The Andaman Times*, which was published from Port Blair in the Andaman Islands. Reading up all about the Andaman Islands from newspapers and books, I decided to go there. The editor, to whom I wrote, was willing to try me out, and so I set sail to Port Blair, this time informing my parents that I had found a job. I was going to be a journalist. They were happy, for once.

42

Babaji at the Taj Mumbai

THE ANDAMAN ISLANDS, WHICH the tourist department touted as the 'Land of the Marigold Sun', were indeed a beautiful place. With my press accreditation card, I had access to parts of the Andaman and Nicobar Islands that were out of bounds for the ordinary tourist. I could go into the Jarawa Reserves inhabited by Jarawas, who were said to be cannibals, and also see the tall, naked tribes called the Sentinelese, who lived on the isolated North Sentinel Islands, and had not even learned to use salt.

I could walk into anybody's office with my press card and was exposed to the political bickering among the local political leaders. I learnt how to gather news and how to edit information to fit the space available, without missing out the essentials. This helped me with my experiments with short story writing. I wrote a short story called 'The Island Boy', which the *Hindustan Times* published in its fiction page.

I also wrote a number of articles for mainland newspapers as Port Blair is a historically interesting place. For instance, during World War II, it was briefly occupied by the Japanese, who used it as a base to bomb Chennai (then Madras). Underground tunnels and bunkers can be found quite close to the city of Port Blair. Port Blair also had the notorious cellular jail, where the British incarcerated hardened criminals, and which was later used to imprison political revolutionaries like Veer Savarkar. There was plenty to write about. Apart from writing, the place was great for contemplation. The beach could be reached from most parts of the city in a few minutes.

I spent a full and enjoyable year in the Andamans, carefully guarding myself from being made into some rich Mopalah merchant or estate owner's son-in-law. Rich settlers on the island were always on the lookout for young, educated, and good-looking men from the mainland to marry their daughters. The girls were indeed beautiful and smart, but I had been warned, and so I took precautions.

The only unpleasant incident was that I contracted severe amoebiasis drinking unfiltered water. I escaped from the other possible danger, cerebral malaria, using mosquito nets at night. Nothing of great spiritual significance occurred. At the end of the year, I resigned and set sail for Calcutta. It was a three-day sea voyage.

Reaching Calcutta, I once again visited Belur Mutt and the temple of Kali at Dakshineshwar. I also visited the headquarters of the Yogoda Satsang Society at Dakshineshwar and had a private discussion about kriya with a senior American swami of the order—the soft-spoken Swami Shantananda, a thorough gentleman.

Returning to the city, I heard from an acquaintance that Sri Satya Charan Lahiri, the great-grandson of the famous Kriya Yoga Master, and disciple of Sri Guru Babaji, was staying with a follower of his. I met Sri Satya Charan Lahiri and had an hour-long discussion. He was a gracious and cultured man, and provided me with many hitherto unknown facts about the great Shyama Charan Lahiri Mahasaya, his great grandfather. We also discussed Kriya Yoga and he agreed with me that it could not be taught through correspondence courses, and required intimate personal contact between the teacher and the student.

Laughing heartily, he told me how a lady went to him during one of his visits to Mumbai, and told him how she had gone to the Himalayas and met Sri Guru Babaji, whom she referred to as Mahaavatar Babaji, the term coined by Swami Yogananda Paramahansa. She told him that she spent three hours meditating with him. Minutes after narrating the story of her encounter, she had asked Sri Satya Charan Lahiri to initiate her into Kriya Yoga. He refused. 'Even Babaji,' Satya Charan

Lahiri said, shaking his head sadly, 'has been turned into a business proposition. Mark my words,' he continued, 'in times to come, every Tom, Dick, and Harry is going to claim direct links with Babaji, and make good business out of it.'

From Calcutta, I went to Banaras. This was my second trip to Banaras, and apart from my wish to visit the temple of Kashi Viswanath once again, I wanted to go to Sarnath, where Buddha preached his first sermon and set in motion what he called the 'Wheel of Dharma'. On the way, I visited the Krishnamurti Centre and the Vasanta College and School, run by the Krishnamurti Foundation at Rajghat.

Finding that I had saved enough money to travel for some time, I hit upon the idea of going to Mumbai and visiting the Elephanta Caves. Babaji had told me long ago that the caves were used in ancient times for initiation ceremonies, as were the cave temples at Bhanjo near Anantnag in Kashmir. They were a short distance from the Gateway of India by boat. I got into one of the many boats used by tourists, and soon reached the caves.

The Elephanta Caves, known in Marathi as the Gharapuri caves, are located on an island in the Arabian Sea. The original Sanskrit name, Babaji had told me, was Agraharpuri. Agrahara means 'the most important necklace,' and is used to denote a place where a community of Brahmins lived. This, Babaji had explained, was because in those days, only the highly evolved initiates in the spiritual mysteries were called Brahmins and a community of such teachers lived in the caves. Neophytes were brought there to be initiated into the mysteries.

The Portuguese for some reason named the caves Elephanta, and defaced many of the sculptures by using them for target practice in the seventeenth century.

The rock-cut complex, with a main chamber and other courtyards and subsidiary shrines, contains magnificent reliefs and sculptures, and houses a temple to Shiva. Inside the chamber, Shiva is represented as *Ardhanarishvara*, his left side representing female energy, and the right representing Shiva in his male aspect.

This, Babaji had said, is a symbol of the perfect yogi, who balances male and female characteristics in himself, brought about by the conjoining of the *ida* and *pingala* energies on both sides of the spine, thereby opening the central channel called the *shushumna* in the cerebrospinal system. The enlightened yogi was one whose central channel was open, so that the great creative energy, *Shakti*, could without obstruction dance up towards the supreme presence, Shiva, to be embraced by him at the crown chakra. This union of great ecstasy transformed man into a superman, with greatly expanded consciousness.

Outside the cave was the twenty-feet tall sculpture of Trimurti Shiva, who combined the symbols of creation, preservation and destruction. In the hall was the sculpture of Shiva dancing in ecstasy as Nataraja, the king of dancers. I marvelled at the wonderful sculptures, and memories of having seen them sometime in the distant past flashed through my mind. For a while, I was lost in contemplation. Then, reminding myself that I had to go back to the mainland, I climbed into the boat and went back to the Gateway of India.

From the Gateway of India, one can see the magnificent Taj Mahal Palace Hotel, an architectural marvel through whose portals monarchs, business tycoons, politicians and leading lights from diverse echelons of society had passed for over a hundred years. For the citizens of Mumbai, it was no less a monument than the Gateway of India. I walked up to the entrance of the Taj Mahal Hotel and stood looking at the liveried guards, and wondering if I should go in and have an expensive coffee and a look around. Just then, a sleek black and chrome Mercedes glided up to the entrance and stopped. The uniformed chauffer jumped out and opened the doors. From the front door emerged a clean-shaven, middle-aged man in a suit who, from his complexion and general bearing, I guessed was a Parsi. From the back door stepped out a beautiful young lady in well cut, light brown Western clothes; and a tall, extremely fair and handsome Sikh, in a dark blue three-piece suit and a turban of the same colour. The Sikh gentleman and the lady wore sunglasses.

It was the Sikh gentleman who riveted my attention. Something about him appeared quite familiar. Was it the dignified way he walked, or his six-feet tall figure, or his extremely fair complexion and handsome features? I was trying to figure it out when he removed his dark glasses and I saw his eyes. He was actually looking at me. There was no mistaking those eyes, it was Babaji himself, my friend and Master. It was such a funny situation, Babaji disguised as a sardar that I began to shake with laughter. The sardar whispered something to his companions, and they went into the hotel. He walked towards where I stood. 'Stop giggling, Madhu,' he said. 'And don't prostrate in public.'

With great effort, I controlled my laughter and asked, 'Why on earth are you masquerading as a sardar, Babaji?'

'Come,' he said, and we crossed the road and came to the Gateway of India. 'You saw my companions; they are Parsis and belong to a very wealthy family, highly westernised. The husband presides over a big industrial empire and the wife, the young lady who was educated abroad, has turned into an alcoholic. I was her father's guru, and at his deathbed I promised to look after his only daughter. I am keeping my promise. She thinks I am a Sikh businessman with spiritual powers, and accepts the fact that I was her father's guru. What mystifies the couple, are my youthful looks, considering that I had known her father for over fifty years.'

'Is she better now?' I asked.

'It will take a little time but she will change. I adopt a method that will astonish you. I sit down with her and have a drink with her occasionally. Soon she will stop drinking voluntarily. Strange method, but after some years you will probably do the same thing for certain special people linked to you from your past lives. Right now, I shall join her for a drink at the bar. So, have you visited the Elephanta Caves?'

'Yes, Babaji, and saw all the marvellous sculptures.'

'All right, I am going now. Do you still feel like going into the Taj and having a cup of coffee?'

'No,' I said, 'on second thought, maybe I won't.'

'Okay then, and before you leave Mumbai, do visit the dargah of Haji Ali. Then go and spend some time in Delhi. You will find a journalist's job. After a year or so, go to Chennai and meet

Jiddu Krishnamurti. He is the last important person you are to come into contact with. Krishnamurti will provide certain inputs necessary for you to fully mature spiritually. Whilst you are in Delhi, go to Kashmir and visit the cave temples near Anantnag. Now you touch my feet, but don't prostrate.'

Sardar Babaji walked away and entered the Taj Mahal Palace Hotel. I visited the Haji Ali dargah built on a small rock island in the Arabian Sea, quite close to the shore. A road runs all the way from the mainland.

After a tasty Maharashtrian lunch at a small wayside restaurant at Dadar, I booked my ticket to New Delhi. Luckily, a sleeper ticket was available for the very next day. I slept the night in my lodging, not far from the Mumbai Central Station, and took the train to New Delhi the next morning.

43

Meeting Laxman Joo and
J. Krishnamurti

GETTING OFF THE TRAIN at the New Delhi Railway Station, I found myself a room in a small lodging in the Paharganj area. After a quick bath, I took an autorickshaw to the office of an English weekly called *Organiser*. I didn't know then that it was the mouthpiece of the ultra-right Hindu organisation called the Rashtriya Swayamsevak Sangh, or RSS. As far as I was concerned, that was the only address I had in Delhi, since my friend Mr Nair had wound up *Accent* magazine and gone back to Chennai, and the Punjabi businessman who was Babaji's disciple had passed away.

It was through Mr Nair that I had been introduced to the Chennai correspondent of the *Organiser*. This gentleman, whose name I forget, had persuaded me to write an article about the meaning of Hinduism, and why, in spite of my being born a non-Hindu, I was proud of being called a Hindu, as I belonged to the great and ancient land called Hindustan. After this article, which the *Organiser* published under the title 'Why I am proud to be called a Hindu', I had contributed a few more articles on Hindu philosophy and religion, and was in touch with the then editor, the late K.R. Malkani. He had said in a letter to me that if ever I was to visit Delhi, I should meet him.

Mr Malkani, when I met him, turned out to be a pucca sahib, thoroughly Westernised, and quite different from the Muslim-hating, anti-Christian types associated with the RSS. Of course, there were exceptions like Nanaji Deshmukh for instance, a very senior RSS man, impartial to the core. It was to Nanaji Deshmukh that Malkaniji took me for an introduction. He also introduced me to his young sub-editor, Mr Balashanker, who like me, was from Kerala.

Mr Balashanker found me accommodation in Delhi. I was to share a house with a group of young RSS men from Kerala who ran their own kitchen. It was here that I was first exposed to the ideology of the RSS and its inner workings. They had developed a superb network. There were RSS men in the most unlikely places one could think of. To give you an example, one of the RSS boys I shared accommodation with in Delhi later on became one of the staff members at the home office of Prime Minister P.V. Narasimha Rao, and wrote to me saying that he had seen Rao listening to my cassette on the Bhagawad Gita.

Similarly, the media, judiciary, the armed forces, the bureaucracy—everywhere, there were some RSS men or sympathisers. Whatever one might say regarding their ideology, I found them hardworking and thoroughly disciplined.

Nanaji Deshmukh took an instant liking to me. After seeing samples of my writing, he asked me to report the following Monday to Devendra Swaroop Agarwal, who was the director of the Deendayal Research Institute (DRI) and editor of DRI's quarterly research journal called *Manthan* (The Churning). Nanaji himself was the founder and chairman of DRI.

Mr Agarwal, a history professor in the DAV College, interviewed me and I was appointed to assist him in editing the English version of *Manthan*. My office was beside his at the high-tech headquarters of DRI, and I shared a cabin with the elderly Mr Chandrakanth Bhardwaj who helped in editing the Hindi version. Since he did not attend office often, I usually had the cabin all to myself. A well-stocked library and tea anytime on demand were the added attractions, ideal for a young mind given to reading, thinking and writing.

Both Devendraji and I had lunch at Nanaji's residence on the fourth floor. If he was in town, he would eat with us, and the lunchtime conversations would be quite informative. Nanaji Deshmukh was a veteran RSS stalwart, who had, for a number of years, been a Member of Parliament, elected from the Jan Sangh party, which was the political front of the RSS. He was responsible for roping Jayprakash Narayan, the ageing socialist, into the revolutionary movement against the dictatorial, emergency ordinance declared by the then Prime Minister, Indira Gandhi.

This resulted in the toppling of the Indira Gandhi government, and the declaration of general elections in which the Janata Party came to power. Nanaji was the general secretary of the party, which was an unprecedented conglomeration of Rightists and Socialists. The Janata rule lasted merely for two or three years; internal dissensions and greed for power of the few brought an end to what started as a novel experiment.

Nanaji resigned from the party and retired from politics. He turned to social work and worked wonders in that field. He differed from ordinary, run-of-the-mill politicians in that he acknowledged his mistakes, and had no ill feeling even towards Mrs Gandhi, against whom he had fought. In fact, I remember him telling me that she was a great leader who was misled by a certain caucus to commit the mistake of declaring an emergency.

Working with Nanaji, and sometimes travelling with him, I came into contact with a wide spectrum of political, social and cultural ideologies, workers and leaders, that opened my mind to a hitherto unknown world of those who were at the helm of affairs of the state. From RSS leaders like Balasaheb Deoras and K.S. Sudarshan at one end, to socialists like George Fernandes and others at the other, all were Nanaji's friends and associates, and I was able to interact with them.

Within a year I was appointed Joint Editor of *Manthan*'s English version, and learnt a lot about the politics of religion whilst reviewing books and working on certain themes for the journal. When not working, I spent my time visiting the ancient monuments that Delhi is full of, and travelling to Agra, Fatehpur Sikri and other places of historical importance. I also visited Haridwar, Rishikesh, Mathura and Brindavan, which were not too far from Delhi. Neither in Haridwar nor in Rishikesh, could I get hold of Babaji, although I visited all his favourite haunts. That, however, did not affect me much. I was on my own, and that was also Babaji's intention, to make me stand on my own feet.

I was eternally thankful to him for making me independent, and for having bestowed on me the gift of meditation. I was meditating all the time, uninterrupted, with eyes open or closed, but I also strictly followed the regimen of sitting down to meditate every day at dawn, and giving exclusive attention to the core of my consciousness. I managed to hide any extraordinary capacities that manifested from the general public. Life was great—I was working for a living, and enjoying a blissful spiritual state internally, side by side.

After a while, I started feeling a little suffocated with working in the narrow field of a research journal, and wanted to try my hand at real-time journalism.

At a conference on communal harmony at the India International Centre, I met Ganesh Shukla, who edited a weekly tabloid called *New Wave*. I had read the tabloid, and though it seemed a little left-oriented, I liked the content and the style. When I expressed my desire to work for *New Wave*, Mr Shukla readily agreed. The next day, I resigned from *Manthan* and joined *New Wave*. My editor was upset, but Nanaji understood why I wanted a change.

Whilst working for *New Wave* as a correspondent, two important events directly connected to my spiritual life took place. One was my visit to Kashmir and my meeting with a great master of Kashmiri Shaivism, Swami Laxman Joo. The other was a short encounter with J. Krishnamurti at the Constitution Club in Delhi.

Kashmir, apart from being a land of marvellous beauty, was known as the cradle of Aryan civilization since ancient times. Even the great Pythagoras, the mathematician, declared that he was indebted to the 'Brachmans of Kashmere' for the mathematical and spiritual knowledge that he possessed. The great Chinese traveller and historian Hiuen Tsang who went to Kashmir (in 631 AD) to improve his knowledge, praised the Kashmiri pundits for their vast learning and erudition. On-Kong, another Chinese traveller who went to Kashmir in 760 AD and lived as a Buddhist *bhikshu* says that there were more than 300 monasteries in Kashmir, engaged in the indepth study of religion and philosophy.

Again, Kashmiri Shaivism is a profound approach to the philosophy and practice of the followers of Shiva, and may be called Kashmir's unique gift to mysticism and its practice.

As far as the scenic beauty of the Kashmir valley goes, one has only to go once to this beautiful state to agree with the description of the Mughal Emperors who described it as 'paradise on earth,' saying, in Persian, *"Agar firdaus bar rue zamin ast, hamin ast, o hamin ast, o hamin ast"*—if there is paradise on earth, it is this, it is this, it is this. Bound by Tibet in the east, Chinese Turkistan and Russia in the north, and Afghanistan on the west, its life and culture is a rich blend of varied influences. Great Sufis like Shah Hamadhani contributed to this composite culture. Very few know that the first-ever translation of the incomparable Upanishads in Persian, brought out by the saintly Dara Shikoh—brother of the despotic Mughal emperor Aurangzeb— was planned and executed by him, while living in Srinagar and being deeply involved in the study of Kashmiri Sufi teachings.

My special interest in visiting Kashmir was to try and meet Sri Lakshman Joo, the great yogi, and visit the temples of the fifth and sixth centuries at Bhanjo near Anantnag, which Babaji had mentioned. These temples were once used for secret initiations into the higher mysteries of religion. In ancient times, even the Hierophants of the old Egyptian pyramid temples came from so far away to be initiated into these mysteries. According to legend, even Jesus Christ spent some time in Kashmir.

After visiting the caves, I went to many Sufi shrines including the famous Hazrat Baal and climbed up to the hills of Adi Shankaracharya, where the linga installed by Sri Shankara still exists.

But by far the most important happening was my meeting the great adept of Kashmiri Shaivism, Sri Laxman Joo.

It was around 3:30 p.m. on a Sunday that I reached the ashram of Sri Laxman Joo, popularly called Swamiji. I was told that it was a day when Swamiji met the public. The beautiful ashram with a colourful garden was his private residence and stood facing the Dal Lake on the mountainside near the Mughal garden of Nishat Bagh. The setting was panoramic. The place was filled with people of all kinds, young and old. I joined the crowd and stood waiting for Swamiji who, Babaji had once told me, was the greatest living authority on Kashmiri Shaivism, and not merely in the theoretical sense.

After a short while, the crowd suddenly stopped chattering. Looking up, I saw him—a thin, almost six-feet tall, clean-shaven and extremely fair man with grey cropped hair, wearing a Kashmiri pheran, stepping down from the porch. He looked around seventy, his gait was quite youthful, and there was something aristocratic in the way he carried himself. I stood quietly amongst the crowd and bowed down to the great one, wondering if I would ever get the opportunity to meet him personally. To my great surprise, after briefly exchanging pleasantries with some of the people who had gathered, and blessing them, he came straight to where I stood, and with a beaming face, held my hand. His eyes looked into mine as if they were searching for something. A blissful thrill passed through my entire body and I shivered.

I think it was the turn of the people who had gathered there to be surprised, when he, still holding my hand, said, 'Come, let us go,' and led me to the building called the meditation hall. Once inside, he sat on a Kashmiri rug and gestured for me to sit in front of him on another rug placed close by. He leaned forward and and said, 'Come closer child, I have been waiting for you. Don't believe me? Ummph! Doubting Thomas.'

From inside his pheran, he took out a blackish object and held it in front of my eyes, 'Do you recognize it?'

I was stunned. It looked so much like the Rudrakshas that Babaji wore around his neck, big and almost black. 'Given to me by Baba Maheshwarnath when I was twenty years old, and which fact, no one knows except you, now that I have told you. A year later, I published the

Bhagawad Gita with Abhinavagupta's commentary. It was Baba's wish that I should do it. I am glad your master sent you to me. Though Babaji is not my personal guru, I hold him in no less esteem than my master Swami Mehtab Kak or my grandmaster Swami Ram. You are blessed that your master found you and re-established your link with Sri Guru.'

With tears in my eyes I said, 'Swamiji, what more can I say, you seem to know all about me.'

We discussed certain aspects of Kashmiri Shaivism and its practice for half an hour. He suggested certain changes in my Kriya routine and asked me to read the *Pratyabhijnahrdayam*, the *Vijaña-bhairava* and the *Paratri'sikavi-varana*. Before terminating the meeting, he handed me two small booklets, his English rendering of the Sanskrit texts *Bodhapancada'sika* and *Paraprave'sika*, which were translated as *Fifteen Verses of Wisdom* and *Entrance into Supreme Reality*.

I prostrated at his feet and left. 'When you see Babaji, give him my pranams and may Amriteswara Bhairava, the Lord of the Nectar of Liberation, liberate you,' he said. These were his parting words.

From Kashmir, I returned to New Delhi.

Two weeks after returning to Delhi, I heard that J. Krishnamurti was giving evening talks at the Constitution Club grounds for two days. I could not make it for the first day due to various reasons, but on the second day I reached a few minutes before the talk started. The audience was indeed an elite one; there were business tycoons, industrialists, politicians belonging to different parties, intellectuals, scientists, and the media. As a journalist, I managed to find a good seat from where I could see the speaker clearly. The audience waited for him silently.

At six o' clock on the dot, he walked in, immaculately dressed in a light brown silk kurta and white pyjamas, and sat cross-legged on the platform. With his grey hair and handsome face, he looked like a modern-day Buddha as he folded his hands in greeting and began to speak. No introductions, no lighting of lamps, no drama. He went directly to the subject. I remember his opening words uttered so many years ago distinctly: 'I would like to point out that we are not making any kind of propaganda for any belief, for any ideal, or for any organisation. Together, we are considering what is taking place in the world...'

There was total silence for about an hour, as Krishnamurti laid bare the anatomy and physiology of violence, and how, for centuries, religion too had encouraged and abetted violence. He was urging human beings to recognise how violent they were deep inside their minds, and pleading with folded hands to see for themselves the incalculable harm violence had brought about—and to consciously shed all violence in day-to-day living.

It was not an exposition of any ideology or philosophy but a journey into the subconscious and the unconscious, a journey of self-discovery. So immersed was the audience in the talk that for a few minutes even after Krishnamurti had stopped talking, nobody stirred. Then he folded his hands in namaste and got off the platform. That was when something of a very personal and intimate nature happened to me. Whilst walking away he suddenly stopped, turned around, and for a few seconds looked directly into my eyes. Then, he turned and walked away.

I felt a tangible force entering my system. Even as I caught a bus and returned to my room, the effect of the strange energy remained. It was as if I was drunk with a certain subtle bliss, which could not be explained. As I entered my room, I remember my friend Sheridan, who lived upstairs, and who later became personal secretary to President Abdul Kalam, asking me if I had had a drink. I was tottering. That feeling remained throughout the night, and I fell asleep only towards dawn.

The very next day, I tendered my resignation and quit *New Wave*. The day after, I took a train to Banaras. In Banaras, I got permission to stay at the Juna Akhada. Close by, at Rajghat, was the Krishnamurti Centre but I felt no inclination to go there. Instead, I spent one whole year walking along the numerous ghats, and occasionally visiting the temple of Kashi Viswanath. I was revelling in absolute, unconditional freedom.

44

Vasant Vihar

ONE FULL MOON NIGHT, while watching a boat going past the Manikarnika Ghat, I felt an irresistible desire to personally meet J. Krishnamurti. The next morning, I went to Rajghat and met Mr Upasani, then the head of the Krishnamurti Centre. On enquiry, he informed me that Krishnamurti would be arriving at Chennai in a week or so. He suggested that I should go to Chennai before that and meet Mr Achyut Patwardhan, the well-known freedom fighter and then the vice-president of the Krishnamurti Foundation. He could probably arrange a meeting with Krishnamurti.

I arrived at Chennai after a few days and, instead of going to my parental home, I headed straight to the headquarters of the Krishnamurti Foundation at Greenways Road. There, at the office, I requested an appointment with Sri Achyut Patwardhan. I was asked to wait in a spacious hall. In about half an hour, Mr Patwardhan walked in.

Having heard of the legendary Achyut Patwardhan, the freedom fighter who had, as part of the Quit India movement, walked up to the headquarters of the British Empire in India along with his colleague Aruna Asaf Ali, pulled down the Union Jack and hoisted the Indian national flag while still very young, I had expected to meet an impressive, well-built man. The man who came in was small and almost mouse-like. But his eyes were sharp and alert, and the seventy-odd years sat lightly on him. He was sprightly and very courteous. He had done his homework before meeting me. Upasini from Rajghat had talked to him on the phone about me, and he had checked up with Nanaji Deshmukh in Delhi, whom he knew very well. He was satisfied with my credentials and background, and was very cordial.

Krishnamurti would arrive, he said in a month. Meanwhile, I could stay in Vasant Vihar, as the headquarters was called. He would try and arrange a private interview with 'K' for me. I thanked him and agreed. I was allotted a small room near the dining hall, and ate at the dining hall with Achyutji. Sometimes there were a few guests at lunch or dinner. The campus was vegetarian: no alcohol and no tobacco, which suited me fine.

In the evenings, I would go for a walk with Achyutji in the five-and-a-half acre, wooded campus, or at the sprawling estates of the Theosophical Society nearby, where we would be dropped by a car and picked up again.

We became good friends in spite of the differences in our age and social status. He was more than thrice my age and well known in political and social circles, yet we discussed a variety of subjects. I had much to learn from a man of his stature. One story of his that I can never forget is how, as a young man, he sought K's permission to join the Indian freedom struggle spearheaded by Mahatma Gandhi. K is supposed to have told him that, for him, 'freedom' was absolute freedom from prejudice, division and violence, and if the freedom struggle was going to achieve that, 'do it, if you feel like it, don't ask me.'

Then, after the British quit, came the partition of India and Pakistan, and the consequent gory violence and bloodshed. Achyutji had met K after that, and K asked him rather sarcastically if the senseless violence and bloodshed of partition was true 'freedom'.

While I waited for Krishnamurti to arrive, I read up all the literature available on him and listened to the audiotapes of his talks. Before I describe my personal meeting with Krishnamurti, I would like to provide a brief profile.

It all started in 1873, with the arrival of Helena Petrovna Blavatsky, an emigrant from an aristocratic Russian family. Together with

Colonel Henry Steel Olcott, with whom she joined in investigating occult phenomena, she started the Theosophical Society. HPB, as Blavatsky was known, was quite a controversial figure, whose so-called materialisation of objects by occult means was considered by some as divine and by others as mere conjuring tricks. Aldous Huxley dismissed her as a charlatan and a complete hoax.

HPB claimed that she was acting on behalf of mysterious Himalayan masters who had ordered her to found the Theosophical Society. Two of these masters, she referred to as Morya and Kuthumi Lal Singh. She said she had lived with them in Tibet and in the Karakoram range, and that one of them was her personal guru.

With her flamboyance, undoubtedly vast knowledge and magnetic personality, she attracted the great orator Annie Besant, an atheist, a member of the Fabian Society and a close friend of George Bernard Shaw. Annie Besant, who was given a copy of the *Secret Doctrine* written by HPB to review, was so taken up by the book that she soon became Blavatsky's disciple. Annie Besant played a very important role in Krishnamurti's life.

Another person who played perhaps the most important part in Krishnamurti's life was C.W. Leadbeater, a disrobed priest of the Church of England, a well-read and many-faceted personality, whose writings on the occult, though fascinating, have left many wondering if the contents were fact or fiction.

C.W. Leadbeater (CWL), who with his flowing white beard and sharp features resembled a biblical prophet, also met HPB, became her disciple and soon was recognized as a prominent theosophist. After Blavatsky's death, CWL was the man who claimed to be directly in contact with the theosophical masters of the White Lodge and dispensed initiations and blessings on their behalf. Annie Besant leaned heavily on him when it came to occult matters.

CWL was mostly responsible for spreading the idea amongst the theosophists that the time was ripe for the descent into flesh of the Maitreya Buddha, the great lord, the future Buddha, the messiah of the age. This descent was unique in that the great lord would take over or possess an already born human being's body, which was pure and virtuous and specially trained. For this reason, prominent theosophists were on the lookout for a suitable young man who could possibly be the vehicle for the Lord Maitreya.

The Theosophical Society, while HPB was still alive, had established headquarters in a 300-acre estate at Adyar in Chennai. The magnificent, wooded compound on the banks of the Adyar River, with its European-style buildings, even boasted its own private beach. It was here, by the riverside, that CWL discovered Krishnamurti and his brother Nityananda at a very young age, and declared that the boy Krishnamurti's aura which he claimed to have seen using his clairvoyant powers, was pure, virtuous and bright, and therefore suitable for being taken over, and used by the Lord Maitreya.

To make a long story short, the buck-toothed, lice-infested Krishna and his younger brother Nitya were taken away from their father Narayanaiah, a retired minor government official, and trained by CWL and others chosen by him, until they learnt to become and behave like pucca sahibs. Krishna, who was considered a moron before he was adopted by the theosophists, never passed exams or qualified for Cambridge or Oxford, whilst his brother Nitya, being quite bright, became well educated. However, when the theosophists took them to the West, the two young men, backed by theosophical propaganda, became quite popular.

Krishna, being the future messiah, was of course treated like a prince and wore Saville Row suits, drove expensive cars, and in general, was the toast of the upper-rung social circles of England, Europe and the USA. Tragedy struck when Nitya died of tuberculosis. Krishna, who assumed that the theosophical masters would not let him die, lost all faith in what theosophy—at least of the CWL variety—stood for, and began to move away from the hierarchical setup.

Finally, on 3 August 1929 at the International Convention of Theosophists held at Ommen, Holland, Krishnamurti cut himself off completely from the Theosophical Society and its ideas, dissolved the Order of the Star of which he was the head, and declared that,

'Truth was a pathless land and you cannot approach it by any path whatsoever...'

To a shocked audience, including Mrs Besant, he said, 'I have now decided to disband the Order as I happen to be its head. You can form other organisations and expect someone else. With that I am not concerned, nor with creating new cages, new decorations for those cages. My only concern is to set men absolutely, unconditionally free.' Mrs Besant never recovered from the shock and soon passed away.

Krishnamurti, with a few friends, of whom Rajgopal, another CWL find, was the most important, set up what was called Krishnamurti Writings Incorporated, which supported his lectures and other activities worldwide. It was Rajgopal who expertly edited the first collection of Krishnamurti's talks called the *Commentaries on Living*.

Years later Rajgopal fell out with him, and after an extended period of acrimony and legal tussles, Rajgopal was sidelined. With the help of Krishnamurti's new and politically powerful friends, the Krishnamurti Foundation India, the Krishnamurti Trust England and the Krishnamurti Foundation of America headquartered at Ojai, California were set up. These organisations published his transcribed talks and looked after all of Krishnamurti's activities in India and abroad.

It was at the Indian headquarters of the Krishnamurti Foundation, Vasant Vihar, not far from the headquarters of the Theosophical Society, that I waited for Krishnamurti to arrive.

Sometime towards the end of November, Krishnamurti arrived in Chennai. It was a midnight flight and I could only get to see him at lunch the next day.

Padmakar Patwardhan, the younger brother of Achyut Patwardhan, and his south Indian wife Sunanda, who edited the *Krishnamurti Bulletin*, had come back from their travels a few days earlier. In spite of their suspicious nature and tendency to keep ordinary people like me away from Krishnamurti, I was allowed, on Achyutji's recommendation, to join the small group that ate with Krishnamurti at the dining hall.

Many more days remained for the public talks and gatherings at Vasant Vihar, and there were very few inmates at that time. There was not much talk at lunch or dinner. An occasional guest who could be a potential donor, or some influential VIP who could be useful to the foundation, was invited to have a meal with Krishnamurti. I was given a seat as far from Krishnamurti as possible. Finally, three or four days after Krishnamurti's arrival, I was informed by Mrs Sunanda Patwardhan that Krishnaji, as she addressed him, would see me privately, in his bedroom upstairs for half an hour or as long as he wished. I knew that only Achyutji could have managed to get me this opportunity.

The bedroom upstairs was considered sacrosanct; no stranger was allowed even to climb the stairs, and so I was thrilled to be accorded the privilege. As I entered the room nervously, I saw Krishnaji sitting cross-legged on a rug on the floor. 'You can shut the door, sir,' were his first words, 'and come and sit down here.' Carefully, I sat on the edge of the rug.

'No, no, come here,' he said and indicated that I should come forward. I sat facing him, just a few feet away. For a minute, he held my left hand and then let it go. I was not overawed or intimidated by his presence; on the contrary, I felt I was sitting with a good friend. Even in his eighties, he was truly handsome. Although I had seen him a few times from afar at the talks in Chennai and again at Delhi, for the first time I understood what George Bernard Shaw must have felt when he went to see him and commented that the young Krishnamurti was 'the most beautiful human being' he ever saw.

'Don't they say "sit near" in the Upanishads?' he said with a mischievous smile. 'I haven't read much, of course.'

'I can't believe that, sir,' I said. 'Surely, in your theosophical days, you must have studied the Upanishads.'

'I don't know. Perhaps I did. I can't remember clearly,' he said. Changing the drift of the conversation abruptly, he said, 'tell me about yourself. Achyut says you were travelling in the Himalayas with a guru. Who was he and what did he do? You know, I don't believe a guru is necessary.'

I said, 'Sir, with due respect, I don't agree. I think a teacher is necessary as long as one doesn't become completely dependent on him.

Babaji, as I call my guru, was from the beginning, very clear that one should stand on one's own feet and not be dependent. Also, he had no organisation or banner, and did not even have a roof over his head. He wandered from place to place and stayed often in caves.

'I have heard your story about how even Truth, when organised, loses its truthfulness; and yet, you head an organisation called the Krishnamurti Foundation. Babaji had nothing. He was an independent human being.'

Krishnamurti, I must admit, listened to me carefully and seriously, instead of asking me to get lost, which he could have done easily.

'You are right,' he said. 'Honestly, I am quite fed up with all this drama. You know, I walked out of the Theosophical Society with its initiations and hierarchies many years ago. If you are going to stay a while, you'll see. I will probably dump this too when I can no longer carry on. Don't you tell anyone I said that, alright?' he said and laughed, tapping my shoulder.

'Now, if you are quite satisfied with what you learnt from what was that... Babaji, why are you here?'

'Sir, Babaji suggested that I meet you.'

'But, why on earth? Anyway if you wish to, you may stay on for some time. From what I heard, it looks like you are a wanderer, and so I don't know how long you'll stay, but that's not an issue.'

'I don't know myself, sir, and I don't want to commit myself.'

'Fair enough. But tell me, did your Babaji mention anything about the theosophical masters, the White Lodge and all the rest of the stuff, you know.'

'There are great masters in the Himalayas, sir. Babaji himself was one, and his teacher, whom we call Sri Guru, I have myself met—and one or two of his disciples. But Babaji believed that Blavatsky exaggerated a bit, and after her others a bit more, and finally the caricatures that emerged were completely different from the originals.'

Krishnamurti rubbed his palms together, looked very thoughtful and said, 'Exactly what I thought. This man Babaji seems quite an interesting fellow. So what do you propose to do here?'

'I will listen to as many cassettes as possible,' I said. 'And do any work allotted to me. I would love to transcribe too.'

'Have you read *Commentaries on Living*?'

'Yes, sir. Once.'

'Read *First and Last Freedom*.'

'Yes, sir. And sir, may I ask you a question?'

'Yes, Mum... I can't get your name straight.'

'Mumtaz,' I said.

'Yes, yes. M would be easier.'

'Sir, you talk about the sexual relationship, love, jealousy, anger and so on as if you have such an intimate understanding of all that. Most people think you are celibate. How do you know then?'

'Sir,' he said with a look that was intense and serious, 'firsthand experience is the only learning experience. How does the world know anything about my personal life? I don't care what people think, but remember, I don't talk about things I don't know personally. Draw your own conclusions.'

'That brings me to one more question, sir,' I said. 'Do you think marriage is essential for one's spiritual growth?'

'Honestly, I don't know what you mean by spiritual growth,' he said, 'but it is better to marry or experience sexual relationships than be obsessed by it all one's life. It's better to marry than to burn.'

Not wanting to impose myself and take up the valuable time of such an important person, I folded my hands and said, 'Namaste, sir. I won't take any more of your time. Thank you very much.'

He too folded his hands most graciously and said, 'One more little thing before you go. You will find some people here who would tell you, "we have known Krishnaji for over thirty years" or some such thing, and volunteer to interpret the teachings for you; gently ignore them. They probably haven't understood a thing.'

I was taken aback and remembered a warning that Swami Ranganathananda had given me when I joined the Ramakrishna Mission as a young brahmachari many years ago. 'An ashram is a small world,' he had said, 'and you will meet all kinds of people. Don't labour under the illusion that they are all great sadhaks, or spiritually advanced souls. You do your work and your *sadhana*, and keep your eyes open.'

I thanked Achyutji for having arranged the interview, and avoided revealing to curious questioners the details of my meeting with Krishnamurti. However much I would have loved to meet in private with Krishnamurti, I was denied access by the powers that be. My movements were, in fact, scrutinised closely lest I climb up to Krishnamurti's room unnoticed. I continued to utilise my time in reading, listening to the tapes, and taking walks. At times, Achyutji would ask me to join him for a walk, and we would discuss diverse subjects—Hindu philosophy, Mahatma Gandhi, socialism, the freedom movement, theosophy and, of course, Krishnamurti. Soon, the Patwardhans began to trust me and give me administrative jobs to do.

As the time for the talks neared, more members of the Krishnamurti Foundation from India and abroad trickled in. Pupul Jayakar, the other vice-president of the Foundation, who was a very old associate and friend of Krishnamurti arrived. One had only to see her rather imperious manners to guess that she was politically powerful. Indira Gandhi, then prime minister, was a close friend of hers, and she was herself chairperson of the Festival of India with the rank of a cabinet minister. I must admit that she was very gentle and loving with me, but I could not help noticing that she was still in the process of assessing my value vis-à-vis the organisation.

Many others came, including governing body members of the foundation, and principals and teachers of its various schools. I became very friendly with the headmistress of the Rishi Valley School, Mrs Rebecca Thomas, a very efficient lady, and her husband Mr Thomas who was the burser—a thoroughly cynical though practical man, who tried to keep himself away from the Krishnamurti ideologies. My friendliness with these two was partly because they hailed from Trivandrum, the place of my birth, and therefore we could converse in Malayalam. Language often brings people together as nothing else does. As it turned out Mr Thomas knew my family well.

Among the few people I could relate to was Radhika Herzburger, Pupul Jayakar's daughter; a truly genuine, unassuming and gentle soul. She had a doctorate in Buddhist Studies and was married to Professor Dr Hans Herzberger, who taught Symbolic Logic at the University of Ontario, Canada.

Intellectuals, socialists, educators, Buddhist scholars, theosophists, and people from the elite sections of society walked in and out of Vasant Vihar. I was told that the foundation's governing body members were a different class altogether, the chosen few, and therefore had to be given preferential treatment. Some of the members, who I met later, were really quite nice, but there were a few who believed that they were above everyone else.

The talks were well attended, and looking at Krishnamurti sitting cross-legged on stage, with Buddha-like stillness, I wondered if he was the same person who cracked jokes at the dining table. Once the talks were over, Krishnamurti would go off to the Rishi Valley School, from where he would return to Chennai, then fly back to the United States. The crowds vanished. Achyutji, his brother Padmakar and wife Sunanda went away to Rishi Valley with Krishnamurti, and I was virtually left alone except for the office and kitchen staff, and one Mr K Krishnamurti, who was a sub-editor with the *Indian Express* newspaper and spent weekends at Vasant Vihar helping with the transcripts and correspondence. He could be defined as a true devotee, who hung on to every word that Krishnamurti uttered.

Krishnamurti returned from Rishi Valley after ten days and left for California. The Patwardhans returned to Chennai. Soon, they entrusted me with administrative work as they had become quite friendly. Occasionally, I would visit my parents who lived at Leith Castle Street, not very far away. My sister had been selected for the Indian Administration Services. Later, she got married to a brewer and shifted to Bangalore. My youngest sister was in college and lived with my parents.

One year passed thus, and Krishnamurti came again. This time, I accompanied the Patwardhans to receive him at the airport. With him came Dr Parchure, his personal physician, and his close friend Mrs Mary Zimbalist, the daughter of Sam Zimbalist, the Hollywood producer who made *The Ten Commandments*. I also met many others associated with the foundation, both from India and abroad. Krishnamurti, by then, recognised me on sight and would sometimes talk to me for a short while. I accompanied him on his walks within the compound and showed him what improvements had been made to the buildings and so on. One day, I had gone up to fetch him for lunch and casually mentioned my interest and proficiency in magic.

'Can you levitate?' he asked me, probably expecting a negative reply.

'Yes, I can.'

'You can't be serious,' he said.

'Sir, if you let me, I will demonstrate the illusion tomorrow at lunchtime in the dining hall,' I said.

'Done.'

The next day, I set up a special bench near the dining table, and in the presence of Krishnamurti and a dozen guests, I can't remember who exactly, I covered myself with a sheet, lay on the bench and levitated. I heard Krishnamurti exclaim loudly, 'Jesus, he did it.' I can still remember the look of total disbelief on his face when I explained how the trick was done and how simple it was. 'You fooled me there,' was all he said.

Once again, the talks began. In the mornings, there were question-and-answer sessions. I was kept quite busy, and part of my job was to look after the foreign guests. After the talks, Krishnamurti left for England, the guests departed, and once again there was peace and quiet. I postponed my plans to wander again, when Krishnaji turned around before he left for the security check at the airport and said, 'Hope to see you when I come back.'

Over the years at Vasant Vihar, I was exposed to a great variety of people: the elitists, the true devotees who considered Krishnaji to be divine, the non-believers, the intellectuals, the art crowd, mostly hoping for some favours from Pupul Jayakar, who was connected to the high

and mighty, and a few true spiritual seekers confounded by the maze
they had entered. They were a pretty harmless and peace-loving group,
except a small core group who, for want of a better word, can best be
described as 'ultra Krishnamurtites'. Not having made an in-depth study
of India's hoary traditions, they sought to cover up their ignorance by
quoting Krishnamurti, who considered knowledge of the ancient texts
unnecessary. Having studied the Hindu books of wisdom in depth
under Babaji's tutelage, I was pained by this attitude that disregarded
tradition and discipline altogether.

On the whole, the ten years of association with the Krishnamurti
organisation was indeed a great learning experience. For the moment,
I was quite excited about the talks, and was involved in a small way in
helping with the day-to-day arrangements.

Sometime in April 1985, I received intimation from Babaji, sent
in his own inimitably mysterious style. I was standing at the gates
of Vasant Vihar one evening, debating if I should go out for a walk
or read the *Essence of Rumi* by John Baldock, when I saw a sadhu in
ochre robes coming up the road. As he came close, I saw that he was
barefoot, clean-shaven and tonsured, and had a glowing young face.
On his forehead, he wore the ensign of the Vaishnavite sect drawn with
sandalwood paste. He came right up to me and said, 'Radhe Radhe' in
greeting. 'Radhe, Radhe,' I replied, and quickly touched his feet. Luckily,
no elitist followers of Krishnamurti were around to see me indulge in
what they would have thought an idiotic gesture.

Without any preamble, the monk came straight to the subject.
'Babaji wants you to see him in four days. You will find him at Mouni
Baba's cave. Start as quickly as possible. *Radhe Radhe*.'

With that, he just walked away and disappeared at the end of the
road. I immediately made arrangements to go. First, I informed the
secretary that I had to go to the Himalayas urgently and had to take
leave for two weeks. Leave granted, I went to the railway station and
bought a ticket to Delhi for the next day.

45

Babaji Leaves His Body

ON THE DAY I reached Rishikesh, I headed straight to Mouni Baba's cave. Babaji was alone. *'Alakh Niranjan,'* he greeted me. I prostrated at his feet. 'Mouni Baba has gone to Uttarkashi,' he said. 'So, long time no see; you look good.'

'Yes Babaji, a very long time. Maybe you want me to prove that I am not dependent on you, but it's so wonderful to be here, and you look just as resplendent as ever.'

'Alright, that's enough, you embarrass me. Now listen, there is important work to be done and you must do it. I have decided to leave.'

'Where to, Babaji? I will come with you.'

'No, my child, you can't come. You have work to do. I wish to leave my body.'

I reeled as if a thunderbolt had struck me, 'But Babaji, I…' No more words came out of my mouth. I just stared wide-eyed at him.

'Now pull yourself together young man, I thought you were a yogi. Okay, take a few slow breaths, now exhale, right, that's it. How do you feel now?'

'Okay Babaji, much better but I was shaken by the suddenness with which you said it. I am ready. Tell me what I have to do.' I was fighting hard to keep the tears from spilling out of my eyes.

'My work is over and you have lots to do. First, I'll explain certain important matters to you briefly, and then tell you how to dispose of my body when I am gone. Other than Sri Guru, and my friend Nagaraj, you are the only one who knows about my departure. Listen carefully now.'

He gave me some instructions on the finer points of Kriya practice and initiated me into the final Kriya, which is practiced by yogis at the time of death. When the yogi decides to die, he practices the final Kriya, shuts off bodily functions, and quietly exits the body. Then, he gave me permission to initiate anyone I wanted into Kriya Yoga, as long as they satisfied just two conditions—sincerity and truthfulness.

After that, he put me into a trance and I went once again back into the past, this time in greater detail. My connection with Sri Guru Babaji, who was then playing the role of a great Nath yogi, went back to the time when I was a fiery warrior belonging to the lunar race (the Yadu Vamsa) claiming descent from Sri Krishna, and engaged in setting up the desert kingdom of Jaisalmer. He was my guru then, for the first time.

When I came out of the trance, Babaji told me that because of my *runa bandhan*, karmic connections, I would later in life have associates and disciples who belonged to the erstwhile royal families of India. Babaji said that I would have to take responsibility for the lives of many who were linked to me intimately in different roles in past lives, and that I would recognise them when I saw them, and that I should in no way refuse anyone who asked for help.

He also reiterated that I should marry and that married life would help me become mature enough to handle emotional situations. 'Remaining unmarried,' he said, 'is not a special qualification for a spiritual aspirant; and in any case, it doesn't apply to you. Most people who will come to you in future are going to be married, and you can't advise or help them if you yourself don't know what married life is.'

Babaji also insisted that I should start writing my autobiography, a little before making a trip to Kailash and Manasarovar, and complete it within a year of my return from there. Certain other things that he revealed are confidential, and I was sworn to secrecy.

Having finished all that, he began to give me instructions on what to do with his body once he abandoned it.

'Please Babaji,' I said, 'before you proceed, are you sure you want to do this? Can't you please wait for a while? Please…'

'My son, you know that when I do something, there are solid reasons for doing so. I have decided to go ahead. Eighty percent of my mind's faculties will be transferred to you but you have the rather difficult task of camouflaging your capacities, and pretending to live like anybody else. I am confident that you can do it. Sri Guru will arrive soon and bless you.

'After I go, you go back to the Krishnamurti Foundation. Krishnamurti is soon going to be taken away too. His purpose is served. You watch all that happens after that keenly. Remember that I always live in your heart. Now, here is what you should do.'

I was shown an isolated spot in the forest close to Mouni Baba's cave, at the foothills of the Neelkant Hill. Babaji provided me with a crowbar, spade and pickaxe. I was to dig a large pit of certain dimensions and, in spite of my inexperience in the matter, had to do it single-handed. Babaji would provide my mind with the necessary skill, and my body with the necessary strength to manage it.

In two days, I had the pit ready although my hands were thoroughly calloused. On the third day, which was a Thursday, Babaji gave me a few more personal instructions, and the same night, we walked to the place where the pit was dug. The full moon shone brightly from a clear sky. A cool breeze was blowing. "We will wait for Sri Guru," said Babaji.

Soon a globe of light like the one I saw at Arundhati Cave appeared on the horizon. As it came close to the full moon, it looked as if there were two moons. As it hurtled towards us it became bigger. This time the landing was smooth. No thunderclap, no noise whatsoever, as it descended in front of us.

The glowing globe opened, and out stepped Sri Guru, followed by an exquisitely handsome naked man with a shining blue complexion. After we had prostrated, Sri Guru said to me, 'You have met Nagaraj before, only this time he is in a different form. The beings of Sarpa Loka can change their forms at will. Now to business.

'We have decided to transfer certain *tattvas* from your teacher's body and mind to yours. This is required because you have a great deal of work to do in the scheme of things. Your teacher worked silently without a banner or an organisation, but you will have to work differently. Till 1991, you will work silently like your teacher, and after that gradually, you will become known to more and more people. Don't shy away. That's required for the work. You will see how terribly self-centred and violent humanity is going to be even in this blessed land. Do you agree, Mahesh?'

'Yes,' said Babaji. 'I wanted the words to come from your mouth. Now it's time, please bless and keep me with you.'

With Sri Guru, Nagaraj and I watching, Babaji climbed down into the pit, sat in padmasana, and inhaled and exhaled vigorously for a few seconds. His eyes were fixed to the centre of his forehead. After the last exhalation, which was the strongest and most powerful, he fell silent, and his body became totally motionless.

A rainbow-hued light emerged from the crown of his head, and entered my heart. My inner identity was transformed forever. Henceforth, Babaji's energies worked through me. Then, I saw a white light emerging from his head and ascending skywards. In a few seconds, it had disappeared in the horizon. Sri Guru said, 'It's over now. Do what you have been instructed to do. I have to leave now, and you know how to get in touch with me.' I prostrated to Sri Guru and Nagaraj. They got into their *vimana* and were soon gone.

I worked the whole night, filling the grave. The first spade full of earth was indeed painful for me to fill, but I was myself surprised at the unemotional and cool way in which I filled the grave with soil.

Soon, the pit with Babaji's body inside was filled and covered completely. As instructed, I hardened the surface, laid patches of natural grass on it and poured water. Since Babaji had prohibited the building of a tomb or even fixing a simple stone slab to identify the grave, I simply prostrated at the sacred spot and left.

It was dawn when I returned to the cave. The rising sun painted the skyline orange. Birds chirped. The wind blew softly. Suddenly, my heart was soaked with sorrow, and my body shook as I wept unashamedly. Tears of love, gratitude, and separation, flowed copiously. I lay down on my blanket and, tired as I was, fell asleep, still crying. It was a deep dreamless sleep. I woke up healed, calm, and ready to shoulder my responsibilities.

46

The Passing Away of 'K'

FOR TWO DAYS, I wandered around Rishikesh. On the third day, I took the train to Delhi, and from there a bus to Amritsar. I had always wanted to visit the Golden Temple of the Sikhs at Amritsar. Babaji had great regard for the Granth Sahib, the sacred book of the Sikhs, and the main centre where the book, regarded by the Sikhs as equal to God and guru was worshipped, was the Harmandir Sahib, the Golden Temple.

Started by the fourth guru of the Sikhs, Guru Ram Das, and completed by the fifth guru, Guru Arjan, the beautiful temple with golden domes stands in the middle of the spring-fed lake called the Amritsaras (Nectar Lake). The town of Amritsar derives its name from this lake and is very close to the Pakistan border at Wagah.

I entered the temple at dawn. The soul-stirring rendering of the Granth Sahib by the raagis at the Harmandir Sahib plunged me into deep ecstasy. That day I heard them sing the songs of Kabir incorporated in the Granth Sahib: 'That heart where love has not entered is like a crematorium, it is dead....' After paying my respects to the holy Granth, I ate the sweet kada prasad.

Catching a bus, I travelled to Delhi. In Delhi, I went straight to the railway station and bought a ticket to Chennai in the unreserved compartment. It was a tiring two-day journey during which I could sleep very little. The rich and powerful have no idea how the ordinary citizen, especially from the poorer sections, travels—it is a nightmare!

Going back to Chennai, I settled down to the routine at Vasant Vihar. At first, it was difficult, but soon I got over the tension of pretending that I had merely gone on a holiday to Rishikesh, and that nothing of consequence had occurred.

In October that year, I heard that Krishnamurti was ill but would nevertheless come to India. On his arrival, he first went to Varanasi for a series of discussions with a group of Buddhist scholars. Among them was Pandit Jagannath Upadhyaya who was to bring out a critical edition of the *Kalachakratantra*, a Mahayana text which was believed to be the teaching of the Maitreya Buddha. Sandung Rinpoche, at present the head of the Tibetan-government-in-exile, was another scholar who participated. No satisfactory answers were provided for Krishnamurti's questions—'Is there something sacred, something long lasting... in India, in this part of the world? And if it is there, why is this part of the world so corrupt?'

But it was clear that he was ill, and was looking closely at the question of death, and what happens after that. Before coming to India, at Saanen in Switzerland, he had said that the 'valley is saying goodbye'. During the last talk in Saanen, he retold the story of Nachiketa, the boy who was sent to the house of death in order to answer many questions, a story from the *Katha Upanishad*.

What he had written in 1929 was very much at the forefront of his thoughts:

When Krishnamurti dies, which is inevitable, you will set about forming rules in your minds, because the individual Krishnamurti had represented to you the Truth. So, you will build a temple, you will then have ceremonies ... If you build great foundations upon me, the individual, you will be caught in that house, in that temple, and so you will have to have another teacher come and extricate you from that temple. But the human mind is such that you will build another temple around him, and so it will go on and on.

He was trying hard to shake and shatter the foundations built upon him. But no one other than him was prepared to break the temples where they had become accustomed to feeling safe and secure.

In November, when he reached Rishi Valley, he was exhausted and his health was failing. He began to lose weight at an alarming rate. He called his last talk in Rishi Valley his 'last show'. Over and over, during discussions with the teachers and students, he kept trying to get them to give solid reasons as to why they were different from other schools. It appeared that he was not at all satisfied with the answers.

On 22 December, he arrived in Chennai for the talks. He had lost even more weight and was running a high temperature. He was even wondering if he would be able to go through with the talks. It was evident to those in the inner circle that he was critically ill, and from the hints he himself gave now and then, the picture that emerged was that his life was drawing to a close.

Apart from the tremendous energy required during public talks to reach the inner core of the prejudice-ridden and self-enclosed minds of those he once referred to as 'Oh God! What a generation,' he was faced with the grim task of replacing the complacent and the pretentious among those in the foundation bearing his name. The clamour for succession was on behind the scenes.

Having lost the battle for dissolving the foundation, which none of the prominent members—secure as they were in their positions of power—were amenable to, he disassociated himself from the organisation, saying that he was no more a part of any foundation. Even though I was not a member of the Krishnamurti Foundation at that time, Krishnamurti personally sent word through a good friend that I was to attend the special meeting at the end of which, he disassociated himself from all the organisations that were named after him. I remembered his words uttered three years ago when I had for the first time been given the opportunity to meet him in private: 'If you are going to stay here for a while, you'll see. I'll probably dump this too, when I can no longer carry on.'

He was so seriously concerned that someone would set himself or herself up as his successor that he got the following clause appended to the rules and regulations of the Krishnamurti Foundation: 'Under no circumstance will the Foundation or any of the institutions under its auspices or any of its members set themselves up as authorities on Krishnamurti's teachings. This is in accordance with Krishnamurti's declaration that no one anywhere should set himself up as an authority on his teachings.'

It was during this period that circumstances got me into close contact with Krishnamurti. Since Krishnamurti had successfully dislodged the previous caretakers of the headquarters, including the old secretary of the Krishnamurti Foundation, the new dispensation had to depend heavily on me to run the day-to-day administration. The new secretary appointed by Krishnamurti, Mahesh Saxena, a retired Inspector General of Police from Rajasthan, had just taken charge and he too needed plenty of help. Krishnamurti himself was very affectionate to me and gave me free access to his bedroom.

As a matter of fact, he did not want the old dispensation anywhere near him, and told me that henceforth I would walk with him from his bedroom to the podium for the talks, and fix the lapel microphone for him before the talks began and remove it afterwards. He continued to lose weight and his temperature kept rising. The doctor could not pinpoint the reason. During the talks he was sometimes running a temperature of a 104 degrees Fahrenheit, but in spite of that, except for a slight loss of clarity in his delivery, which the public hardly noticed, he was as powerful and incisive as ever.

The last talk was on the 4 January 1986. It started with, 'Will you kindly participate in what he is talking about?' And it ended with 'This is the last talk. Do you want to sit together quietly for a while? All right, sirs, sit quietly for a while.'

That night he was in a delirium, but the next morning, I heard him sitting quietly in his room and chanting one of Tennyson's poems in a manner that made me think he was chanting in Sanskrit.

I felt strongly that he would not last long. There were a few things in his room including an old chair that required attention. When I told him they would be ready when he came back next time, he put his frail arms on my shoulders, looked me in the eyes and said, 'Sir, the circus is over. I am not coming back.' Tears came into my eyes. Coming down from his room, I saw Radhika Herzberger going up the stairs and somehow felt she knew too.

The night he left for Ojai, I was at the airport to see him off. Considering his serious physical condition, the airport authorities had granted permission to drive him down to the tarmac. That was the last that I saw of him. As the car moved out and the three of us who were there, folded our hands in namaste, he returned the salutations, courteous as ever.

In roughly a month's time, on 17 February 1986, he passed away at Ojai. The doctors had diagnosed cancer of the pancreas. In a voice recording that was done just a few days before his death, he had requested that no elaborate rituals be performed over his dead body and that it be sent to the electric crematorium. I am not at liberty to reveal the contents of this tape since it was not meant for public broadcasting, but I cannot resist the temptation of revealing that Krishnamurti himself is on record saying that no one knew what tremendous energies had been working through his body.

47

Marriage and Shifting to Neel Bagh

THE NEW DISPENSATION AFTER Krishnamurti's passing away, with Mahesh Saxena as the secretary, went on smoothly for a while. Being a retired senior police officer, he had excellent administrative skills. He roped me in to assist him and appointed me as a joint secretary, in spite of opposition from certain quarters. I was also elected to the governing body at a meeting following Krishnamurti's death.

But somehow, Mr Saxena was not able to fit into the ambience of the Krishnamurti Foundation. He was from a traditional milieu, and for the first time, Vasant Vihar had a long-haired man in what could be best described as a brown, knee-length bathrobe, strutting around the campus like a policeman on duty. The usual 'Hello, Sir' or 'Good morning' that the visitors and residents of Vasant Vihar were familiar with were replaced with the traditional 'Namaste'.

Soon, in private conversations with me, he confessed that things were not going too well. Accustomed as he was to law and order, and the implicit obedience from those he considered 'subordinates', the so-called total freedom of thought and action was beginning to bug him. That combined with bouts of depression and obsessive behaviour, which he at times exhibited, led me to suspect a personality disorder. Finally, he was done in by a combination of these factors and had to resign and leave for Banaras—but that was much later.

A few months after I was elected as a member of the Krishnamurti Foundation, something occurred which opened a new chapter in my life. A pretty, twenty-five-year-old woman came to Vasant Vihar. Her name was Sunanda Sanadi, and she had been an English teacher at the Rishi Valley School for a few years. She was a postgraduate in English Literature and was exploring the possibilities of finding a non-teaching job in Chennai. Her father, a retired army officer, and her mother lived in a suburb of Chennai called Purushawalkam. I had, in fact, seen her once in Rishi Valley, though we had not formally met, and one of her former students had expressed the opinion a few months earlier that Sunanda was an excellent teacher and a good human being.

Part of my responsibility at Vasant Vihar those days was to coordinate the publication of the *Krishnamurti Bulletin*. I thought that, being a literature student, she could help out. Mr Saxena agreed readily. Initially, she was supposed to reside in the headquarters during the week, and go home on the weekend. It worked well for her.

I had had relationships, though not so intimate or physical, with a few women since my youth, but had not paid much importance to them. I was already thirty-five, and although I had no inclination to get entangled in human relationships, Babaji's thoughts regarding marriage being the ideal situation for me and a necessary step to the evolution of my consciousness kept going through my mind. Sunanda was sincere, loving, pretty, and came from a good family.

When I had once discussed marriage with Krishnamurti, he had quoted St Paul, 'It is better to marry than to burn.' I was not exactly burning, but within a short time of working together, Sunanda and I realised that the gentle breeze of love and affection was blowing. We decided to get married, but it was not so easy.

For one, she came from a Saraswat Brahmin family from Udupi (her mother hailed from Dharwad), and I was not only not a Brahmin but also belonged, by birth, to a non-Hindu community. Secondly, I earned a meagre honorarium and did not even have a house of my own. However, together we resolved the issue, meeting with her parents' condition that the marriage ceremony be a Hindu Vedic one. I admire the fact that she not only reposed so much faith in a stranger like me, whom she had known only for a short while, but also that she took a step that required exemplary courage given the circumstances. I must also admit that without the open-mindedness of her parents, this would not have been possible.

As I write this, we have completed twenty-three years of married life and have two grown-up children. I can't say we have not had differences, but on the whole we have been a well-knit family, resolving problems together and loving each other dearly.

Coming back to Vasant Vihar, we were a young and enthusiastic couple, working and living together in the beautiful five-acre estate, but soon we found that things were not going too well. For one, Mr Saxena's health—physical and psychological—was deteriorating day by day, and we found him becoming obsessively suspicious of people who were close to him. I personally felt that one of the factors that aggravated his condition was the inability of his tradition-soaked mind to adjust to the Krishnamurtite way of thinking. He was also becoming increasingly hostile to me, as he had never been in favour of my marrying Sunanda, or for that matter getting married at all.

Meanwhile, Sunanda became pregnant and we were also beginning to wonder if Vasant Vihar would be a suitable place to bring up a child. It was during this period that a godsent opportunity to move out of the place presented itself. One night, I dreamt of Babaji blessing both of us and saying that it was time to move out. The next morning, we came to know that the Neel Bagh School was going to be purchased by the Rishi Valley School, and that they were looking for someone to live there and manage it.

The Neel Bagh School was located in seven-and-a-half acres of lovely wooded property near Rayalpad, deep in the rural districts of Karnataka, but close to the Andhra Pradesh border. Rishi Valley, which was in Andhra Pradesh, was just an hour-and-a-half away. David Horsborough, a Scot with a fair knowledge of Sanskrit, an excellent craftsman, carpenter and educator, had purchased the land, built a lovely English style, mud-walled cottage, and settled down there initially. The school had grown around his residence. It was a free school for the poor children of the neighbouring village, and David—who had worked in Rishi Valley in the early days and then with the education section of the British Council—offered not only free education to the village children, but also trained excellent teachers in innovative educational techniques.

Unfortunately, David died of cirrhosis in his early sixties. His descendents could not manage the property and the school, and wanted to relocate to England. It was at that point that Rishi Valley stepped in and decided to acquire it. It was a very scenic place, very rustic, and although all the buildings were of mud, they were built to British specifications by David's architect friend Mr Baker, and even boasted of bathtubs, and western toilets with wooden seats.

It was Dr Radhika Herzberger, the director of Rishi Valley and my dear friend, who spearheaded the move to acquire Neel Bagh. When I discussed the matter of shifting to Neel Bagh, she was only too glad. She understood how we felt, and so with Sunanda pregnant, we moved to Neel Bagh.

The ten years we spent in Neel Bagh are very important to me. It was our first private home after marriage because we were residing in a lovely independent cottage. Sunanda was busy with the academics and I looked after the administration. Also both our children, our son Roshan and daughter Aisha, were brought up there, till they reached the age of nine and seven. Third, it was during the later part of our stay there that I gave my first public talk in Bangalore and continued giving talks. Fourth, it was here that the Satsang Foundation was formed. Fifth, it was here that Vivek Mahendru from Delhi, came to see me with my old friend Radhakrishnan from Trivandrum, and later on played an active role in Babaji's work. It was also here that I wrote my first book, *The Little Guide to Greater Glory and a Happier Life*. Last, but not least, it was during my time here that I resigned from the Krishnamurti Foundation.

48

Neel Bagh and the Satsang Train

FROM BOTH THE SPIRITUAL, as well as from a worldly point of view, the ten years spent in Neel Bagh were indeed significant, and in some way, rewarding. Situated deep in a rural district, with so many trees and abundant greenery all around, Neel Bagh was ideal for my meditative mind. Being also the first home after we got married, it helped us understand each other and build a proper relationship. As for our children, they grew up in a free atmosphere close to nature and loved it.

Once a week, I rode to Rishi Valley on my motorbike, took culture classes for the ninth standard and attended any committee meetings. Soon, I got myself a secondhand car, which was all that I could afford in those days. We often drove to Bangalore, where my in-laws and parents lived, stopping on the way beside a beautiful lake not far away to watch the white birds and monkeys. We loved the life there, and Sunanda, who was the headmistress, loved the school. Indira Seetharaman, a teacher trained by David Horsborough, assisted her ably. Her husband has been a dear friend ever since.

I wrote The Little Guide to Greater Glory and a Happier Life, but had no intention of publishing it as yet, as my public teaching phase had not begun, and I kept my knowledge and experiences to myself as far as possible. In retrospect, I think that if Babaji had not given me the green signal, I would have gladly gone about incognito, living blissfully with no headaches whatsoever. But that was not to be, for Babaji had other plans for me.

Although I kept my spiritual experiences and adventures to myself, and most people I came in contact with those days knew nothing, some of my old friends, schoolmates and college mates were aware of my spiritual inclinations and explorations. One of them, Prem Kukillaya, who was then working in Bangalore, visited a jeweller, Mangiah Chetty & Sons on Jeweller's Street on some errand. The younger of the two brothers who ran the shop was Mohankumar. While speaking with him, Prem noticed a book by Swami Muktananda lying on the table. When asked about it, Mohankumar said that it was a spiritual book and that he was interested in the subject.

Prem casually mentioned to him that an old friend of his, who was not even born a Hindu, was deep into Hindu philosophy and spiritual matters, practiced yoga, had been to the Himalayas, and also knew some kind of magic. Mohan evinced keen interest in meeting me and was told that I lived in Rayalpad, a remote village, a three-hour drive from Bangalore. He was told that I visited Bangalore now and then, as both my parents and in-laws lived there. Those days, there was no telephone in Neel Bagh, and so Prem promised to convey Mohan's interest in meeting me the next time he saw me.

Three weeks later, I went to Prem's office in Bangalore en route to my in-laws home, and heard the story of his meeting with Mohan. Afterwards, I forgot all about it. On my next visit to Bangalore, I went to Commercial Street to buy oil paint and brushes from Reliance Stationers and remembered that my wife had given me some of her mother's jewellery to be cleaned. Looking around for a jeweller, I walked into Jeweller's Street and soon found myself in front of Mangaiah Chetty & Sons. I vaguely remembered Prem mentioning the name of the shop. Entering the shop, I found an old man and a young man sitting behind the desk. The old man was busy counting money. I approached the young man and explained to him what I wanted, and enquired if this was the same shop my friend Prem from Trivandrum had visited.

The young man, who turned out to be Mr Mohan, said that yes, Mr Prem had visited the shop sometime ago, and asked if I was a friend of his. When I told him that I was indeed Prem's friend, he asked me if I had another friend who had gone to the Himalayas. He probably did not think that I, with my jeans and red T-shirt could be the yogi friend Prem had described.

Not wanting to tell a lie, I said I was the one Prem had mentioned, and that was it. Mohan said that he was a member of the local Theosophical Society, and wanted me to give a talk there. I said that I have never spoken in public about my spiritual life and did not intend to do so. He said even something about my travels in the Himalayas would do. I said that I would think about it, and finishing my business with him, walked out as quickly as possible.

My suspicion that Babaji's hand was behind this meeting with Mohan was confirmed by what happened two days later. On the second night after this incident, I had a vivid dream. After a long interval, Babaji appeared in my dream, and he looked so funny that even in the dream I was laughing loudly. I was in some kind of a train on which was stuck a banner with 'Satsang' written on it. Babaji appeared on the platform in a railway guard's uniform, minus the shoes and hat, and whistled repeatedly. The train started moving fast. When I woke up, I was still laughing, but when I realised the implications of the dream, the smile was wiped off my face. I was being green-signalled to go public. Soon the quiet, private life I led with my family would be compromised. I kept my apprehensions to myself, knowing only too well that when the higher forces wanted one to work for a cause, all personal considerations had to be set aside.

Two weeks later, when I went to collect the jewellery I had given to Mohan, and he tried to persuade me to give a talk at the Theosophical Society, I agreed. The very next day, a Sunday, I was taken to the cantonment lodge of the society at five in the evening. That was my first satsang, and at the end of it, the thirty-odd people who had gathered shook hands with me and said that it was one of the best talks they had attended. I silently thanked Babaji. Mr Naidu, a functionary, wondered if it would be possible for me to come for such programmes on a regular basis. The 'Satsang' train was in motion—the whistle had been blown.

At that first satsang, I was introduced to Group Captain Ratnakar Sanadi, a retired fighter pilot from the Indian Air Force. It turned out that he was related to Sunanda, whose father Ramesh Sanadi had retired as a Lieutenant Colonel from the Indian Army. Many informal satsangs were held under the jackfruit tree, in the garden of his big house on Cubbon Road. It was Ratnakar Sanadi who persuaded and encouraged me to publish the Little Guide, which was already in a typed manuscript format.

Publishing the book required a publisher, and the Satsang Foundation was formed for this purpose, and take care of organising the satsangs. I was made the president, Ratnakar Sanadi was the treasurer, and Mohan, the first secretary. A handful of close friends were the first members, but there were hardly any funds even to print the book. An Italian gentleman who simply called himself Maurice, appeared at the right time. He financed the publication of my first book, The Little Guide to Greater Glory and a Happier Life, which as I write, is going into its third edition.

Maurice and Ratnakar were the first to call me 'M' which later was transformed into Sri M or even Mr M. In my mind, I identified 'M' with 'Madhu,' the name given to me by Sri Guru and Babaji.

It was also in Neel Bagh that Vivek Mahendru, then a stranger from New Delhi, met me for the first time. Vivek was a director of a switchgear company, with factories and offices in Jalandhar, New Delhi and Noida. My old friend from the Trivandrum days, Radhakrishnan Nair was his sales manager in Chennai. Vivek was interested in religion and mind power, and frequently talked about it to his sales staff. On one of Vivek's visits to Chennai, Nair talked to him about me and gave him a copy of the Little Guide. Vivek insisted on visiting me the same day, in spite of the 350 km that separated Neel Bagh from Chennai. I was leaving for Bangalore that afternoon, and we travelled together discussing various spiritual matters. After that, we met often and he remains a good friend.

In like manner, the book found its way into many peoples' homes and soon a dedicated group gathered around me. The Satsang family kept growing.

49

The Kailash-Mansarovar Yatra

ONE IMPORTANT PERSON WHO came across my book was Dr Karan Singh of the royal family of Kashmir. He was a rare example of a prominent politician, a great scholar, and a sincere spiritual practitioner, all rolled into one. He had also met and had interactions with many spiritual masters, and had been initiated by Sri Krishna Prem of the Mihirtola Ashram in the Himalayas.

During one of his visits to Bangalore, Dr Karan Singh located Mohan Kumar from the information given in the *Little Guide*, and contacted him over the telephone. On finding out that I was in Bangalore, he insisted on meeting me. A meeting was arranged at noon at the Raj Bhavan, where he was staying. We hit it off from the very first meeting, and I found him a very gracious and unassuming person who exuded the courteousness that marks a descendant of an illustrious royal family, with its age-old traditions. He was also a remarkably learned and knowledgeable person on spiritual as well as temporal subjects, and carried it off with great dignity and humility.

He was my first link in what later turned into a vast network of connections with the erstwhile royal families of India. Perhaps my past life connections with royalty explain the interest shown by their descendants. It was Dr Karan Singh who arranged for my first satsang in Delhi in the Ramayana Vidyapeet, owned by his trust. Later on, he wrote the forewords to both my books, *The Jewel in the Lotus* and *Wisdom of the Rishis*, and continues to keep in touch. I have a special place for him in my heart, and never miss an opportunity to spend some time with him, or have a meal with him, when in Delhi.

Around the time I met Dr Karan Singh, I resigned from the Krishnamurti Foundation. There were many reasons, but the most important ones are the following. Since the Satsang Foundation had already been formed, with different aims and objectives from those of the Krishnamurti Foundation, and I would be giving more time and energy to it, I thought it would be unfair to continue to be in the Krishnamurti Foundation. Then, since the passing away of Krishnamurti, my interest in the organisation had diminished, although my respect and regard for Krishnamurti remained. I felt that the spirit had vanished and only the shell remained.

I sent in my resignation after first informing Achyut Patwardhan. He said that Krishnamurti had commented after my first meeting with him that, 'this bird won't remain long in your cage.' However, Sunanda and I continued to live and work in Neel Bagh. One month after my resignation was accepted rather reluctantly, I made my first teaching trip abroad.

Dr Ramananda Prasad, a senior scientist at NASA who founded the Gita Society of America and distributed free translations of the Gita, on the same lines as the Bible Society of India's distribution of Bibles, came to know of my existence through my good friend Mohan Kumar. He met me in Bangalore and invited me to the United States. He said he would organise talks and discussions in different places although he resided in Freemont, California.

I agreed, this time without waiting for any particular sign from Babaji because, by then, I knew that the work had started, and 'M' would no longer be able to maintain his privacy. So, in the year 2000, I travelled to the USA for the first time. My dear old friend Thomas Kurien bought me the tickets from Chennai to San Francisco. This was my first journey abroad. Soon, my good friend Hans Kelichhaus—an old friend of the

Mahendru family who was introduced to me by Vivek—invited me to Aachen in his home country of Germany. In a short while, I was travelling to Germany and the United States almost every year.

The teachings were being broadcast, but in a private and subtle manner. It was Babaji's way of doing things. 'Quality,' he used to say, 'not quantity. Spiritual evolution is individual and cannot be a mass phenomenon. No meditation technique franchises can do much good. Each individual is special. No poster blitz and poster wars when your work starts.'

Slowly but steadily, the work was growing, and so was the Satsang Foundation. My children were growing up too. At that juncture, the Rishi Valley School began to run out of funds to conduct the free school at Neel Bagh. A buyer was interested in taking it over and running it. When I was informed, I gladly agreed. For quite some time, I had begun to feel strongly that I had to move out and give more time to the activities of the Satsang Foundation.

Radhika Herzberger wanted Sunanda to go back to teaching in Rishi Valley, and it was agreed that both our children would get free education up to the twelfth grade there. I, not wanting to work for anybody other than Babaji, decided not to go to Rishi Valley, and once more found myself as in my wandering days, faced with the situation of not knowing where to stay once Neel Bagh was sold.

Like the great Jewish teacher and spiritual master Jesus, I rejoiced in the thought that 'The snakes have holes and the foxes have dens, but the son of man knoweth not where to lay his head'—but not for long. A year earlier, I had bought a little more than a quarter of an acre of land on the outskirts of Madanapalle, the small town I had to pass almost every week on my way to Rishi Valley School and back. The land came cheap because it was away from the busy centre of the town, and not too far from a Lambani tribal settlement, which was not considered an ideal neighbourhood. The Lambanis were believed to be thieves and robbers. I, on the other hand, was very happy that the land was outside the commercial hub of Madanapalle, nestling in a valley surrounded by hills and paddy fields. As far as my Lambani neighbours were concerned, I believed that it was wrong to label any community using such derogatory terms, and had no problems living near them. I had bought the land on an impulse and did not know what I was going to do with it. Now, it turned out to be a good buy.

It would have taken about a year to go through all the red tape involved in transferring farmland and registering a sale deed in the rural district where Neel Bagh was located. So, I invested all my savings, borrowed money at a high interest from a moneylender at Madanapalle, and started constructing a house on the land I bought. I was able to finish a modest dwelling place within a year, and as soon as Neel Bagh was sold, moved into the house, named 'Snow White' in remembrance of the eternal snows of the upper Himalayan ranges.

My wife and children moved to Rishi Valley School, and I shifted to Snow White. The Madanapalle house soon became the centre from where the activities of the still fledgling Satsang Foundation would spread its wings and fly worldwide. It was here that the Satsang Vidyalaya, a free school for the underprivileged, had its humble beginnings with one classroom, fifteen children and no teachers. As I write this, it has grown into a beautiful centre for learning, imparting excellent education in all its aspects, for free, to about 120 children.

A few years later, the Peepal Grove School (PGS), an ICSE boarding school, was born.[1] Located in an idyllic setting amidst hills, forests, and a little lake not far from Tirupathi, the PGS is, as Dr Abdul Kalam, former President of India, described in his interaction with students during his visit, 'a very beautiful place, where you are fortunate to grow up and develop your creativity.' Here, children learn not just academics, but also about the multidimensional reality we call life. I often picture Babaji sitting under the peepal tree and explaining the meaning of *Ficus religiosa*, the tree's botanical name, or identifying which species of bird sat up in its branches.

---

[1] The Peepal Grove School (PGS), was founded in a beautiful valley with many peepal trees, gifted by Smt. Varanasi Rukmini Ramasamy Reddy, my friend Ramesh Reddy's mother.

The various activities of the Satsang Foundation were moving forward slowly but steadily: the schools, the Manav Ekta Mission, which strives to bring people together as human beings, and my travels in India and abroad to personally guide those who were interested in the search for the True Reality behind all appearances. All this was made possible by the coming together of individuals who were ready to support the cause.

For want of a better word, I use the word 'providers' to describe them. It was the same term used by the great Ramakrishna Paramahamsa to describe Mathur Babu and other wealthy people who provided him with what he needed to fulfill his mission. Some provided funds, some volunteered to help, sacrificing their temporal conveniences and precious time. And a few true seekers came, whose predominant trait was the search for the 'Truth'. From the spiritual point of view, this last category was the most important to me, although I was karmically indebted to, and eternally thankful to all whom Babaji sent to further his plans, in which I was a mere instrument.

I shall not name anyone in particular because I know they would be embarrassed, and also so many would have to be named that the list would become endless. I can only say that Babaji's blessings are abundantly showered on all these beings, and that they, on account of that infinite grace, shall not miss the goal but move steadily towards it. As for me, I am Babaji's slave, and would labour, day and night if required, to walk with them on their difficult though glorious journey.

As part of the spiritual journey, I began some years ago to take groups of close friends on a pilgrimage to Badri, Kedar, Gomukh, Rishikesh, Ajmer, Dakshineshwar, Kanyakumari, Balaknath, Gorakhpur, Ayodhya and other places. The journey to Kailash and Manasarovar was, by far, the most difficult, and for me very significant. I am sure that the fifty-odd people who accompanied me also felt how different it was from the other trips we had made in the past.

If you recall, I had travelled halfway to Kailash with Babaji many years ago, and had to return without completing the journey due to ill health. Babaji had said I would to Kailash go many years later, accompanied by a lot of people. At that time, I had wondered what 'a lot of people' meant.

A good friend took the initiative and organised the trip against all odds. I shall not describe the journey in detail, and the difficulties encountered by the city dwellers who accompanied me because a travelogue has already been written about the journey by a good friend. However, I must describe certain personal experiences which I had.

The first was when Mansarovar Lake came into sight. As soon as I laid eyes the sacred turquoise-hued lake, I knew that this was not the first time I was seeing the the source of the Brahmaputra, which flows through Tibet into India. A thrill passed through my spine as I stood looking at the waters. Scene after scene regarding my past flashed through my mind. I saw myself as a yogi wearing just a white cotton loincloth and meditating in a cave at the foot of the snow-clad Gurla Mandhata range. Mount Kailash towered at a distance to the right.

As I prepared to take a dip in the lake, I saw a young ascetic, barely in his teens, hair matted, wearing a kaupin and carrying the insignia of the Nath Panth—a pair of fire tongs called the *chimta*—come out of the water. He was exceedingly handsome and a smile hovered on his lips. From the blank expression on the faces of those who stood near me, I knew that they saw nothing. It was a special vision bestowed on me for whatever reason.

I stood, attentive and respectful, waiting for him to come out of the waters. Passing me, he said, 'I am Siddhinath, the disciple of Jalandhripa and Guru Gorakh. Sri Guru is waiting for you. *Alakh Niranjan,*' and walked away. Nobody heard or saw anything, and when I bent and touched the ground with my forehead in prostration, they thought I was offering my prostrations to the lake and Mount Kailash. After that, I had a dip and so did the others. It was cold, but most invigorating and purifying. I felt transported to a different plane.

Then, at Yama Dwar, we came face to face for the first time with the great Kailash, sacred to the Hindus, Buddhists and the Bonpas of Tibet. As the great snow-clad peak towered above us, an extraordinarily deep meditative mood enveloped me.

Some of our group had to wait for ponies and porters to be organised. Others like me decided to walk the *parikrama*, but we waited at Yama Dwar for half an hour. I sat down on a rock facing Kailash and dived deep into myself. I heard the sound of the little drum called the *damaru*, which Shiva Mahadev holds in his hand whilst dancing the *Tandava Nritya*, the dance of destruction, in my inner ear—*dug dug dug dug*. This was soon replaced by the sonorous *bhum bhum bhum* that seemed to explode inside my head. With my inner eye, I could perceive a strong, conical, whirlwind at a distance. It was moving towards me, threatening to take me with it. Suddenly, I heard the loud greeting of the Naths—*Alakh Niranjan*—and the typhoon disappeared. The whirling stopped, there was absolute silence. I opened my eyes, said 'Sivoham' and began to walk. 'Sivoham' remained with me throughout the journey and even afterwards.

The third experience was on the second day of the parikrama when, having traversed the Dolmo La pass (around 18,500 ft above sea level), we reached the campsite at around 8 p.m. We were tired and exhausted, for the oxygen levels were very low, and we had walked twenty-two kilometres that day along a really difficult tract.

After settling down in my tent, I instructed our friends not to disturb me after dinner. Many of us suffered from nasal bleeding. I wiped my nose clean, emptied my bladder near the rocks, and zipping close the flap of the tent, sat in padmasana, my attention fixed on the ajna chakra. Blood rushed to my head and a streak of lightning shot up my spine. Within seconds, I was out of my body clothed in a blissful silvery sheath.

This new luminous self passed swiftly through several planes where glorious beings dwelt, and reached a wondrous realm that glowed with a silvery blue, soothing light. Two large blue cobras guarded the patio of a white crystal palace. They swung their hoods nodding to me to enter. In a central hall, on a raised crimson couch was Mahadev, the Great Being, manifested as the Luminous Void, changing every now and then into the resplendent form of Shiv Bholenath, with the crescent moon on his head and a black cobra around his neck, his body snow-white, and his third eye looking like a blue pearl.

Beside him on either side sat five persons: Babaji, someone who looked like a biblical prophet, a Nath with his chimta, a bearded man with a white turban whose eyes were the most peaceful and compassionate that I have seen, and another man with Mongolian features, matted hair tied in a knot, twirled up moustache, and wearing a loose red robe. All of them possessed silvery luminescent bodies like mine. The fragrance of jasmine filled the air. I prostrated many times and then sat cross-legged on the floor. Babaji broke the silence.

'Madhu, welcome to Kailash! This is the great Jewish master called Esa or Yesu; the Nath is none other than Sri Gorakhnath; the one with the loving eyes is the great Nanakdev; and this one with the moustache and red robe, the inimitable Padmasambhava, Guru Rinpoche. All of us here are the disciples of Sri Guru Babaji, who is none other than the luminous void, Adinath, Shiv Mahadev who sits on the throne. The great Pir Sainath and the venerable Sheikh Khwaja Moinuddin Chisti, also known as Garib Nawaz, could not be present here but have conveyed their love and blessings to you. Greetings and blessings also from all the great yogis and masters like Shanker Bhagwadpad whose abode is Kailash, and who chose to not manifest themselves here today.'

'Babaji,' I said, 'thank you and Sri Guru for letting me enter here. I think I will stay on here, and like you, I have no interest in going back to the earth, covered by the darkness of *kaliyug*. I think I have done enough, and those who you sent to me for guidance, can now take care of themselves. You, I know are always there, to help them.

'My body is already sixty years old and before it falls seriously ill or becomes weak, I think it is better to drop it. I do not want to be physically dependent on anyone.'

Babaji said, 'You are again in a similar situation as you were when I asked you to leave me and go to the plains. Once again, I say that you should go back. Your dependants and associates, spiritual or temporal, are still not evolved enough to fend for themselves. Your wife, whom you married of your own choice, still needs you, and so do your children. Family responsibilities of both the temporal and spiritual family are still not over. Hold on and don't be in a hurry.

'Also, you have not decided on who would take over and continue your spiritual responsibilities. Till such time you better stay there. There is no problem. You have free access to this realm to come and go as you like. That's what we think and that's what Sri Guru thinks, but you are free to take your own decision as always.'

I stood silent, head bowed. Guru Rinpoche spoke, 'Adopt the Bodhisattva path, Madhupa; the Bodhisattva is ready to be born again and again to take others to Nirvana. The Arhant merely seeks his own salvation. *Om Vajrasattva Hoom.*'

The great Yesu spoke, 'Let your body be even crucified if that means help for even a single soul, O son of Man.'

Nanak Dev said, 'The Supreme is full of grace. May you be instrumental in the descent of that grace. *Satnaam, Hari Hari, Ya Rab.*'

Shiv Gorakh said, 'The dhuni is to continue till you find a caretaker who can be trusted to keep it lit for eternity. *Alakh Niranjan, Bhum Bhole.*'

I said, 'As always, I am your obedient servant. I have realised that the subtle ego that is satisfied with individual salvation had lingered up till now, deep in my psyche. Today, it has been pulled out by its roots, and burnt in the fire of wisdom that glows in the dhuni of the Naths. *Jai Bholenath, Bhum Bhole*, glory to Jagannath, the Lord of the Universe, Rab-il-aalimeen. I shall go back right now. Bless me, Sri Guru.'

The sweet voice of Sri Guru came from the effulgent void, 'Madhu, Sri Madhu, I am always with you. You are a spark of my inner fire. Go now in peace and bliss.'

I prostrated, chanting *Sri Gurubhyo Namah!* Instantly, I found myself back in my body which was still in the padmasana posture inside the tent. I looked at my wristwatch. The time was one minute past midnight.

My head throbbed with a severe headache that came on suddenly, and then my nose began to bleed copiously. I had to use all the towels I had to wipe the blood. When the flow of blood ceased, my headache vanished. It was as if all the blood that had rushed to my head had been allowed to flow out. I washed my nose and face with water from my water bottle, stretched my legs, and folding them again in padmasana, went into deep meditation. This time, I could feel myself in everyone around me, including the yaks and the ponies.

In the morning, we walked the last stretch of the parikrama and reached Manasarovar without any major mishap, except that one of our group fell off his pony and hurt his rib and back. Although the doctor, a good friend who was accompanying us, was quite concerned, I knew he would be fine by the grace of Sri Guru.

50

The Journey Continues

THIS IS THE CONCLUDING chapter and it is going to be quite short. I write this sitting in my tent in Haridwar. The cool waters of the Ganga are not far from here. We are a big group of almost eighty-five gathered here to attend the Purna Kumbha Mela, or full Kumbha Mela, which occurs once in twelve years. We are here to spend a few days amidst the hundreds of holy men who come in from all quarters of India, and the thousands who come to take their blessings and bathe in the sacred river. Our tents are situated in a quiet place, away from the hustle and bustle of the mela, and yet close enough to walk over and participate in all the activity when and if we so desire.

As I wind up my autobiography, I shall now spell out a few important points before coming to the thanksgiving. I say this sitting before the dhuni, with the Fire and the Supreme Being as witnesses.

Do not accept as authentic, any biography that may come after my time which contains material that does not factually agree with what I have written here in my autobiography, especially if the facts are twisted to glorify me.

The other important point is this: *I have, as of now, not selected anyone to be my spiritual successor.* There are sincere and devoted souls who are close to me, but I have not found anyone ready yet to take on that stupendous responsibility. Perhaps someone amongst them might develop the requisite qualifications, or a new and mature soul who has past links with me, as some of the present group have, might appear. I shall wait patiently and give clear indications when the time is ripe.

A very important aspect about the spiritual-successor-syndrome that needs to be clarified: If by any chance I do not designate someone as my spiritual successor before my death, I warn our friends not to accept anyone who claims to be my spiritual successor, on account of having seen me in a dream saying so, or proving his or her credentials through spirit writing or some such nonsense. I hereby declare that I shall not ever use so-called mediums of whatever kind, to instruct people or express my thoughts.

Those sincere, able and kind souls who take up administrative positions in running the affairs of the Satsang Foundation and its schools should, under no circumstances, consider themselves as my sole spiritual heirs unless I categorically spell it out before my body ceases to function.

Having said this, I must now thank all those who helped me in executing Babaji's plan.

First, I thank my mother and father, who brought me into this world so that I could do the work allotted to me. I call them my first providers. I thank my wife for bearing and putting up with the eccentricities of a crazy husband like me, and my children for understanding and sympathising with my peculiarities. Then, I thank all the providers, spiritual and temporal, who came to my help from my childhood to the present, supporting my work so selflessly.

To all these souls, and also to those who are silent and unknown, I offer my repeated prostrations, bow down again and again, and kiss their toes in utter humility. May Sri Guru bestow his boundless grace on them.

This is the end of this autobiography, but I pray that it becomes the beginning of a fascinating spiritual journey for you.

In love and friendship, M.